When Writers Read

When Writers Read

Jane Hansen
University of New Hampshire

Heinemann
Portsmouth, NH

Heinemann Educational Books, Inc.
70 Court Street, Portsmouth, NH 03801
Offices and agents throughout the world

Chapter 12 originally appeared in Jane Hansen, Thomas Newkirk, and Donald Graves (eds.), *Breaking Ground: Teachers Relate Reading and Writing in the Elementary School* (Portsmouth, NH: Heinemann, 1985) and is copyright © 1985 by Jane Hansen.

The following have generously given permission to use quotations from their work:

The quote from Ruth Hubbard in chapter 3 is reprinted by permission of the author.
The poem "The Little Boy" appearing in chapter 5 is reprinted by permission of the author, Dr. Helen E. Buckley, Professor Emeritus, State University of New York, College at Oswego, New York. (From *School Arts*, October 1961, a Davis Publication.)
"Crisis in Confidence, Life in a New School, or Reflections on Open House" by Liz Turner, appearing in chapter 7, is reprinted by permission of the author.
Matthew's journal entries appearing in chapter 14 are reprinted with permission.
The quote by Leslie Funkhouser appearing in chapter 14 is reprinted by permission of the author.
Byrd Baylor, excerpted from *The Desert Is Theirs.* Copyright © 1975 Byrd Baylor. Reprinted with the permission of Charles Scribner's Sons.
Justin's piece, "Ship Ahoy," appearing in chapter 15, is reprinted with permission.
Brian Ogden's "Harold (A Dolphin Tale)," appearing in chapter 15, is reprinted with permission.
Amy Burtelow's "My Life as a Mustang," appearing in chapter 15, is reprinted with permission.
The chart in chapter 18 by Millie Woodward and Leslie Funkhouser is reprinted by permission of the authors.

On the cover: Becky Palmer, Jacquie Woods, Michael O'Keefe, and Peter Fiske (left to right) engage in a reading/writing conference. Photo by James Whitney.

Library of Congress Cataloging-in-Publication Data
Hansen, Jane.
  When writers read.
  Bibliography: p.
  Includes index.
  1. Reading (Elementary)—United States.   2. Language arts—United States.   3. Education—United States—Experimental methods.   I. Title.
LB1573.H1754 1987   372.4   86-29556
ISBN 0-435-08438-0

10 9 8 7 6 5 4 3

Designed by Maria Szmauz.
Printed in the United States of America.

Contents

Twenty

Twenty-One

Twenty-Two

Acknowledgments

I am extremely fortunate to have many people who encourage my learning. Several people at the University of New Hampshire interact to continuously learn about reading and writing, and I thrive in this climate of exploration.

First, I thank Don Graves. I have worked more closely with Don than anyone else as his world of writing has opened my world of reading. He has let me figure things out for myself, not becoming frustrated with how slow I am to see what to him is often obvious.

Ruth Hubbard is the person I have worked longest with at the University of New Hampshire. She worked as my research assistant during my first year at UNH (1979–80) when she was a master's student in reading. We did an instructional study on inferential comprehension with fourth-grade students and teachers. The next year we did a similar study with fifth grade. During 1981–83 when I studied reading and writing in Ellen Blackburn Karelitz's classroom with Don Graves, Ruth was a public school teacher. Then we both worked as part of the Mast Way project to continue the study of reading and writing. This year (1986–87) we are both part of the new Stratham study of evaluation in reading and writing. Both of us have learned a tremendous amount about writing and reading and, like Don, Ruth has been patient when I drag one foot in my twelve years of experience as a traditional elementary teacher. Next year I look forward to learning with her as she conducts the research for her dissertation.

I have learned from other professors, especially Don Murray and Tom Newkirk. Don suggested the title for this book. (Thanks, Don!) Tom was the first person to ask me to teach writing, and I continue to teach in the New Hampshire Summer Writing Program under his direction. Also, he suggested the book that he, Don Graves, and I edited: *Breaking Ground*. Someday I'll think of something to do for Tom besides inviting his family to my house for Thanksgiving.

Many teachers own portions of this book. I will be forever grateful to Ellen Blackburn Karelitz and Phyllis Kinzie, in whose classrooms I worked most directly. I thank the entire Mast Way staff; they are still so gracious and let my UNH reading students continue to work in their classrooms. They teach these university students, me, their own students, and other teachers who visit Mast Way. They also conduct workshops and speak at conferences. My learning and theirs are closely intertwined.

Other teachers who teach in nearby schools in New Hampshire and elsewhere share stories about their students with me. I learn from them both on social occasions and at professional gatherings. Their names are sprinkled throughout this book. Many others influence me when I return their phone calls, read their letters, and travel to their faraway places.

The PhD students in our new reading/writing program stimulate me. Besides Ruth, I want to acknowledge Tim Rynkofs, Mary-Ellen MacMillan, Judy Fueyo, Peg Murray, Elizabeth Chiseri Strater, Meg Peterson, Brenda Miller, Tom Romano, and Lorri Neilsen. They do wonders. They challenge me—I mean, argue—and they tell me I'm great. They read constantly, write, conduct countless research projects, and work with teachers. The world needs to watch out for them.

Many teachers, students, and professors have read drafts of every chapter in this book. They responded to my thoughts and writing in helpful ways, and I want to thank them for the time they spent conferring with me either over the phone, in writing, or, most often, at the Bagelry: Freddie Furnas, Kay Whitten, Ellen Blackburn Karelitz, Jill Waddell, Pete Schiot, Sarah Opdycke, Margaret Bruell, Tim Rynkofs, Marcia Taft, Peg Murray, Pam Bradley, Mary-Ellen MacMillan, John Lowy, Ruth Hubbard, Jan Roberts, Judy Fueyo, Liz Turner, Florence Damon, Don Murray, Pat McLure, Don Graves, Leslie Funkhouser, Millie Woodward, Ellen Blanchard, and Ann-Marie Klein.

Everyone always thanks their family with these words, "If it hadn't been for the support of. . . ." Well, I say likewise, but I'm sure Tom will be glad when I give this manuscript to Heinemann and become my normal, relaxed, quiet, peaceful self.

Dori is my secretary and runs the Writing Process Lab. She is always nice to me, no matter what. She hates typing references, especially on December 22, but when she completes her degree this year she will no longer have to put up with professors who always want things done yesterday. Dori lived in my house when I was on sabbatical to write this book and, except for breaking the water pump, she gave this 200-year-old house the tender loving care it must have. Plus, she loves Ole, the dog who owns my husband and me.

Everyone at Heinemann has bent over backwards to make this book readable and to get it out quickly. I especially thank Philippa Stratton. It's so nice to have her only a few miles away.

When Writers Read

One

Writers read with conviction.

I learned this in the fall of 1981 and it set off a chain reaction of discoveries about how children learn to read.

Prior to 1981, I taught reading the same way Mrs. Hughes taught me in kindergarten in 1948. I can remember sitting in a small circle on the bare wooden not-cold floor. I turned my wire-rimmed eyes up at a huge book on an easel. My teacher stood beside it with her long wooden pointer and I read, "See Jane. See Jane run." I was Jane. I liked our giant book and my workbook with its brown cover and brown edges on the pages. My mother saved it, and I've looked back to see that I circled lots of little pictures and didn't get any wrong. I gave my little students similar work when I first taught in 1964.

I joined the Peace Corps and lived on Bromley Mission in Liberia, West Africa. The Episcopal church supported my school, and I found a ditto machine in my bedroom! I gave my fifteen first- and second-grade pupils at least one purple sheet every day and they circled lots of little pictures. I didn't have a big book for them but we did have discarded reading books from California and each child read about Jack and Janet. I liked it OK, but I liked my afternoon job better.

I appointed myself afternoon school librarian after I found a tiny room full of books from American attics. I never saw so many outdated physics texts in my life and certainly not in an elementary school library. We had no money for children's books, but Monrovia, the capital city, had a children's library. Every other week I rode in the mission van to check out another armload of books for my school library, and during the next two weeks, my little girls checked them out on our own real library cards. Over the next several years when I taught back in this country, I continued to use library books.

I read to my students every day, but not during reading class. Therefore, when I became a Title I reading teacher, real books left my teaching. I spent all day, every day, with worksheets, Dick and Jane, and children with problems. My nagging concerns about reading instruction came to a head.

In 1975, the last year I taught elementary school, I can remember sitting on the carpeted floor behind a second-grade teacher's desk with a small circle of children in front of me. I held the Distar manual and they repeated, ''ham-bur-ger,'' after me, as they learned to hear parts of words. Later they learned to hear single letter sounds and, even later, to blend those sounds into words. I didn't like it much. Neither did they. They squirmed, the most I'd let them move, but I got up and left. I went to get a PhD, to find a better way.

In 1978, for my dissertation, I collected data on second-grade children for eight weeks. I taught three reading groups in a corner of the hallway under the stairs to the second floor in White Bear Lake, Minnesota. The children sat at a table and I stood above them so they could hear me over the noises around us. I taught the children to answer inferential questions about The Dog Next Door and other stories in their reading book. The children learned to answer my questions and I felt terrific. Young children supposedly couldn't do inferential thinking very well, but I'd found out that they could. I came to the University of New Hampshire thinking I knew something.

My confidence lasted two years.

Even though I knew young children could do more than we usually thought, I saw children who opened my eyes farther. From 1981–83 I spent two days each week in Ellen Blackburn Karelitz's first-grade classroom in Somersworth, New Hampshire. When it was time for reading, her children sat all over the room, in twos, threes, and alone—reading books. Two of them even wore earphones in the old, footed bathtub. These children hadn't gone to kindergarten. Some of them couldn't even write their names, but they could read. For years I had heard, ''Start where the children are,'' but I never had. These children taught me their definition of reading, ''We look at books, show them to other kids, point to things in the pictures, explain them to each other, and wonder what the words say.'' They giggled, hurried around the room, and enjoyed reading. I loved responding to their queries about the words.

They wanted to learn to read those books and I could help. I answered their questions and watched their interest in reading grow throughout the year. In the past I had often seen children's interest wane. The big change in what I believe about reading began. A new awareness started to grow inside me.

I Learned About Writing

On the first day of school, I'd asked some of Ellen's students if they could write, and they said, "Yes." This not only surprised me, because I knew they couldn't, it also inspired me to look again at the dictum, "Start where the children are." Ellen did and I followed her lead. I gave them blank paper and they wrote. Most of them drew pictures, but I didn't say, "Hey, you said you could write. You'd better do it." I said, "Tell me about your picture," and they did. They could talk and "write." I wanted them to write more, so I listened, learned to limit my vocabulary to, "Uh-hmmmmmmmmm," and they talked and talked. The more I listened, the more they talked. The more they talked, the more they wrote. They wrote every day and I never told a child what to write about. I finally threw away the boxes of frayed pictures I'd collected for years to use as story starters. If the children didn't need them, I certainly didn't.

I Learned About Reading

One boy wrote a three-sentence story on the first day of school and, after school, Ellen typed it on the primary typewriter, one sentence per page. The second day he illustrated it and read it to the class:

> The fire engine is red.
> The fire was gigantic.
> The fire engine went FAST!

His picture for the last sentence covered two pages—and most of the words. The children loved Brian's book and quickly chose it from the book shelf during reading. "Hey, Brian, what's this say?" they would ask. Brian became the first child to teach reading in the room, soon to be followed by his classmates, one by one. No wonder they liked to read. They had tons of help at their fingertips or within hearing distance. The room was full of teachers.

I Learned About Teaching

I taught with all the others, and I tried to take on some of their characteristics. First and foremost, they were excited about learning. So was I. I had never been in a classroom where children authored books for each other to read and also helped each other read any book from the bookshelf they decided to tackle. I had never seen anything like this before. I responded to their energy with more energy and with help.

I learned a new definition for teaching: help. The children knew what they wanted so I threw away my agenda and followed theirs. That's how they taught. None of them worried about what to teach the others. They simply provided the help requested, if they could.

I supplied the help beyond their classmates' expertise and learned to ask what they wanted to learn next.

I Learned About Learning

I remember so clearly the day Daniel sat with the book he'd chosen to learn to read. He hesitated on a word and held up his hand to silence my open mouth. "I know it!" he blurted, walked away, and came back with his writing folder.

Daniel's writing folder looked like Daniel. Hair here and there, papers here and there. Shirt hanging out, papers hanging out. Daniel was in his own world. He whipped through his writing, obviously looking for a certain sheet he would recognize by sight. He found it and triumphantly pointed to the word *were*, but he couldn't read it. "I know it," he insisted. He found the beginning of that piece of writing and read until he came to *were*. He did know it. He found it again in the book, read it, glanced at me, and kept reading. Daniel knew what kind of help he didn't need. In his classroom the children met with each other and their teacher to share what they read and how they learned to read it. This talk about their reading strategies helped make them aware of what to do when they got stuck, and their confidence grew when they purposely used a strategy to figure something out by themselves. Their growing sense of themselves as learners provides the theme of this book.

Independence. I have probably always thought that my goal was to have my students become independent readers, but I didn't understand the word. I taught my class to learn from me. Now I'm learning to teach students to depend on each other, me, and themselves. During the year I worked in Daniel's room I found an ancient truth that tells what I belatedly learned.

A leader is best
When people barely know that he exists,
Not so good when people obey and acclaim him,
Worse when they despise him.

Fail to honor people
They fail to honor you.

But of a good leader, who talks little,
When his work is done, his aim fulfilled,
They will say,
"We did this ourselves."

Lao-tzu (604 B.C.)

I started to learn about reading through writing, so I'll write about writing before I bring in reading.

When I went into classrooms where children wrote and responded to each other's chosen topics, many children and teachers said, "Writing is my favorite time of day." I had to find out why they liked writing.

As it turned out, the students liked writing because it was "their" time of day, and the teachers liked writing because their students liked it. When they wrote, the students made more decisions than at other times of the day, and this authority, given to them by their teachers, pleased them. I thought it was fine for them to like writing, but since I spend my life in the world of reading, I'm afraid I felt jealous. Students should also like reading.

Students told me, "I like to read but I don't like reading." Teachers told me, "Reading is dull to teach and boring for the students."

I knew these things and decided to learn about writing to get some cues about how to teach reading better. I had much to learn because writing is a complicated process. Many others have already written about writing, so I'll condense what I've learned into one five-part chapter. Then, I'll write an entire reading chapter about each of these five sections. In these five chapters, I'll show how what I learned about writing changed what I know about reading.

Time

My understanding of writing began with the word *time*. In the writing classrooms where I have worked, both teachers and children use their time differently than either they, or I, did in former years. Traditionally, we assigned a topic once every two weeks, our students wrote about it at home the night before the due date (or we assigned it and they wrote about it right away during class), they handed in their papers and walked away, we took the papers home, marked the errors with our red pen, returned the papers, the students felt rejected, and we assigned another topic. That writing program also included exercises in handwriting, spelling, grammar, and punctuation. However, over the last fifteen years, many researchers (e.g., Atwell 1987) have accumulated more realistic information about what writers do. The writing teachers I learned from provide many opportunities for their students to compose.

Students write often and on a regular schedule.　Writing is hard work and requires much practice. All the information in this book comes from classrooms where children write four or five times a week. Not only did I work in Ellen Blackburn Karelitz's first-grade classroom, as I mentioned in chapter 1, but during 1983–85, I spent two days each week in the Mast Way Elementary School (grades K–5) in Lee, New Hampshire. During the 1984–85 school year I focused my time in Phyllis Kinzie's fourth grade. The teachers couldn't always schedule writing every day, but ideally, students write daily. When they write often, many writers start to look at their world as an arena of writing topics and usually come to writing class with a topic in mind.

Students can plan their writing because they know on which days they will write, at what time, and how they will spend their time during writing; whether, for example, they will write first, have a small group conference, or have an all-class conference. Whenever the time to write arrives, the children either start new pieces of writing, continue on with yesterday's, or return to an even earlier draft.

Writers may keep a piece of writing alive for a long period of time.　Third-grader Amy started a piece of writing, "My New Cabbage Patch Kid," in September, but when she didn't get the doll, she discontinued her draft. In February when she finally got the Cabbage Patch Kid she returned to her draft. A piece of writing can go on for months or years if a writer chooses—and if she keeps every draft in her folder so it's there if she wants to come back to it. We don't think of the writing period as a daily block of time. Rather, it's a block of time that begins on the first day of school and continues from day to day.

Writers spend most of their time working on the information in their writing.　Our focus has changed from several years ago when we stressed mechanics over content. As teachers we now establish the importance of meaning by our initial response to our students. The first thing we do is confirm their message, "Chad, you said your dog is a mixture of black lab and Chesapeake Bay retriever."

"Yes, the brown on his neck is the Chesapeake part. . . ."

We spend the majority of our time listening to our students elaborate on the data in their writing. They know that their information is what counts.

Writers spend some of their time sharing, seeking help, and responding to others. Writers have "conferences," the label we give to response sessions. We teach students to confer with each other because we don't want to be the only ones they turn to for response. We used to have our students write only for us, but that distorted part of the nature of most writing. Authors don't write for an audience of one. They write for many readers and, therefore, our writers can't write only for our response.

The writers in the classrooms where I have worked share both their own writing and the writing of professionals with their classmates and with younger and older students. They learn content from each other, generate ideas, learn new mechanical skills, and strive to keep each other's interest high. They hold all-class conferences, small group conferences, and individual conferences. Students and teachers have more personal contact with each other in this kind of classroom than in classrooms without an oral response network. Not only do we know each other; we also know about each other's writing. We know the history of most pieces of writing—where Chad got his idea, where he is in his draft, and what he intends to do next. Students also know about their teacher's work.

Teachers spend time writing and sharing. We write and share our writing with our students. Matt, a fourth grader, explained what he thinks when Phyllis Kinzie writes, "It's sort of like she's telling you what to do. Besides, she writes pretty good stories." The writing teacher finds time to write and share with her class. This gives her credibility as a writer with her students—and with herself.

Most of us feel nervous about writing because we have had sparse, often negative experiences with writing. To make us even more insecure, we have no teachers' manuals for this new kind of response teaching and never will because of the nature of the approach itself. When we listen to a student read his writing, whether alone or in a group, we make instructional decisions based not on a curriculum guide but on what the student can do and wants to do next. When we write and talk about our writing, as our students do, we learn about writing and how to share it. In other words, we spend our preparation time differently than in the past. We prepare by writing, reading, and taking part in conferences with our own peers. Of all the things the teachers did during the two years I worked at Mast

Way, the teachers' writing group was the most powerful influence on their teaching. I will write more about this group later because it warrants separate space of its own.

Choice

The notion of Time interacts with that of choice. In writing, students usually compose drafts on topics of their own choice.

Writers know that it is their responsibility to decide what to write about. Many of us didn't let our students choose their own topics when we first taught, and we still find it hard to give our students this freedom. However, when I conduct workshops for teachers, we choose our own topics and discover the richness and variety of our choices. Someone writes about Japanese cooking, others about ceramics, the Peace Corps, how to raise bluebirds, the awful conditions in homes for the retarded, and a dangerous sailing excursion. Within a half day the teachers sense the benefits of topic choice. Because they have decided what to write about, they care more about their writing than they would if I had chosen any one of these topics and assigned it to all of us.

Thus, as teachers, we learn to step back and write with our students. We can't assign topics because then we create a teacher-centered classroom, which contradicts our aim of independence. Students can't see themselves as independent learners if they only begin to write when they hear the teacher's assignment. Independent learners are self-starters, who learn from the consequences of their choices. If they choose poorly, they can discontinue the draft. When they choose well, they can take credit for it and feel a sense of accomplishment.

Writers write best when they write about what they know or want to learn. Topic choice gives students the chance to do their best, even though it can be hard for them to identify hot topics. Many children come to us with a poor self-concept; they don't think they know anything, or they assume that the things they do know are unimportant and uninteresting. Students gain confidence when we have a genuine interest in them. We do believe they know something, and this sets the stage for the writing process to begin, as the children themselves come to realize.

Third-grader Chad said, "I had to know a lot about stamps," when researcher Tom Romano asked, "What's the most important thing for a writer to know?"

Chad explained further, "You gotta know a lot of stuff about your story. . . ."

Because children know about their own personal experiences, we usually start a writing class with personal narrative so that students can gain confidence in their knowledge base and become acquainted with each other. Again, we realize the value of personal exchanges from our own writing. A teacher in a workshop I conducted in West Bedford, Massachusetts, responded, "I've known these other three people in my group for years, but I know things about them after just one morning of writing that I never knew before. And we each felt our piece of writing was uninteresting, but the others always thought it was interesting. We each felt good. This must make students feel good about themselves."

As writers, we do need to feel that we have a contribution to make, something to give to others. We write something we think is unique, not something someone else has already written, but it may be difficult to find a topic. In classrooms we often begin the first day with talking. When each student has told the others at least three things he knows, we say, "Write about one of those things," and the students can. They realize that everyone knows they have things to write about.

Writers have a daily decision to make, "Do I want to continue yesterday's piece of writing or start another?" Chad wanted a conference with an adult every day to get him started. In early November, Tom Romano decided to teach Chad to write marginal notes at the end of each writing period to tell himself where his thoughts were when his time was up. Then, at the beginning of writing the next day, he could read his own notes to himself instead of depending on someone to get him started.

By late November, Chad could not only continue a piece of writing, he could also start a new piece without consulting a teacher beforehand. He began a scary story about clams that he had heard at home. He was moving toward independence, learning to take responsibility for his own writing just as we want students to do. The kind of direct instruction provided by Tom Romano helps discontinue their notion of the teacher as authority and start to rely on themselves. However, not even professional writers consider themselves self-sufficient. Therefore, we teach children to recognize when they need help and to consider various sources of help

Many ideas for writing topics come from classmates. When someone shares a ski adventure, six classmates may write ski narratives. At other times, children convene sessions to request help on topic ideas. In Phyllis Kinzie's fourth grade, a child who can't get started calls two friends to meet with him. Prior to the conference, the child lists three possible topics, even if he doesn't feel enthusiastic about any of them. One day Matt called Todd and Mark to listen to his ideas: my new football, the snake I caught, and my new dog. The new football turned out to be more interesting to his dad than Matt; the snake had a thorn in it and Matt couldn't remove the thorn, so that story didn't satisfy his friends; but Matt's new dog sounded interesting. Matt went off to write.

Children also get ideas from professional authors. Someone may read Eric Wilson's *Murder on the Canadian* and write a mystery; or an illustration in a picture book may remind a child of the butterflies in her stomach when she rode a Ferris wheel; or perhaps Melissa reads poetry and then writes her own poems. Both teachers and students share the writing of professionals daily within the writing program, and this writing opens options from which to choose topics, genres, and strategies.

Choice goes beyond topic choice. In January 1985, second-grader Mike read a draft to his class:

Sharks

Sharks are very dangerous.
This shark is swimming after a man.
Sharks live in the ocean.
As you can see, this shark is eating a big fish.
I like sharks.
The end.

"Comments, questions, remembers or reminders?"

His friends made comments, such as, "Mike, that word 'dangerous' was a good choice. I know; I've read about sharks, and they are very dangerous."

Leslie Funkhouser, his teacher, had a comment and a question: "Mike, I liked the way you used the words 'as you can see.' How did you think of those words to begin your sentence?"

"Well, Miss Funkhouser, I was looking at this book from the library on sharks. I saw the words 'as you can see' and I know how to read them so I decided to put them with my idea for the picture. 'As you can see, this shark is eating a big fish.' And you know what? I made a very good sentence!" Mike notices writing when he reads and chooses to try the language of other authors.

Decisions about how to put together a piece of writing and what information to include present writers with a constant barrage of problems to solve. In November of third grade, Amy explained what she does if she gets stuck when she's writing, "I usually think of either the ways I could change it so I could put something that I know would make sense, or I go and I read what I've written so far to the class, or I ask a friend." The ability to weigh input from friends becomes standard behavior in many conferences.

Children consider the usefulness of what their friends want to know when they wonder if they need to clarify their writing. For example, when Chad shared his mystery in December, he answered several questions, but when he continued to work on it he ignored "Where did the story take place?" and "Where did you get the title?" because he didn't consider those pieces of information important to his story. He also rejected "How did you feel?" because he felt he'd included his feelings. He did find two questions helpful, "Why did Randy scare you?" and "Why did you have a movie projector in there?" and inserted facts to clarify these points. By sharing his writing with friends, Chad discovered more options than the teacher alone could provide.

Response

Response rests on Time and Choice. We respond to topics students choose and by responding, we teach. Thus, we teach writing from students' drafts. At first we may doubt our ability to respond, but we learn to respond, initially, to information, and devote a smaller percentage of our attention to mechanics than previously. Also, we respond not only when the students have finished their writing but along the way, while they are in the process of working on a draft. We don't spend our time doing something else when our students write. We move among them, teaching. This responsive teaching requires a shift in approach for most of us.

We listen for what our students know.   This presents the biggest change for us, because we grew up in a tradition that looked for what students didn't know. Our red pens found negative things to highlight. Now we not only look for the positive, but we listen as well as look. These changes often mean that we reeducate ourselves.

A redefinition of good writing initiated the shift in composition instruction from a skills emphasis to a meaning emphasis. (See Calkins 1986 for more about writing instruction.) We now realize that a messy draft may be a better piece of writing than a neat one, as illustrated by these two examples; the first by Suzanne, the second by Daniel:

My name is Suzanne.
I am six years old.
I go to school.
I have a dog.

WEN RAN	When rain comes down
KUMS DAN	
IT DANS	It dances in the puddles
IS IN THU PUDLS	
AND	And splashes in the air,
SPLAZI IN THU	
IR PSSSSS	p-s-s-s-s.
IT SPASHI	It splashes on the window
ON THU WIND	
GOO PAT PAT PAT	Goes "Pat, pat, pat"
IND I KEHS	And I catch it in my mouth.
IND MY MUSH	

WEN I WOK IN THU P UDLS	When I walk in the puddles
I TRI TO SPLASH T	I try to splash it.
WEND I K UM HOM	When I come home
I ?? CLOSSSSSSS	I change my clothes-s-s-s-s-s.
I LUV I	I love it
I LUV IT	I love it
I LUV IT	I love it
I LUV THU RAN	I love the rain.

The second composition is better because it contains several vivid pieces of specific information. We see perfect mechanics in the first and may feel a tug toward it, but mechanics do not bring a flat piece of writing to life.

We respond to the potential in the writer's voice.   When children share, we listen for sparks of interest in the writer's tone and watch the writer's face. If we see or hear a difference in Suzanne when she mentions school or her dog, we comment on the one that showed more spark: "You smiled when you said you like school." Suzanne may respond with additional information about what she likes. If not, we ask, "What do you like about school?" Perhaps we can't sense where the potential lies. If this is the case, we may respond, "You wrote about school and your dog. I'd like to know more." Suzanne's preference for school shows if she chatters about painting at the easel but says little about her dog. Or maybe this is a piece she wrote when she was bored, and she has little to say about any of it. In that case, Suzanne would begin a new piece of writing. We approach writing conferences such as Suzanne's without an agenda, find out where the child is, and help the child move ahead.

We teach by helping the students generate options.   We try to sense the urgency, the driving force. If Suzanne talks excitedly about the huge rainbow she has painted, her teacher may tell her to put her finger on the spot in her writing where that information would go if she decided to add it. Suzanne may or may not want to add it, but, regardless, we want to teach her about two options: She may decide to add or not to add. Suzanne also needs to consider what to write about in case she chooses to abandon her current draft. She might talk about something new, such as her family's outing to buy kites for her and her sister. When the student knows what decisions she faces, the teacher leaves her to consider her options on her own.

The response system confers responsibility on writers.   Like other writing teachers, Suzanne's teacher approaches her students to find out what they're writing about. She does not come thinking, "I wonder what I can do to help." The conference resembles a conversation, with the piece of writing the conversation starter. She acknowledges what the child knows and asks questions to learn more. This extends Suzanne's awareness of how much she knows and helps her realize that she may have more to write about. But the teacher doesn't dictate, nor do the other students. We all remember the important, imaginary, always-present protective shield that surrounds each writer and provides her with her own sphere of influence.

Suzanne not only decides what she will write about, she also chooses what form the writing will take (whether narrative or poetry, for example), what information she will include, who she'll share it with, and whether she will bury it in her folder or label it a final draft. She makes these decisions for the same reason I make cheesecake from scratch. When guests say it's terrific, I can say, "Thank you. I did it myself."

The test of whether the response system works is whether the students want to write. It's not fashionable to consider the affective domain as the driving force in school, but we do in writing. If writers want to write, they will invest more effort in it and learn more. Affirmative response increases the chance that students will believe they have something to say. Some of our understanding about the impact of response comes from studies of language acquisition (Bissex 1980).

Adults respond to the messages young children try to communicate, not to the errors they make in their attempts. Toddlers' early words confuse us, but we concentrate on trying to figure out their intent as we listen to their tone and watch their body language. We respond to what we think they are trying to tell us. If we respond to children in an encouraging way, they try again. The more supportive we are, the more likely it is that they will want to experiment with language, both oral and written. The bottom line in the writing conference is, "The writer wants to write again."

Structure

The oral response system works in tightly structured classrooms. Teachers who like order can often get a writing program organized more easily than those of us whose classrooms tend to get out of hand. It helped me to learn this, because the structure of a writing class can escape a casual observer, but a parent who spent the day in Ann-Marie Klein's first-grade classroom summarized the work period with these words, "All the children knew what they were doing." On any one day, various writers begin new drafts, share with classmates, edit final drafts, or rework old drafts. They all know why they're doing something and what they might do next. The structure helps them realize their possibilities and assume control of their forward direction.

The structure provides options. This may be a new definition for us. We have tended to think of well-structured situations as those in which we listed the students' assignments on the chalkboard. When they needed to start something new, or needed direction in the midst of a task, they turned to us. More specifically, we initiated the work, the students did the work for us—alone so we would know how much they knew—and we evaluated how well they had carried out our plans. We now reject this structure because it gives us a writer-with-no-authority model that undermines the basic nature of writing. Authors are Authorities. They make decisions.

Writing is not formulaic. Writers often create and solve problems when they compose. We avoid like death any system that encourages writers to handle all pieces of writing similarly. For example, orthodoxies that dictate a first draft, second draft, and final draft for any piece of writing take away the writer's right to recognize when to revise. Students often do realize they have a problem but can't think of a solution. In such situations, we teach students not to be satisfied with work they know could be better. They know their classmates' areas of interest and expertise, and we expect them to get up and solicit help when they're stuck. This system encourages productive work habits, but we can't have excessive movement, so writers learn to solve many concerns themselves and to discover which problems aren't problems.

Spelling during drafting is one example of a nonproblem. Invented spelling, or functional spelling, opens the world of writing to both adults and young writers. They can use any word in their speaking vocabulary. This myriad of possibilities brings more richness into their writing than if they used only words in their spelling lexicon. They go back later to check for correctness. Thus, we place fewer restrictions on our students, but in so doing, we expect them to do more.

The structure places control at the tip of the writer's pen. The writer tells me what's good about her writing. For example, a different scene could have transpired with Suzanne's writing when I asked, "How's it going, Suzanne?"

"This is my best writing—ever."

"Oh, tell me about it."

"It's long. I never wrote anything with four lines before."

"That's a lot. Will you read it to me?"

Suzanne could then have told me about the rainbow she painted, plus the towers she and her friend Suzie built in the block corner, but I wouldn't pose the possibility of additions. Writers set their own standards, and Suzanne knows she's accomplished something new and is moving ahead. As I leave Suzanne, I would ask, "What will you do next?"

"I'm going to write a new, longer one," might be her answer. Or,

"I'm going to put in something about the blocks so this one will be even longer." Or, "I'm going to write a new one about the blocks. I'm gonna think of a title for it. I've never written a title before." Suzanne evaluates her progress, and we have to find out from her whether she is progressing. Her evaluation reflects what she values and what we value.

In this case, we value the writer's control. We dispense knowledge, but we try to give it only after we've found out what the writer wants; then we try not to command. We either generate options or, ultimately, we say, "Well, what would be a couple ways you might handle that?" Sometimes a child comes with a problem, "I can't think of a lead," but the child learns not to expect solutions from the teacher. The child doesn't mean, "Tell me what to write for a lead." Writers want ideas but they maintain control.

Community

The members of the writing community rejoice in each other's accomplishments. We don't withhold information from each other because we fear someone else will do as well as we do. We share and others share with us. We want to learn, and through sharing we know what others know. This notion of everyone as a possessor of knowledge for everyone's use differs from our previous systems, which insisted that every student keep to herself and which also established hierarchies of haves and have nots. In the classrooms described in this book, the community, a collective of diverse information, underlies the success of the writing.

Writers value their own contributions. Some children think they don't know anything, but we know better. We find out what they know and go on to tell them what we learned. In addition, we make their knowledge public. Everyone in the community knows about Lynne's Himalayan cats and Carlyle's passion for science fiction. Everyone knows that Janice can come up with catchy titles and Bud can keep *there* and *their* straight. (For helpful editing information, see Zinsser 1980.) These writers know they have information that others can use. Their classmates ask them questions and come to them for help.

Writers value the contributions of others. Writers know they don't know everything. They use writing to help them explore and learn about topics and concerns of interest to them. They want to carve out their own territory and expect others to do likewise. Lynne knows how important her Himalayan cats are to her and she assumes that other students also have something to write about. Writers want to find out what others will share, and their writer's curiosity inspires them to ask questions. In these sessions, the knowledge of the authors dominates the classroom. We have what Jan Roberts calls an author-centered classroom, which can be expanded to an author-centered school if the teachers also write.

Teachers who share writing with each other know each other both as people and professionals. They see beyond their isolated classrooms. Likewise, they don't want their students to work at isolated desks or in isolated groups. They work to break down any barriers that keep writers from each other.

One possible barrier is the teachers themselves. We often feel that our knowledge is paramount and set ourselves up as the channel through which everyone passes. However, when we trust children to share appropriate information, we refuse to answer questions that someone else in the class can answer. In so doing, we encourage children to seek information from each other. When they do, they use the building blocks of a community—chunks of each other's knowledge. Besides individual interaction, we may establish small writing groups to work together for a period of time, but not indefinitely because writers benefit from varied feedback. Also, the daily whole-class conference provides a time for everyone to learn from, and receive help from, the group in all its diversity.

The children look to each other, other writers, and their teacher, for suggestions and support. They like working together. When Dave Overand, a grade-six teacher in Edmonton, Alberta, created a writing community in his class, his students liked it. At the end of the year, when they wrote for their grade-six yearbook, many of them chose a favorite subject his students in previous years had not chosen. They liked writing.

References

ATWELL, NANCIE. 1987. *In the Middle*. Montclair, N.J.: Boynton/Cook.

BISSEX, GLENDA. 1980. *GNYS AT WRK: A Child Learns to Write and Read*. Cambridge, Mass.: Harvard University Press.

CALKINS, LUCY. 1986. *The Art of Teaching Writing*. Portsmouth, N.H.: Heinemann.

EMIG, JANET. 1982. *The Web of Meaning*. Montclair, N.J.: Boynton/Cook.

GRAVES, DONALD. 1982. *Writing: Teachers and Children at Work*. Portsmouth, N.H.: Heinemann.

MURRAY, DONALD. 1985. Under the Lightning. In *Writers on Writing*, ed. by Tom Waldrep. New York: Random House.

ZINSSER, WILLIAM. 1980. *On Writing Well*. New York: Harper and Row.

Time | Three

Pam Bradley, grade-four teacher at Mast Way Elementary School, says, "Reading a book is different from reading a story. You have to follow one thread and remember it from day to day. You have to read books in order to know how to read books" (Whitney and Hubbard 1986).

Pam's students read books as the core of their reading program. The number one item on their list of Things to Do During Reading is: Read. When reading time arrives, they read.

This was a big change for Pam, as it would be for me. When I taught, I wrote "Read a book" at the bottom of the day's reading schedule on the chalkboard. My students read if they finished their work. I planned their tasks but didn't assure them time to read. Now I would do things very differently, but to move the last item to the top of the list requires a huge shift in my approach to reading instruction.

My new thinking crept in as I learned about writing. One facet of writing instruction is Time. Writers write. Similarly, readers read, or at least I thought it made sense to entertain that possibility. What we do when we teach reading reflects our understanding of what we do when we teach writing.

Writing instruction rests on certain principles about how people learn, and if we believe in them we need to reassess our reading instruction. If what we know about writing doesn't bring changes in our reading instruction, then we don't really understand writing. Typical reading instruction cannot exist alongside writing instruction; they are philosophically incompatible. Unless we change the way we teach reading, in time, writing instruction will falter in our classrooms because we do not believe in it and do not reinforce it when our writers read the work of other writers. Those of us who find we do believe in the learning principles that underlie writing will evaluate every aspect of our teaching. In this book I won't go quite that far, however. I will connect our understanding of what people do when they learn to what we do when we teach reading.

A Different Pace

Readers need long blocks of uninterrupted time. This is a new concept for elementary reading periods. If you had visited my classroom in the sixties and seventies, you would have seen perhaps seven items on the board for my class to do during the sixty to ninety minutes I devoted to "reading." This gave them nine to thirteen minutes per task. I didn't teach my students the definition of "reading" I use in the real world where, as a reader, I read many things and love the luxury of time with a book. People who do spend time with books label themselves "readers" and we want students to think of themselves as readers. At Mast Way, when the children started to spend time with books, they referred to themselves more and more frequently as Readers.

Beginning readers as well as students in the upper grades quickly become Readers. Recently, I explored whether very inexperienced readers could cope with entire books. I went to a primary ESL (English as a Second Language) classroom in Rhode Island. I could hardly understand the little girl with me, but she brought me a picture book of opposites by Margaret and Gilbert Riswold. The librarian had read it to the class and Povang shared it with me. She knew a few of the pages:

> Balloons are smaller   bigger
> high   low

I read the other pages to her and we shared the book again. After the fourth time, she read it alone and beamed. I suggested that she share it with a friend. They read it together and another child joined them. I left as they reread the book and taught others to read it.

This was Povang's first book, and she learned to read it in a few minutes. Then she taught others. All children's work is to learn to read, and when one of them can read a book, the others gather to learn from their friend. This is how they spend much of their time during reading. (They also need specific skills, which I share in later chapters.) They read and read and read. They devour books, whether they are six-year-old ESL students, fourth-grade students at Mast Way, or Tim Hillmer's junior high English students in Boulder, Colorado.

Readers need time to choose books.   Within the period set aside for reading books, students can browse. This is normal behavior for readers. They take several books off the shelves as they look for "just the right book for this moment." They page through these books, consult with other readers, read parts of a book, and either decide to try the entire book or continue their search. The process of selection is part of reading. We have neglected this in the past, but as we learn about the reading process from writing and from readers, we know that writers take time to explore topics just as readers peruse books.

When reading begins in Jan Roberts's third-grade class, some of the students go off to the library to pick a book to read. Others remain in the room to continue reading books they have already started, choose books from the classroom library, or swap with friends. The selection of a book is important. It's not a task to be relegated to tiny spaces of free time throughout the day in between other work. Children's devotion to their books may depend on whether they choose wisely. The teachers I learned from teach their students how to select books and include time for this within the reading program. I will devote part of chapter 4 to Book Choice.

Readers need time to think.   Once a student has decided to pursue a book, he needs time to enjoy it. As he reads he looks out the window, reflects, and dreams. His mind meanders and discovers something unexpected because he has time to explore connections. He has time to appreciate this book. Time is a requisite of thinking, and we learn to honor the time thinkers need. Vera John-Steiner (1985) writes about the pace renowned thinkers used in their childhood, when adults encouraged their drive to know and imagine. As children, these thinkers worked with one idea for days, weeks, years. These opportunities helped them establish the thinking behaviors they used throughout their lives.

Joel, a boy in Phyllis Kinzie's fourth grade, enjoys the kind of childhood in which imagination lives. In April he shared a book he authored about the waterbugs on the pond behind his house. He studied them and named his book *Taxi Cabs* because "they zoom around with others on their backs." Later, he shared with me a draft he had just started about a spider he saw that morning when he waited for the schoolbus. The spider was tiny, and it was spinning a big web under the brace of his mailbox. Joel, who had watched him work, said to me, "I didn't think he'd have that much web in him!" Joel was "writing" when he let the spider amaze him. Joel has time to wonder.

We try to create environments in our classrooms where students can explore their thinking. Ruth Hubbard (1985) wrote about such an environment in Pat McLure's first grade one Monday morning in March.

Like a young turtle, Bobby tucks his head into his jersey, covering his chin with the material, then slowly extends his neck and stretches back his head. A hastily torn off sweater has mussed his hair, causing red tufts to stand out in all directions, but he is oblivious. His body moves slowly, absently, lost in thought, staring straight ahead instead of down at the open writing folder before him.

The noise of my scraping chair breaks his trance and his eyes meet mine.

"You look like you're thinking hard this morning."

Bobby nods and licks his chapped lips. "I'm trying to remember what it was like at the soccer game I was writing about."

"How do you do that?"

A pause. "Um . . . think about it. Try to remember . . . I sort of see it, but I can't remember if there was another guy on the other team THERE." His finger jabs at an open space on the white soccer field. "I think he SHOULD be there." His voice trails off and he rapidly sketches in the outline of a bulky player, upside down, lunging toward a ball.

"We almost got a goal," he writes slowly, sounding each letter aloud.

Bobby is hard at work, reasoning, remembering, thinking. . . .

. . . there's time for the kind of serious work Bobby is engaged in. An efficiency expert would no doubt rate Bobby's efforts as time off task, as doing nothing of significance. Yet Bobby was incredibly conscientious in his writing efforts, trying to recreate realistically the scene he was writing about. He worked to organize his drawing and words to represent the action that took place. To the product oriented, Bobby accomplished little this morning—about ten written words in all and a hastily penned sketch. But what about thought production? If it were possible to graph that, I'm sure Bobby would have shot off the chart.

The children learn that it takes time to do something well. Their teachers give them the time to take on new challenges.

Readers need time to interact with other readers. Students seek help from friends. When I tell about these interactions, someone often responds with this fear: "But, don't a few children always get interrupted with questions? How do they get their work done?" Ann-Marie Klein says that this isn't a problem in her grade-one classroom. Children do not seek help from any one child (for more about interaction in the classroom, see chapter 6, "Structure"). Because of all the sharing, children can think of more than one classmate to go to for help. Interaction works. When we teach readers to ask for help, they get more done because they can solve problems on the spot and thus move forward.

Young children usually need help with words, but some children will get bogged down because of comprehension. Or they will not exactly have trouble with comprehension but will stop to wonder what a book might mean. They question what they read because they learn in writing that authors expect questions. They feel bad if their audience doesn't question them. If their classmates don't ask them very many questions, they interpret this as a sign of lack of interest in their work. Questioning remains an inherent part of their response to the writing of professional authors (for more about Response sessions, see chapter 5).

These questions also help them set their own purposes. As Pam Bradley says, "They don't need a teacher to set purposes. This makes them more independent."

Readers need time to show their excitement. Often they interact informally. Children turn to their friends with "Hey, listen to this!" and share a section they really like. When Larry Wolfe restructured his grade-two reading program in Concord, New Hampshire, his explanation on the first day included this comment: "If you read something you want to share with someone, you may." Further into the year he reflected, "It's amazing how these second graders love reading after only eight weeks."

If Larry squelches this excitement, he runs the risk of inhibiting the growth of an independent reader. Consequently, he sets up a reading program where students have time to share their enthusiasm.

Time to Read

Students in elementary schools in this country read for approximately 12 percent of the time set aside for reading (Anderson 1985). That's not much. Instead of reading, they spend most of their time doing worksheets, workbook pages, and other written work. They typically read one story per week from their basal. That's an average of about three pages or less per day. The world of reading doesn't view reading class as a time to read, even though quantity of reading correlates with vocabulary power better than anything else. The issue of time on task looms in front of us.

I started the chapter on writing with a section on "Time," an uncommon concept when recent writing research began in the seventies. Then, students typically wrote only once every two weeks. When we decide to update our writing instruction, therefore, we first set aside time for our students to write. We make the same decision when we decide to base our reading instruction on the same principles as our writing program: we set aside time for our students to read.

Readers read. When Linda Rief, a grade-eight English teacher in Durham, New Hampshire, established as the core of her literature program a time to read books, her students spontaneously wrote her thank-you notes. Her students knew she was taking a bold step in deviating from the norm, and they appreciated it. Linda was inspired to take her risk when she read about Nancie Atwell's eighth-grade students, who read an average of thirty-four books a year (Atwell 1986). Similarly, teachers of young children can let them read lots of books.

At the end of the 1984–85 school year, the first year Jan Roberts gave her third graders lots of time to read, she reflected back to the beginning of the year. "It wasn't natural to them to read during reading and that really bothered me. I wanted to make it so they were reading when, in fact, we were reading." She didn't want her students to say what sixth graders elsewhere said in interviews with my education students: "I love to read, I just don't like reading class. . . ." Jan's students soon realized that they were reading more than in previous years, and they thought the time was worthwhile. In November 1984, Melissa already thought her reading had improved, and she said it was because she read more. One important reason to continue to let Melissa read relates to her confidence. She thinks she spends her time wisely when she has a book in her hands. This perception helps many students keep on track. But if Melissa was one of those students, it took Chad longer to find his way.

When Chad entered third grade, he didn't consider himself a reader. He didn't become involved in his reading until January. Then, during one week, he read *Tony Dorsett*, *Soap Box Racing*, *Skateboard Mania*, and *Fast, Faster, Fastest*. His mother said that he began to read at home for the first time. By the end of the year, more of Jan Roberts's students were readers than in previous years, but it took some of them a while to overcome negative perceptions of themselves, a problem less frequent among younger students.

Ellen Blackburn Karelitz accepted her first-grade children's definition of reading. During reading time they looked at books, told the story of a book, and read the repetitive parts of books. They also listened to books at two centers, one with records and one with tapes. They spent a lot of time with their friends, telling/reading/listening. Many of the books they read on their own were among those Ellen had read to them.

Teachers and students read to each other. Teachers of all grades create time to read to the entire class, to individuals and to groups. In a sense, this is not new behavior for us, but the context is new, as teachers point out to me. In the fall of 1985 when I spoke at the University of Northern Colorado in Greeley, a first-grade teacher commented, "We have read to our classes for years, but not during reading time. One day last week I did and I felt guilty. . . ." Her comment was on target. Yes, we have read to our classes for years, but the teachers at Mast Way consider this a part of their reading program. They read to their classes during the time of day labeled "Reading" and/or "Writing" because the writing of authors such as Betsy Byars belongs within the reading/writing program.

Children as well as teachers read books aloud. This is new to me. I never planned time for my students to share books they liked. I used to read to my class every day, and that was the only assured place for books in my classroom. Now I see books in the hands of students as well, and they not only read them to themselves and with each other, they read to the class. Most classes hear more books shared by children than by the teacher. If we as teachers limit the sharing of literature only to ourselves, we convey a different message about books than if everyone has equal rights and privileges.

In Phyllis Kinzie's fourth grade at Mast Way, students and teacher read to the class daily, and they read pieces they had written as well as works by professionals. This confirmed the children's own status as writers and readers, rather than setting them apart from professionals or their teacher. They read literature not only because they liked it, but because they could listen to how other writers put words together.

Jenny Mosely, a fourth-grade writer in Phyllis Kinzie's class, showed me how literature can "help you learn to write." One day in the spring of 1985, Jenny shared a draft of her fiction with the entire class in what these children called the Big Conference. Here is part of Jenny's writing:

"Who's there" they answered

. . . Help!'' cried Mary but there was no one
around no one to help her no one to hear
her she was all alone; her friends had been
taken away by someone; "why had they
not taken me" Mary thought. Well now it
was up to her to find her friends. She
started then stoped she thought back
at what had happened where had
the smoke come from? the scary
thought startled her; she went on the
search again so scared that even the
hairs on her skin stood on end. As she
went on all alone thoughts were growing in
her mind. . . .

During the conference, her teacher asked a question: "How do you figure out what to write next in a story?" Jenny's reply disappointed us and wasn't helpful to her friends: "Sentences just pop into my mind." I went to Jenny later and, initially, she couldn't shed light on her success. Her breakthrough was too new. "I've never written anything before where the parts fit together so well," she explained with a bewildered look on her face. I persisted, "I really wonder how you learned to do it."

Jenny sat, thinking seriously, as visitors tell us the Mast Way children do. They know it's important to try to understand what they do. Good sentences don't just pop off the ends of pencils. If you want them to appear again you need to hypothesize about their travels. Jenny finally answered, "It must be because I'm reading *Tom's Midnight Garden.* . . . When you read famous authors like Philippa Pearce you notice how their words fit together. . . ." "Do you suppose you could find an example in *Tom's Midnight Garden*?" I asked with feigned calmness.

Jenny paged back and forth and finally found a paragraph. "It's disgusting, but I noticed these words. I could really picture this: 'Tom found himself looking out over a meadow. There were cows in the meadow: some still at their night's rest; one getting up, hind-legs first; and one already at the day's work of eating. This last cow stopped grazing to stare at Tom, as though she thought she must still be dreaming. Stalks of grass hung from the sides of her mouth, and a long trickle of saliva descended from her lip and swung slightly in the morning breeze that was getting up.'"

Later, when I told Phyllis Kinzie, she said, "Somehow I'm sure that's an influence of literature, with its rich language and cadence. . . . I've been trying to get them to hear what they read." I couldn't help but remember the day Phyllis read to her students from Eudora Welty's *One Writer's Beginnings* (1984), a beautiful book about the importance of listening when we write. Phyllis wants them to learn about writing from as many writers as possible. The more children listen, talk, write, and read good books, the more they may enjoy the music of language. They may learn this best from teachers like Phyllis Kinzie, who have read every book in the library.

Reading teachers are readers.   I wonder about this in terms of what we know about both writing and reading. An important characteristic of a writing teacher is that she writes; teachers who write in their classrooms and share their drafts with their students confirm this. Recently I talked to a writing supervisor who works in junior high schools in Florida. She said writing sometimes wanes in the classrooms of teachers who don't write. "If a teacher hasn't personally felt the meaning of writing, how it helps her know herself and other people, writing dies in her classroom. And reading works the same way. It's what it means to be literate. Writing and reading keep us in touch with ourselves and others."

We know that it is vital for a writing teacher to write, and therefore, in our search for reading/writing connections, the Mast Way teachers assumed that it is equally important for a reading teacher to read. Teachers who already love reading so much that they always have time to read may engender enthusiasm in their students more easily than teachers who don't. We can learn the influence of our own reading demonstrations in much the same way that we experiment and learn the importance of our writing. Our students tell us that we improve our credibility when they know we write, but those students also say that we do not read. The world of reading instruction has never studied the significance of the teacher's own reading as an aspect of reading instruction. I think we must begin to take its possible importance seriously.

Teachers in my workshops bemoan the small amount of time they read. In the fall of 1985, teachers brought the book they were currently reading—a "real" book, not a textbook for a course—to my writing/reading workshop. They shared their novels, biographies, and mysteries in small groups, and then I asked for feedback. One of the first comments was, "We ended up talking about how much we wish we had time to read more."

Our students, also, wish they had time to read more. And we can give them time. Our ability to find time for them to read begins with our belief in the importance of reading.

We can't do everything. If we worry more about worksheets than about books, we will choose to assign seat work, but if we care more about books, we'll learn to teach reading from books rather than from worksheets. One of my purposes in writing this book is to show how teachers can teach reading from the books the children choose to read.

Maybe, if we give our students time to read, they will develop the good reading habits we wish we had.

A Consistent Time to Read

Leslie Funkhouser's grade-two children walk into their classroom at 8:30 and begin to read. Children in other classrooms have different schedules, but they know when they will read, when their time ends, and when they will read the next day. They can look forward to picking up their book where they left off, or they can think about starting a new book.

When students have an unending block of time that only temporarily ends today and picks up tomorrow where it leaves off today, they can read entire books. They have the nerve to take on big tasks because they know they'll finish them. Having a consistent time means that other things don't interfere.

Reading happens every day. We are busy, and busy people are always doing something. What we do to keep busy shows what is important to us. A child whose teacher keeps him so busy with other things that he doesn't have time to read, starts down a different road than the child whose teacher says, "We have lots to do every day and some things won't get done on some days. One of the things we'll always do is read."

Time is precious. We don't want to waste it. We want our students to spend their time wisely. If we have to announce, "It's time for reading," we have yet to teach our students to start reading on their own. They still depend on us to initiate their reading process for them. Scheduling a consistent time to read enables students to get a book and read when reading begins each day.

This predictability creates habits. Pam Bradley's students become like her: "My refrigerator may be empty and my laundry not done, but I have time to read. My students always have a book with them. They weren't getting very far in their books so now they carry a book back and forth in their backpacks. They read at home every night. They know where their book is. It's in their pack. They may have lost their lunch ticket, but they know where their book is. They read it in the bathroom, in bed, and on the bus. They develop stronger feelings for a book if they stay with it. It's like if you have only one friend, you put everything into that friend. You read often and don't get bogged down."

When visitors come into the Mast Way classrooms, they see children reading, but the scene evolved slowly and the teachers' comfort grew gradually. Change happens in a pokey way for most of us. In the fall of 1985, after our two-year reading/writing project had ended and the teachers were continuing to explore reading and writing on their own, I stopped in to visit. Leslie Funkhouser made this comment: "I've been letting my students read since March of 1984, but only this fall am I not nervous when visitors don't see my students with worksheets. I always thought they had to do that kind of work during reading. Now I feel comfortable when they see my students reading books."

References

ANDERSON, RICHARD C. 1985. *Becoming a Nation of Readers*. Newark, Del.: International Reading Association; Urbana, Ill.: National Council of Teachers of English.

ATWELL, NANCIE. 1986. Making Time. In *To Compose: Writing in the High School*, ed. by Thomas Newkirk. Portsmouth, N.H.: Heinemann.

HUBBARD, RUTH. 1985. Monday Morning. In *Teachers and Learners*. Durham, N.H.: Writing Process Laboratory, University of New Hampshire.

JOHN-STEINER, VERA. 1985. *Notebooks of the Mind*. Albuquerque, N.M.: University of New Mexico Press.

WELTY, EUDORA. 1984. *One Writer's Beginnings*. Cambridge, Mass.: Harvard University Press.

WHITNEY, JAMES, AND HUBBARD, RUTH. 1986. *Time and Choice: Key Elements for Process Teaching*. Videotape. Portsmouth, N.H.: Heinemann.

Choice | Four

On the first day of the school year in 1984, Leslie Funkhouser explained the reading program to her second-grade class: "You will choose your own books. . . ."

Emily hadn't been in first grade at Mast Way School and questioned Leslie, "I choose my own books?"

"Yes, Emily."

"All the time?"

"Yes, Emily."

"Everyday?"

"Yes, Emily."

Emily's body swung into one big grin.

Children want to choose their own books, but we are afraid to let them. We think they won't read and the classroom will be chaotic. Further, even if they read, we don't know how to teach them to read from the books they choose.

When I taught I didn't let my students choose the books from which I taught them to read, and I was typical. I depended on my guidebook for my ideas, and my students depended on me to tell them what to do each day. When I study writing, however, I see the importance of the writer's choices, and know that similar decision-making skills would also help readers. Even with a firm background in writing, we make a giant decision when we decide to set independence as our goal in reading.

In the previous chapter, I wrote about what I consider the first characteristic of independent readers: they read. In this chapter, I'll explain why it's important for them to read books of their own choice during reading class. The books they choose are not for supplementary reading but serve as the core of their reading program.

Readers Decide What to Read

The reading process begins when a reader chooses a book. The ability to select a book is an attribute of independent readers. Obvious as this may sound, I didn't give it serious thought until I learned the significance of choice in writing.

Topic choice underlies book choice.   Choice is one of the parts of a writing program the teachers and students value most. Paul Gish's fourth-grade students in Edmonton, Alberta, told me, "The best thing Mr. Gish does as a writing teacher is he doesn't tell us what to write about." Similarly, one of Mark Milliken's eighth-grade students in York, Maine, said to me, "We have more freedom this way. When the teacher tells you what to write about you get glued to something you don't like."

Any topic assignment will place most students at a disadvantage. Recently, I led a workshop in Winston-Salem, and the teachers wrote on topics that varied from their first time behind a steering wheel to their father's death, the family chores they did in high school, fishing in San Diego, and the newly restored Mast Farm Inn. They could all write about something they wanted to think about. Similarly, book choice helps ensure success (Harms and Lettow 1986).

The additional freedom offered by choice increases the probability of accomplishment for a reader. In second grade Emily cares about her books, wants to learn to read them, and puts forth more effort than when she must read a book she doesn't like. She had only spent one year in a reading program without choice and did not appreciate the restrictions. Her first-grade teacher may be one of the many teachers who asks herself the most common question of elementary teachers (Crismore 1985): "How do I get my students to read?" Teachers are painfully aware of how little interest students often have during reading. We want to increase their enthusiasm (Hale 1986).

The library becomes the center of the reading program.   A reader has a better chance of finding a book she likes if she can choose from seventy-five rather than five.

The classroom library pulls me toward it whenever I enter a classroom. When I taught, I planned my library first when I designed my room and put everything else in place to complement it. I'd still do that. Sometimes, however, teachers tell me they have a hard time getting books for a classroom library. One middle school teacher wanted to fill the bookcase in his classroom and searched closets throughout the school. He found enough books to fill six shelves.

"No one was using them," he said. Ellen Blackburn Karelitz checks out boxfuls of books from her community library for her classroom library. Most teachers check out books from their school libraries to put on the shelves in their classrooms and most also acquire a permanent collection for their own rooms. Children need lots of books to choose from and once we've decided to give them time to read, both children and teachers devote energy to collecting a wide range of titles.

Students also use the school library. More and more schools have well-stocked libraries accessible to the children at all times. The accessibility helps children, because they may want to select books before reading, during reading, and after reading so they're ready for the next day. The role of the school librarian is pivotal, which is why we included Marcia Taft, the librarian at Mast Way, as one of the key figures in the Mast Way project. The more often the library door is open, the more chances the librarian has to foster book choice. (Later, I will devote a chapter to the librarian's role.)

Children today use their community libraries more than in the past. As they read more and more, they want certain titles or new titles and gradually increase the frequency of their visits to the public library. When we elevate the act of reading books, we increase the excitement of frequent trips to the library.

We acquaint children with books.   After we have figured out a way to place books at their fingertips, we help students become familiar with many of the titles they might like to read. One way we do this is by reading to our students. The teachers I worked with read to their students often, and their students frequently reread those books. As one fourth grader explained, "When she reads it, I don't exactly hear it all, but when I read it all I know everything that happened."

Third-grader Chad had another reason for choosing books his teacher had read. He said it helped him read if he had first heard the story aloud. Chad had a few problems with reading, but he talked regularly about his reading process, knew what helped him, and realized he could more likely move ahead if he knew the story line of a book than if he didn't. Chad's preference for books he'd heard didn't surprise us.

Both Pat McLure and Ellen Blackburn Karelitz reread books to their first-grade students, and the children often chose those familiar books as their first books to learn to read because they needed a starting point. If they had heard a book, they could at least tell it, which is reading to beginners.

The teachers don't always read entire books. They read leads, endings, and well-written parts from books they think the children haven't read, as well as parts from familiar books. They don't necessarily say, "I'm reading this to you because I hope one of you will choose it," but often the students do.

I now use the teachers' ideas for my workshops and often read from adult literature, such as Russell Baker's *Growing Up*. We enjoy the excerpt about the day Russell's mother bought him his first pair of long pants and the description of the seat of the trousers after the tailor had altered the man-sized pants to fit Russell's sparse frame: "so much fabric had been removed from the seat that the two hip pockets were located with seams kissing right over my spine." Many teachers have read this book and enjoy thinking about it again. Others have not read it, and some decide to do so, even though my primary purpose is to share good writing, rather than to promote a particular book. I found something I enjoyed and want to share it. Likewise, our students feel our enthusiasm for books and want to experience that joy.

The children learn about good choices from their classmates.   They share books and parts of books when the class comes together for their Big Conference. The teachers establish these share sessions on the first day of school and every day thereafter. The students need many ideas, and they often choose books because friends have read them.

In October 1984, when Jan Roberts's students had chosen their own reading material for only two months, researcher Tom Romano interviewed students to find out what they were reading.

Ed had *Fishing Manual*.

Randy worked on *Reggie Jackson*.

Johanna chose *It's So Nice to Have a Wolf Around the House*.

Courtney chose *Mystery of Witch's Shoes*.

Marc had *The Space Shuttle*.

Melissa read *Wobbly Tooth*.

Jen read *Amazing Bone* and also had *The Mouse and the Motorcycle* on her desk.

Cheryl chose *Hector Horton's Flea Circus*.

Aaron chose *Our Universe*.

Nathan read *Clifford Gets a Job*.

Brent worked on *Apollo Soyuz*.

Jan commented on the variety. "How hard teachers work to motivate students to read widely, especially biography, and here we're not doing anything but letting them choose and share," she said.

Only two weeks earlier, Jan had expressed concern to a visitor from Maryland. At the time, Jan said that her students found it hard to choose an appropriate book and mentioned her own struggles with how to teach book choice. Jan worked with her third graders for two months before she felt comfortable with their ability to choose. During this time she came to realize the importance of their sharing. Finally, when they had shared lots of books, the children knew of many options, and book choice was no longer a daily concern.

Children choose books by author and content. But students do not always choose books others have shared. They also select books because they liked something else the author wrote or because they are pursuing a certain content area. A child may be on a "raccoon" binge and want to absorb as much data as possible. Marcia Taft, the Mast Way librarian, reports that the increase in content area books is even greater than the increase in fiction since children started choosing their own books. They use many of these books as resources for their writing.

Readers often choose to reread books. The children often choose to reread these books many, many times, as Daniel did when he decided to learn to read *More Spaghetti, I Say!* One day when I entered his first grade he rushed to me with the book outstretched. "I can read it perfect now. Wanna hear it?" He had worked on it for days and could now celebrate by reading it to me and to his class. When he shared, one of the children asked him how he learned to read the book. "I practiced it and practiced it," was Daniel's answer.

Children want to read smoothly, and they know they are learning to read when they gradually "overcome" a book. Children need to experience the feeling of reading "perfect," and this can happen when they have the opportunity to reread a book many, many times—a book they choose to reread.

Sometimes a child rereads a book off and on throughout the school year, as one first-grade child did with Sendak's *Where the Wild Things Are*. When Amanda heard Ellen Blackburn Karelitz read Sendak's book to the class in October, she tried to read it but found it much too difficult. She tried it again periodically throughout the year, until one day in April she read it successfully. She used it as her barometer and knew she became a better reader in first grade.

Sometimes students reread a book in successive years. In October, November, and December of grade three, Amy chose to read books she had read or had heard her teachers read in previous years. Although there were not very many of these long-term repeats on Amy's book list, an important aspect of reading is to relax with old favorites and enjoy reading.

Children choose books of various difficulty levels. Mrs. Taft and the teachers often worried about the difficulty level of the children's choices. Leslie Funkhouser decided that her second graders should not only learn to judge the difficulty of a book, they should also read books at more than one level of difficulty. Her students work on hard, medium, and easy books. They label them "challenge books," the "book I'm workin' on," and "easy books."

The Challenge book, or Dream book, may be similar to the book I described earlier when I mentioned *Where the Wild Things Are*, which Amanda worked on for months. When we observed this natural behavior in Ellen Blackburn Karelitz's room, Leslie decided to try to formalize it. She expects each of her students to have a Challenge book and to work on it for a few minutes regularly. This helps them to know they are getting better. We all need to know we are improving—this gives us the incentive we need to keep working.

The "easy" books are books the child can read well and loves to reread, like the books Amy reread in third grade. This rereading is important because it encourages children's enjoyment and solidifies their skills. They refer to these familiar books when they come across new words in other books, which they recognize but can't identify. They find the word in the "easy" book, identify the word in its familiar context, and return to their current book with the word they need. Many easy books contain much repetition (Holdaway 1979). The "easy" books give them the confidence to say, "I can read."

The books they are "workin' on" are a bit difficult but not too troublesome. If a child gets started on one and finds it too problematic, he selects another until he has one he can learn to read without too much struggle. Again, this takes us back to writing. We know that each piece of writing will not become a final product. Even professionals dump some of their work when they know that a particular draft will never amount to anything. It's part of learning about writing to be able to recognize when a draft has potential and when it should be dropped. Readers also discontinue their reading of certain books. This is part of the behavior of a reader, and we teach children to discriminate between books they can learn to read and inappropriate ones.

Pat McLure's first-grade children find one book each week to learn how to read. This book provides a daily accomplishment as students work out the hard spots they encounter here and there. "Challenge" books provide a long-term sense of growth, while "easy" books give children a constant element within their instructional program that emphasizes their competence. They can read successfully. Every day.

Reading at all levels is necessary. The teacher doesn't have to worry about whether her students will tell her the truth when she asks about the difficulty level of their books. Many teachers tell me that they're afraid to give their students a choice of books because the children will choose books that are either too easy or too hard but will always say the book is at the right level. However, if children know we expect them to read at all levels, then they not only learn to judge varying levels but give an honest appraisal. They learn to evaluate their own reading. I will write about this goal of evaluation in a later chapter.

Readers Decide Why They Want to Read a Book

Children assess their reading in terms of their purpose. If Chad reads to find facts about a raccoon's eating habits, he may skip words he doesn't know and never go back to figure them out if he has enough of the message to realize that this isn't the part of the book with the facts he wants. However, when he finds the section he needs, he may read every word.

When I taught, I told students why I wanted them to read an assignment and what information to look for. I set their purpose. When I started to study writers, however, I didn't hear teachers setting their purposes for them. Children not only chose their own topics, they decided what they would do with their information—on whales for example. If a student decided to put his information in the form of a song or only write about one incident—when swimmers found a whale on a beach—the teacher supported the child's intention and helped him to achieve it.

I have learned to find out a student's goal before I help. How else can I help? This is one of those elements of writing that sounds so logical now, but I didn't know it. When Todd wrote log entries about his swim meets, he didn't intend to read them to the class or publish them. He definitely wanted to have the facts straight and had his times from the weekend scratched on a memo beside him. He needed a different kind of help than another boy, who wrote a poem about his success at the meet. Todd wanted to begin a long-term account for himself so he could chart his progress over the years, and I helped him try to design a format he could easily refer to for comparisons. His friend, meanwhile, was reading a book of poetry, and we tapped out the rhythm in several poems to find one that sounded like swimming.

Everyone honors the reader's purpose. As in writing, when students read, their purposes determine the kind of help they need, and both teacher and friends respond to what the reader declares important. One way the children find out each other's intentions is by asking specific questions, such as, "Why did you choose a book about the ocean?" They ask this in individual contacts, small groups, and Big Conferences. The students learn to expect this type of question and prepare their answer. When someone says, "I wanted to learn something new about sharks," it determines a different kind of response than, "I wanted to know the difference between Tiger sharks and Killer sharks."

The children pursue the initial question with further queries: "What did you learn about sharks?" and "How did you find the difference?" Children's awareness of purposes evolves over time as they learn about different purposes from each other.

When one child chose a *Little Bear* book because she wanted to read only one of the stories in the collection, another child saw the world of thick books become territory to explore. Still another child read the words from his favorite song in his music book, "because I already knew it and wanted to learn to read it." The music book then became a book for other children to choose during reading. Sometimes children's purpose in choosing a book is allied with their writing, as when Chad brought a fact book about hockey from the library. He said it would help him with the hockey piece he was writing "about the rules." On a different occasion one child said, "I read Christopher's book because when he read it to the class everybody laughed, but I didn't know why."

Readers change their intentions as they read a book.   Students learn that their purposes sometimes evolve or change as they read a book. Melissa may initially select a book because she's heard of the author, Patricia Reilly Giff, but as she gets into it she finds that she is reading to compare it with another of Giff's books, and by the time she is farther along, her purpose may be to find out how the story will end. These purposes influence what goes through a reader's mind as she traverses the pages and may shape discussion of the book, depending on where the child is in her reading when she shares.

The children regularly think about why they are reading a book. They need to know their goal in order to know if they are getting somewhere. If Chad's purpose is only to find out the weight of newborn sharks, then it matters to neither him nor to his teacher whether he can read other parts of his book. We honor children's purposes because this underlies the worth of their choices. If students start to think that they should choose books with our purposes in mind, their enthusiasm for book choices wanes.

Readers Decide Which Strategies to Use

When we know a student's reason for poring over a book, we can help the student become aware of strategies he might use to achieve that purpose. One strategy might be to skip a word and come back to it after the reader has enough context to guess it. Another might be to use an index. At other times and for other students, the appropriate strategy might be to produce the sound /th/ for the letters *TH* or to ask a friend to help clarify a character's motives in a novel. All the actions readers use to help them accomplish whatever they want to do with the book they have in front of them make up their reading process. Readers increase their chance of success when they know various options they might use to accomplish their goal.

Daniel, a student in Ellen Blackburn Karelitz's first-grade class in 1981–82, repeated first grade and was in her class again. On the first day of school in 1982 he read to his new classmates. After he read, the children sat, speechless. Ellen capitalized on the moment and made a request. "Daniel, I think the children would like to know how you learned to read that book."

"Well," began Daniel in his best professorial voice, "if I don't know a word it sometimes works to skip it. I usually know it when I go back. Sometimes the story rhymes and I can guess those words. Sometimes I sound out a whole word. Sometimes I remember the word from writing and find it in my folder. If I have to, I ask someone else."

When Daniel read, he impressed the class, but his explanation confused them. They knew, however, that Daniel had said something about learning how to read, and they decided to find out what it was. I traced the children's questions throughout the year when they met daily for their Big Conference (Hansen 1984) and discovered a pattern that revolved around the children's desire to figure out what to do when they needed help with a book. Of the various questions and comments the children offered when they responded to another child, the largest proportion during the beginning of the year were some variation of "How did you learn to read that book?"

The children wanted to know as many options as possible so that they could tackle problems they knew they'd have when they took on new books. The struggles ahead didn't bother them. They knew that learning to read was work. But children who know that their efforts will bring the results they want will try and try. When they learn to read one book and can attribute their success to themselves, they have the desire and courage to choose another.

Leslie Funkhouser's second-grade children held regular Big Conferences specifically to share "What I Learned Today in Reading." Anyone who had learned something could tell the class, whether it was information about the eating habits of sharks, about how an author started a new paragraph for each speaker, about the grammatical difference between *better* and *best*, or about the "shun" sound for *-tion*. The children not only thought of themselves as having learning expertise, they also learned about new strategies from each other and used these solutions to expand their own repertoire. On some future day, when their own reading process didn't contain a workable option for a problem, they could turn to each other for help.

Whether students are in the primary grades or graduate school, when they regularly confer about what they do when they read, they get ideas from their peers. My graduate students, for example, share new reading strategies as they teach each other how to read research articles. Phyllis Kinzie's fourth-grade students read transitions at the ends of chapters in their Big Conferences to show how the last few words helped them anticipate the next chapter and thus improved their understanding of what lay ahead. Readers' awareness of their reading process (Hemming 1985) makes it possible for them to read the books they choose.

At the end of 1985, after my year as researcher in Phyllis Kinzie's fourth grade, I asked the children to write to me about what they do when they read and write. Darren's comments about his reading show his awareness of different strategies for different purposes and his joy when he has a book he likes.

If I'm reading an exciting book with lots of detail and adventure I read every little thing.

If I'm reading a boring book with little detail I skim mostly but still get enough in to understand what is happening.

If I'm reading for information I read it very slowly so I can get everything in my mind or on my paper.

If the book is horrible I just read the first hundred words and the last hundred words and try to make up the middle part.

Also when I'm reading I listen for new words to try using them in my own writing or talking.

Sometimes if I'm reading a good book I check the last sentence of the book and try to guess what is going to happen in the book.

Sometimes if the book is good enough I read it over and over again.

References

CRISMORE, AVON, ED. 1985. *Landscape: A State-of-the-Art Assessment of Reading Comprehension Research 1974–1984.* Bloomington, Ind.: University of Indiana.

HALE, ROBERT D. 1986. Musings. *Horn Book* 62, no. 3 (May/June).

HANSEN, JANE. 1984. First Grade Writers Pursue Reading. *1983 Fforum: Essays on Theory and Practice in the Teaching of Writing,* ed. by Patricia Stock. Montclair, N.J.: Boynton/Cook.

HARMS, JEANNE MCLAIN, AND LETTOW, LUCILLE T. 1986. Fostering Ownership of the Reading Experience. *The Reading Teacher* 42, no. 3 (December).

HEMMING, HEATHER. 1985. Reading: A Monitor for Writing. In *Breaking Ground: Teachers Relate Reading and Writing in the Elementary School,* ed. by Jane Hansen, Thomas Newkirk, and Donald Graves. Portsmouth, N.H.: Heinemann.

HOLDAWAY, DONALD. 1979. *The Foundations of Literacy.* Sydney: Ashton Scholastic.

Responsibility, Response Ability, Response

When I think of RESPONSE, I think of turtles.

Turtles slowly move ahead when they think the world around them is safe. At other times, when they fear their surroundings, turtles keep their necks in and make no progress.

Their RESPONSE ABILITY disappears.

Their RESPONSIBILITY returns when they sense it's OK to stick out their necks.

Whether we picture ourselves or our students as the turtles, we each need the nerve to confront the world in order to progress. Our students have lots to learn about writing and reading, and they'll learn it better when their heads bob up and down and side to side, filled with curiosity, than if they retreat. We also want to live in a safe world where we have the nerve to stick our necks out. Like us, our students learn most when people respond to them in a supportive way. This probably applies to most learning.

Thousands of us adult turtles fear writing and have kept our necks in for years because in the past, someone criticized us with blood-red marks and stinging comments that highlighted our errors. The response system didn't help us gain confidence. Now we're trying to teach others to write, and all we know about response is what didn't work. If we're fortunate, we're in a safe place where others support our desire to explore a new way of teaching. We want the responsibility to learn placed on our shoulders.

Gradually, we become more adept in our ability to provide supportive RESPONSE; our RESPONSE ABILITY improves. We start to feel ourselves make a 180 degree turn; we move from our position in front of the students to move among them. We give them the RESPONSIBILITY to explore new territory, and we provide the help they need. We teach. Response brings a new definition to teaching.

Responsibility Between Teacher and Students

It's still strange for me to think of myself as a responder, because for years I thought of "response" as something my students did. They responded to me. I learned to share their role, however, when I listened to writing conferences, whether the sessions involved an entire class, a small group, or two people.

At one time, the most common conference I might have listened to would have been the individual teacher-student conference. This is no longer so. In Ellen Blackburn Karelitz's class I learned the value of the all-class conference (Graves & Hansen 1984) and at Mast Way I learned the importance of the small group within a response network. Whether the gathering involved two people or more, I heard response move in all directions with everyone—teachers and students—responding to everyone else. Students learned to respond from the teachers' demonstrations.

We teach students to tell us what they know.   The children open a reading conference by telling us what they know about their book and, in so doing, gain confidence in their meaning-making ability (Cramer 1984, 253). We do as much as we can think of to bolster their self-confidence. This pledge on our part has a number of ramifications.

When we expect the students to set the stage for conferences, they start to assume some authority. The word *authority* served as the clincher for me.

Throughout the school day, teachers bolster children's sense of authority by giving them responsibilities. The entire day provides the backdrop against which writing and reading instruction happen most readily. Leslie Funkhouser says she constantly asks herself, "What do I do now that I could turn over to the students?"

Her second-grade children organize supplies for new students and make phone calls to arrange guest speakers. Pat McLure's and Ellen Blackburn Karelitz's first-grade children take attendance, lunch count, and milk count, and collect money for paperbacks and permission slips for field trips. They watch the clock, put away their materials, and begin new activities as the class schedule dictates. These students do a lot because their teachers have a basic understanding of how children learn (Vygotsky 1978, Donaldson 1976).

Adults give children supportive response when they learn to talk (e.g., de Villiers & de Villiers 1979). We strain to get the gist and respond, "You want more milk?" We assume that children want to say something meaningful and take their struggle seriously. When adults try to figure out what children want to say, youngsters try again and again. Because we know that language is an art they will refine for years, we celebrate their errors. We hear the mistakes change as the children learn some language patterns and struggle with more complex ways to make meaning. Because we support their attempts, they talk more and learn language faster than if they kept their mouths shut or their necks in.

We respond in the same way to their writing. One day Jessica read a draft about her day at a fair in Maine, and as I listened to her voice, I tried to sense what was important to her. When she finished, I told her what I heard. "You liked the oxen at the fair." Jessica, in turn, picked up on my cue and chatted about the oxen. I could tell that she liked their bells and asked a question: "What were the bells like?" She described them. By talking, Jessica became more aware of what she knows. A child must realize that she knows something in order to write. This is where writing begins.

And this is where reading begins. We respond similarly, whether the children have their own writing or the writing of another author in their hands (Hansen 1983): "Oh, you're reading *The Red Pony*. What do you think of it?" Donovan talks. The conference belongs to him, and he does the majority of the talking. I listen and comment on his message, "It's an unbelievably tragic story, isn't it?" He tells me more. We assume that the children know something and we want to know what it is. The children recognize this, because we always begin a conference by listening to their reflections about their book. We place the responsibility for generating a response on their shoulders.

It's the students' responsibility to respond to what they read, but we teach them how to respond. They acquire their response ability from us. This is the crux of response in reading. This is what we teach when we teach reading.

We also teach children to think about writing when they read, as Jan Roberts does. After Melissa, a third-grader in her class, had read *Mr. Willoughby's Christmas Tree* by Robert E. Barry, Jan asked her what she learned about writing. Melissa answered, "I like how it ended where it began."

The children respond to what they read and we support what they know. We insist that they stick out their necks, but they know we won't chop them off. The children do not come to us so we can check their comprehension. We begin with their information and build on it. They tell us what they know, we honor their knowledge, and they develop confidence in themselves as readers. Reading conferences work when we give our students/authors the authority to make two choices. They choose what books, magazines, and other materials to respond to, and they choose what, within those materials, to respond to. When we respond to them, we support their interest in reading and encourage them to read more and more.

Eventually, when we pull up a chair beside them during reading, we don't have to say a word. They start telling us what they know about their book. By our consistency, we teach them to focus on information. They learn that it's their responsibility to know something about their book, but we also learn a great deal when we listen to find out what their books mean to them. Imagine Ellen Blackburn Karelitz's surprise when Amanda told her that *The Three Bears* was about loneliness. "If Goldilocks hadn't been lonely, she wouldn't have gone in to look for someone." After we know what a book means to a student, then we can give our support to their comprehension.

We teach students to tell us what they want to learn. Leslie Funkhouser, a second-grade teacher at Mast Way, says this about response teaching: "It works if you trust kids to let you know what they need." This is a new twist on teaching for me, because when I taught, I looked in my teachers' guide and decided what to teach next. I've finally learned to meet with students to find out what they have on their agenda instead of bringing my own agenda to the conference. This was a hard step for me to take, but I saw how the teachers at Mast Way set up the environment their students needed to feel free to request information and help.

The teachers asked "real" questions, questions to which they didn't know the answers. In time, the students did likewise. Such questions permit an exchange between us and the children that is very different from the "discussions" I used to convene. I would call children together to check their comprehension, to administer an oral test. I do it differently now, and my change in attitude about questions started with writing, where most of what I'm learning about reading began. I'll never forget the day I started to realize the difference.

I sat in a first-grade class and heard one of the students read:

> My little brother is three years old. His name is Jeremy. He plays with his blocks and trucks all day long.

During the response session, a child asked, "What's your little brother's name?" The author didn't know what to say. Finally, he said, "That information was in my writing. You should have listened." I shrank. That kind of question insults the writer. But I had asked that kind of question for years. That kind of question also insults the reader. I wish that one of my students years ago had had the nerve to say, "That information was in the story. I just read it."

Children's other questions showed me alternatives. "What else does your little brother do?" "How do you feel about him?" "Why did you write about your brother?" "Will you write some more about him?" Children ask similar questions when they respond to another author's writing, as when they responded to Sendak's *Where the Wild Things Are* with, "Why do you suppose Max was acting like a wild thing?" "Do you think his mother doesn't give him any supper sometimes?" Students look at a piece of writing as a springboard for discussion, a take-off point for learning.

Their attitude toward reading changes when they respond to reading as writing. They treat the books they read in much the same way they do their own writing. As Judy Velasquez, a sixth-grade teacher in Healdsburg, California, explains it, "My students start to look at reading as writing, rather than as a series of questions to be answered."

At first, some students look at us with surprise when we initiate this kind of response system. We catch them off guard with our honest questions—questions to which we don't know the answers. However, when they realize that we really do want to find out what they think is important, they start to share with us. We take the learner's stance and they teach. We treat them as authorities.

The notion of "authority" comes from other disciplines besides writing, including the world of cognitive psychology, where I began my study of reading for my PhD. I studied prior knowledge (Hansen and Hubbard 1984) because readers' prior knowledge affects their comprehension. When I couple that research with writing, in which we teach students to exercise their voices and listen carefully to what the author has to say, I see more clearly the influence of prior knowledge on readers. The more our students know, the more they can learn from their books. The more we think our students know, the more we expect them to learn; the more they think they know, the more they think they can learn. Teacher expectations exert great influence on student learning.

We expect children to understand the books they choose, which may include titles we haven't read ourselves. We ask questions and they must be able to explain so we can understand. If we've read the book, then the discussion begins beyond the exchange of information with what the book meant to both of us, the student and the teacher. Because of the difference in our ages, the book most likely meant something different to each of us, and we can both question each other (Tchudi 1985). It's this atmosphere of question-asking that gives students the opportunity to tell us what they want to learn, to ask for explanations, to ask for help, as Derek did one day with me.

He had chosen to read from a book about turtles and came to me saying, "This doesn't make sense." He pointed to a paragraph about the amount of pressure it takes to crack a tortoise's shell. I asked him what he didn't understand and then I explained it.

However, students don't always ask for help. One day when researcher Tom Romano met with Matt and Randy, they talked about *Soup* by Robert Peck. The boys thought Rob had hit a nurse with a ball because they thought that "throwing the ball" back to the other person in conversation meant throwing a real ball. Romano didn't come to this session with a list of questions to ask the boys. He came to find out what they knew. They talked and he listened. When he realized that they misunderstood the words, he explained. He taught.

We teach what our students need and/or want to know about their books. Our goal in reading instruction is not to get our students to value the same information we would from a book about turtles or to get them to interpret *Where the Red Fern Grows*, by Wilson Rawls, the same way we would. We read for different purposes than they do and we understand books at a different level. They respect our additional knowledge and often seek it. However, sometimes we can't help.

One day first-grader Amanda came to me with a question: "I know the horse is friendly and the goat isn't but I don't understand why they become friends." I hadn't read the book, so I asked some questions. Amanda couldn't explain the story well enough for me to figure out why the two animals became friends. Amanda sat. I suggested that she read the book to someone. Amanda continued to sit. Finally she said, "I'll read the whole book to Stephanie. Then me and her can talk about it." Amanda determines what she wants to know and gets help not only from us but from the twenty-five other responders in the classroom.

Responsibility Among Students

The bulk of the response in the reading program is among students, rather than between teacher and students. Opportunities for learning multiply when the students share with and respond to each other. Their responsibilities are similar to those between teacher and student. They respond to what each knows and teach each other in the same settings as the teacher—in small groups, in Big Conferences that involve the entire class, and in pairs.

The students respond to what their classmates know. The Mast Way teachers learned the value of response among students in their teachers' writing group. The feedback they experienced among themselves kept their writing going. As Pam Bradley said, "Without the group, I wouldn't write."

Similarly, for the children, response among themselves keeps their writing and reading going. When a small group convenes, children may share either a piece of their own writing or something written by a professional. Someone may share a draft of her own and someone else Judith Viorst's *Rosie and Michael*. They come to share writing, anyone's writing (Hansen 1983). They may read the entire selection to the group or parts of it, or tell about it. The responsibility for providing a response, in this situation, rests with the group.

They listen and comment: "I liked the poem you used for your lead" or "I learned that Border collies herd sheep. I thought they were just pets" or "I'm glad S. E. Hinton decided to have Tex turn out OK. He had a tough time, with his dad being gone all the time." But isolated comments like these do not comprise an enlightening discussion. Phyllis Kinzie also taught her fourth-grade students to "piggyback" comments on each other. She worked with them on how to take body cues from each other so the conference could flow without people raising hands and being called on.

These group conferences can be quite long if four or more children participate, but often just one child wants to share, so a group meets for that person's sake. One day Chad, Randy, Marc, and Nathan met because Randy had read a book about deer. He started by telling what he learned from the author, and then his friends, their interest piqued, asked him questions. Randy proceeded to tell them a lot about deer and their strategies for escaping wolves. Randy's friends met to learn from him and they did.

In general, students respond to each other, to both the information shared and, on a more basic level, the person who shared. Sometimes we fear that they will criticize each other, but this seldom happens because the students have learned what kind of response they want to their own writing and they want others to respond similarly when they share a book. They share books they like and want others to respond to their enthusiasm just as professional authors do.

We learn a great deal about response from professional authors. Virginia Woolf (1932) wrote, "If you criticise first, you prevent yourself from getting the fullest possible value from what you read. But if you open your mind as widely as possible, then signs of fineness, from the twist and turn of the first sentences, will bring you into the presence of a human being unlike any other." When children share their books, they often read aloud sections that are especially memorable to them. If they meet to share a book everyone in the group has read, they find that favorite sections vary.

We expect this variance. Authors hope their writing appeals to a wide audience. They know that many different kinds of people sit in the audience and that they will find varying significance in their work. Author Jane Yolen (1985) tells us, "there is no real story on the page, only that which is created between the writer and the reader. Just as the writer brings a lifetime to the creation of the tale, so the reader carries along a different lifetime with which to recreate it. Even the author may reread her own story days, weeks, months later and understand it on another level. . . . We bring to tales that most complex of constructs—ourselves. And we *take* from them what we need. It is as true with the writer as the reader."

We teach children to do what the professional authors suggest. Students share their individual creation of one story and come away with an enriched understanding of the book because their friends have thought of extensions beyond the story they would never have thought of. First-grader Daniel put it succinctly, "Of course Scott understood the story differently than me. He's *lived* in Alaska."

Students teach each other. On some occasions readers call specific friends together to satisfy a certain need. One day third-grader Nathan wrote about his move and called together a few friends who had also moved. In time, we hear children open some of their sessions with a request for a certain kind of help. "I'd like suggestions for a title" or "I don't understand the ending" or "I want to find out what each of you thinks is the funniest part." We help children recognize situations in which they might benefit from others.

I initially watched students teach each other in Ellen Blackburn Karelitz's first grade. These beginning readers sought help with the words they didn't know. Ellen realized that they needed to get help in order to learn to read their books, so she taught them whom to ask for assistance. Sometimes they chose to read books written by class members and asked the author for help. At other times they chose a book a class member had read to the class and knew that their friend could help them. Overall, the children sought to work with students who knew something they didn't know. Because they could get help from many sources, their chances for learning increased.

At Mast Way where the research project involved classrooms at various grade levels, the children not only asked classmates for help, they sought help from students at other grade levels. Some teachers worked out a system of regular meetings between their students and students in other classes, while other teachers felt comfortable with a more free-flowing system, in which students went to other classrooms when they knew they could get better response there than in their own class. Because of the sharing among the teachers and classrooms, everyone became aware of students' areas of expertise—who would confer about Porsches, for example. At other times, a young advanced student could learn how to use an index from an older student. Students started to look beyond their classroom walls for help, and opportunities opened to them.

Besides the specific help, the students gave each other the incentive to stay on-task. Their number-one role was to provide support. Whether children met alone with the teacher, in small groups with each other, alone with a friend, or with an entire class, they all knew the bottom line for every conference—the bottom line for teachers of all ages: The reader wants to read tomorrow.

Responsibility to Self

When four third-grade children read *Annie and the Old One* by Miska Miles, Amy's response differed from that of the other children. She was both happy and sad about the ending, happy because Annie understood more about why her grandmother had to die and sad because her own grandmother had died the previous fall. Amy never realized how much she loved her own grandmother until she died. Such personal connections with books help reading become and remain a special pursuit for each child. Children learn to explain their responses, and their friends learn to honor their interpretations. Amy's friends wanted to know more about her grandmother and how Amy felt. They talked about the confused feelings that surround death, something most of them had not experienced.

These children have an interdependent definition of independence. They know they need associates to enrich their own stories (Weiss 1986). Part of their responsibility to themselves urges them to ask others for response. They start to realize their need for co-workers in writing when various friends respond differently to their drafts. The meanings their classmates create continue to reflect a wide span of personal experience when they respond to a final draft by a professional. The notion that reading, like writing, involves creating a personal meaning becomes a reality when we start to look at reading as writing. Teachers feel this when they share books.

In one of the workshops I conducted in Calgary, Alberta, the teachers each brought a book they liked. One teacher shared *The Old Man and the Sea* by Hemingway and said that when she read it in high school she had personally identified with it. That was the first time she had responded to a book, and she remembered her astonishment: "This is what reading is all about!"

Teachers in my graduate reading classes tell similar stories, especially in relation to poetry. Invariably, several teachers in each class say that their teachers taught them to dislike poetry. When they read poems in our reading course, they say, "This is the first time I've ever been told by a teacher to read a poem for myself."

Our belief in whether students should believe in themselves or not shows when we respond to our students. We can decide to support their efforts, or we can decide not to and weaken their self-confidence. In the following poem, we all recognize ourselves in the actions of both teachers. May we strive to be more like the one than the other.

The little boy
by Helen E. Buckley

Once a little boy went to school.
He was quite a little boy.
And it was quite a big school.
But when the little boy
Found that he could go to his room
By walking right in from the door outside,
He was happy.
And the school did not seem
Quite so *big* any more.

One morning,
When the little boy had been in school awhile,
The teacher said:
"Today we are going to make a picture."
"Good!" thought the little boy.
He *liked* to make pictures.
He could make all kinds:
Lions and tigers,
Chickens and cows,
Trains and boats—
And he took out his box of crayons
And began to draw.

But the teacher said: "Wait!
It is not time to begin!"
And she waited until everyone looked ready.

"Now," said the teacher,
"We are going to make flowers."
"Good!" thought the little boy,
He *liked* to make flowers,
And he began to make beautiful ones
With his pink and orange and blue crayons.

But the teacher said, "Wait!
And I will show you how."
And she drew a flower on the blackboard.
It was red, with a green stem.
"There," said the teacher,
"Now you may begin."

The little boy looked at the teacher's flower.
Then he looked at his own flower.
He liked *his* flower better than the teacher's.
But he did not say this,
He just turned his paper over
And made a flower like the teacher's.
It was red, with a green stem.

On another day,
When the little boy had opened
The door from the outside all by himself,
The teacher said:
"Today we are going to make something with clay."
"Good!" thought the little boy,
He *liked* clay.
He could make all kinds of things with clay:
Snakes and snowmen,
Elephants and mice,
Cars and trucks—
And he began to pull and pinch
His ball of clay.

But the teacher said:
"Wait! It is not time to begin!"
And she waited until everyone looked ready.

"Now," said the teacher,
"We are going to make a dish."
"Good!" thought the little boy,
He *liked* to make dishes,
And he began to make some
That were all shapes and sizes.

But the teacher said, "Wait!
And I will show you how."
And she showed everyone how to make
One deep dish.
"There," said the teacher,
"Now you may begin."

The little boy looked at the teacher's dish.
Then he looked at his own.
He *liked his* dishes better than the teacher's.
But he did not say this.
He just rolled his clay into a big ball again,
And made a dish like the teacher's.
It was a deep dish.

And pretty soon
The little boy learned to wait,
And to watch,
And to make things just like the teacher.
And pretty soon
He didn't make things of his own anymore.

Then it happened
That the little boy and his family
Moved to another house,
In another city,
And the little boy
Had to go to another school.

This school was even Bigger
Than this other one,
And there was no door from the outside
Into his room.
He had to go up some big steps,
And walk down a long hall
To get to his room.

And the very first day
He was there,
The teacher said:
"Today we are going to make a picture."
"Good!" thought the little boy,

And he waited for the teacher
To tell him what to do.
But the teacher didn't say anything.
She just walked around the room.

When she came to the little boy
She said, "Don't you want to make a picture?"
"Yes," said the little boy,
"What are we going to make?"
"I don't know until you make it," said the teacher.
"*How* shall I make it?" asked the little boy.
"Why, any way you like," said the teacher.
"And any color?" asked the little boy.
"Any color," said the teacher,
"If everyone made the same picture,
And used the same colors,
How would I know who made what,
And which was which?"
"I don't know," said the little boy.
And he began to make pink and orange and blue flowers.

He liked his new school . . .
Even if it didn't have a door
Right in from the outside!

References

CRAMER, BARBARA B. 1984. Bequest of Wings: Three Readers and Special Books. *Language Arts* 61, no. 3 (March).

DE VILLIERS, JILL, AND DE VILLIERS, PETER. 1982. *Early Language.* Cambridge, Mass.: Harvard University Press.

DONALDSON, MARGARET. 1976. *Children's Minds.* New York: Holt, Rinehart, and Winston.

GRAVES, DONALD, AND HANSEN, JANE. 1984. The Author's Chair. *Language Arts* 60, no. 8 (November/December).

HANSEN, JANE. 1983. Authors Respond to Authors. *Language Arts* 60, no. 8 (November/December).

HANSEN, JANE, AND HUBBARD, RUTH. 1984. Poor Readers Can Draw Inferences. *The Reading Teacher* 37, no. 7 (March).

TCHUDI, SUSAN. 1985. The Roots of Response to Literature. *Language Arts* 62, no. 5 (September).

VYGOTSKY, L. S. 1978. *Mind and Society: The Development of Higher Psychological Process,* trans. and ed. by M. Cole, V. John-Steiner, S. Scribner, and E. Souberman. Cambridge, Mass.: Harvard University Press.

WEISS, JERRY. 1986. Writers and Readers: The Literary Connection. *The Reading Teacher* (April).

WOOLF, VIRGINIA. 1932. How Should One Read a Book? *The Second Common Reader.* New York: Harcourt Brace.

Structure | Six

Reading/writing classrooms are tightly structured. They must be. The classroom is full of decision makers, many of whom may be inexperienced and need guidelines. To complicate matters, many of us are new at this kind of teaching and don't know how to organize ourselves. We feel certain about only one thing: The classroom must be orderly.

It's hard to see how reading/writing classrooms function, because the teachers have established an inner structure very different from the exostructure I always used when I taught. You could hear my management plan when I said, "It's time for reading. Put your math away. . . . I see Fred's eyes. . . . John's row is ready. . . . Thank you. In reading today, the Gobots will do workbook pages 35 and 36. . . ." I then proceeded to outline the work of each group. I didn't stop to think about the importance to an independent learner of establishing a personal work schedule, which allows learners the time they need to accomplish their goals. If they're to feel responsible for their accomplishments, they must have control over their work time.

We help them gain this control when we work among them rather than expect them to work alone while we spend our time elsewhere. When we interact with them, we teach them how to interact with each other in a systematic way. In time, they can rely on each other and we can conduct conferences without interruptions. Further, as they become more adept at making decisions about their work, they can work independently with a better sense of accomplishment than when they relied on us to evaluate all their work.

The Teacher Moves Among the Students

Teachers are the most powerful people in the classroom, and how we physically position ourselves there tells our students how we use our strength. During work time, for example, we have at least three choices. We can: 1) sit behind our desks, 2) work with groups, or 3) move among the students. The teachers in this book moved among their students more than I used to when I taught. The work time is important enough to warrant our presence.

We demonstrate our sense of authority.   When we confer with a student, the student is the authority on the printed material before him. We support the child's efforts and help him with his concerns. At the point of help, we assume authority. First, however, we demonstrate our value of the student and his work. Observers can see our attentiveness without hearing a word we say when we stop beside our students. The children watch us like hawks and figure out our agenda fast. Our genuine interest in a child's work shows when we make our decisions about whether to let others interrupt a conference or not.

In the following example, researcher Lorri Neilsen (1985) shows the respect she holds for David when other children tried to barge in on his conference.

Silent partners

David and I sat at a table in his classroom to have a conference on his story about him, Matt, and two young girls riding off into the woods on an ATC and a snowmobile. . . .

We moved our chairs together and David read. . . .

We heard a voice from behind. "Can I go to the library?" the voice said. David looked at me. I was looking at the paper. The voice grew louder. "Can I go to the library?" The question was obviously directed at me. I looked at David and smiled, pointing at his paper. . . .

Again the voice: "Can I go to the library?" Again, David's eyes. . . .

Again, I pointed and he turned back to the page. . . .

We were both into it now. . . .

Suddenly we heard, "Will you read this for me?" Process interruptus was back. This time David didn't even look at where the voice was coming from. He looked at me. . . .

I pointed to the sentence we were working on. He looked down at the paper. . . . The voice behind David and me grew louder, but we carried on. . . .

I heard one voice say to another, "They won't answer you," and David and I smiled.

Interruptions shatter the respect for authority we want to build. They are not easy to ignore, but ignoring them is much easier than having to live with the consequences of not ignoring them. If we permit someone to interrupt David's teaching session, he starts to think that his knowledge is not center stage. He will question his own sense of authority, and his respect for himself and other students will have a hard time growing. However, when we focus on David, our actions tell the other students that we value their knowledge and will also listen to them.

We don't let "process interruptus" interrupt our session with David because if he can't share his work, then we cannot help him. We cannot teach. However, regardless of how seriously we resolve to eliminate interruptions, we often say, "Fred interrupts constantly. Jennifer always interrupts. Becky interrupts whenever she has a chance. . . ." Eventually, we hear our own words and realize their nonsense.

Children don't interrupt; they try to interrupt. Only if we stop listening to the child at hand do they succeed in interrupting their classmates. We not only think of this in terms of writing conferences but also when we teach reading. The teacher does not permit interruptions when she helps readers choose books, decide on reasons for working on a book, explore ways to reach their goals, or think of some reading-related writing. The students' thoughts are important. In contrast, I taught my students to listen to me. Without analyzing my teaching, I propagated a disrespect for authority.

There's no way I could have known everything. I knew some things, but by presenting myself as an overall authority I set myself up to be knocked down by my students whenever I erred. We now want our students to learn to recognize the strengths of authorities and permit their weaknesses. (See chapter 2 in Perl and Wilson 1986.) We demonstrate this by recognizing strengths and expecting weaknesses ourselves.

We demonstrate how to respond. When we respond to our students, we use a predictable pattern that they can internalize and use when they respond to each other. Teachers will vary in how they structure their responses, but all use a consistent variation on these three areas:

1. They find out what the student is doing right now, such as "Oh, you're reading a Byrd Baylor book. Please tell me about it." Or "I heard you telling Jamie about your *Clifford* book. Please read three pages to me."
2. They find out what preceded where the student is now. They may want to know why the student chose the book or want an explanation of an earlier part of the story.
3. They find out what the student plans to do next. Tony, a third grader, told me he wants to learn how to read more big words and Becky, a fifth grader, told me she wants to learn how to read in her brain better. She wants time to practice silent reading.

Teachers teach the children their format in various ways—within Big Conferences, small group response sessions, or individual conferences. Some teachers start with all three response systems at once so they will reinforce each other. Regardless, the teacher designs the pattern she wants to try and establishes it in her classroom.

If we begin with a demonstration during the Big Conference, we acknowledge the newness of response, share a book, and ask for the kind of response we have decided to seek. The students also share with each other and respond according to the same format they used when they responded to us. The response format gives students slots to fill. They know what to say, and the person who shares knows what the others will say. This predictable structure provides safety and simplicity.

The teacher who establishes a repetitive format will have an orderly classroom faster than the teacher whose students don't know exactly what to say. Teachers may begin with only one element in a response pattern until the students can use that portion without hitches. In some classrooms, by the fourth week of school, the students as yet only say, "The most interesting part to me was. . . ." Eventually, teacher and students will expand the response format, but the initial structure helps to establish a pattern the children can follow from the start, without teacher guidance. Even if we only demonstrate one kind of comment, however, there's always the child who might criticize another child. When this happens, we respond immediately: "Tina, no one responded to me that way when I shared my book, and if someone had I'd have felt awful. I don't respond to you that way, either. We all expect everyone to receive each other's work, not criticize it." Then we immediately return supportive attention to the reader at hand. "I forgot where we were. Let's see. Moira said she had never thought of a person fitting into a dragon's ear, and who else said something?" The children recap and go on.

Students need to hear the teacher approach all of them similarly, and the teacher needs to explain to them what she is doing. She listens while they respond to each other, helps them learn to do what she does, and then leaves them to confer without her while she responds to others.

We demonstrate the discipline of work.   When we extend the notion of a structure beyond the format of the conferences into overall work time, we demonstrate the discipline of work. Each teacher has her own system of organizing the day—whether to start or end with the Big Conference, how to schedule small groups, when to set aside the time to read, and how to incorporate other components. She decides on a format she'd like to try and uses it daily. If it doesn't work and needs to be altered, she shares her concerns with the students. Together they decide on an alternative so that everyone knows what to expect the next day. Learners need to be able to count on their work time.

Leslie Funkhouser's second graders know that reading begins first thing in the morning (Hubbard 1986). Leslie doesn't announce it. When the children enter the room they start to read. They may read alone or with one or two friends. After they're read four books, which may take one day or several days, they write a response to one of them which they may exchange with friends and Ms. Funkhouser. Or, they may write as they go through a book, when something strikes them as interesting. Once a week, each student meets with a small group according to a schedule they control.

The children divide themselves into five nonpermanent groups and decide which group will meet each day, allowing for one group per day each week. A student goes around with a clipboard each Friday to arrange the following week. Leslie's role is to have a book to share and to join as many groups as she wants during the week and for as long as she wants each day. Leslie may bring either a children's book or an adult book to share, most often a children's book. The children can conduct their groups without her, but she often wants to hear them interact, listen to particular children share, or ask questions of certain students. During the group meeting, she records the book titles the children share, the comments specific children offer, and the other children's responses to these offerings.

After lunch, the class assembles for the Big Conference where one child shares. At the end of the Big Conference Leslie addresses the children for the first time all day. There has been no reason for her to do so during the entire reading class or writing class (from recess until noon). They know what to do.

They have a better notion of how to plan their work time than I did when I was their age. The discipline of work time became especially real to me this year while I was on sabbatical at home. Our house is my husband's workplace and he has a schedule. He gets up at a certain time, follows a morning routine, and begins work at his own regularly prescribed time. His system enables him to get his work done. I've devised a similar system for myself, but when I don't seem to accomplish much, I fret about my work plan and devise a new one.

Teachers help their students become productive by providing a work period within which the pupils can plan their own reading. This allows children to struggle with ways to use their time as independent workers do and gradually develop a work plan. They begin to feel the sense of order in the classroom that results from everyone knowing what they will do throughout the day. Each child can explain his or her own schedule. In addition, they know how the teacher will spend her time—when she is accessible and more importantly, when they are allotted time on her schedule.

The Students Work Together

Although the network of help within the classroom seems complicated, in a sense only two things happen. The students learn how to respond to others, and they learn how to initiate sessions so that others can respond to them (Mayher and Brause 1986). They sit in both chairs—they plan the roles of both helper and helpee—and the insights they gain in each chair help them when they switch positions.

Students share their excitement.   They share their discoveries with individuals, small groups, and the class; and the other children respond with support. When a student tells the class he liked *The Wind in the Willows* because of the funny things Toad said, it's their responsibility to say something like, "I also thought Toad was an interesting creature. I thought his clothes were so funny." The ability to respond is the capacity to support the reader's thoughts. But the children can give this kind of response only if they have listened carefully to the story.

If someone gives a generic response such as, "I like what you said about your book," the child on the Author's Chair becomes suspicious and wonders if the responder even listened to his description of Toad. This is similar to what happens when children share their writing. They know that a comment like, "I thought your story sounded nice," doesn't help them with their writing. Thus, they try not to give global responses during writing and, similarly, they learn to give specific comments during reading. There is an element of surprise within the response sessions. We never know what a child will say about a book. That's why all of us—teachers and students—can come to the sessions to learn.

The students ask each other for help.   The kind of help they seek is crucial. They seldom ask each other for help on an assignment the teacher has given because we don't give many. If we did, their problem-solving strategies would be very different, because whoever determines the assignment must evaluate the ongoing process of doing it (Watson and Young 1986). In other words, when students do tasks for us, we are the best helpers. But when students choose what to read, determine why they want to read it, and decide whether they've met their goal, they know where they're going and can explain to someone else what kind of help they need.

First graders often get more excited about pronouncing the words in their books than about the content. Jeannine bounces because she's worked on her book for five days and has finally read the entire volume without asking the teacher for help with a single word. Many children helped her with words and she can tell you who taught her *were* and who taught her *there*. She asked quick questions of her peers and received on-the-spot help. Other readers make different requests.

When Jon wants help with specific information, he approaches a friend who uses the library a lot. "I can't find out how much baby blue whales weigh. Can you help me?" His friend takes him down the hall and explains the card catalogue while he finds two possible sources. On another day, Jon tries again and can figure out the Dewey numbers but still needs his friend's help within the card file. Gradually, he becomes an independent information-seeker who can, in time, help another child. The chain extends.

The busyness of children working, sharing their joys and asking for help, involves more movement than we usually picture. As we get used to a mood of activity we become suspicious of repeated scenes of quiet workers. We think:

"Aren't they trying to figure out new things?"

"Have they all chosen such easy work they have no questions?"

"Isn't anyone excited about anything?"

But we must remember that one of the reasons we encourage interaction is to allow the children to learn how other students tackle a problem. When they have built up a repertoire of strategies, they can solve more and more routine problems on their own.

The Students Work Alone

Our goal is not that children should work alone at all times, but that they know when to work alone and when to go for help. As our concern for order implies, we worry that students who interact won't get their work done, but this does not have to happen. One of the strugglers in Leslie Funkhouser's second grade read sixteen books between December 16 and January 23. That's almost a book a day when you count the number of days left after the holiday break. That young man worked hard and got a lot accomplished because he knows how and when to solicit help.

The children don't want someone to tell them what to do, and similarly, they learn not to tell others what to do. We teach them to approach their problems in reading just as they grapple with rough spots in their writing. They ask their friends to help them generate options so that they can make their own decision about what to do. They negotiate the meaning of a text or, if their problem is word recognition, they might ask, "Do you know this word?" If yes, then, "Don't tell me. What are some ways I can figure it out?" They want to know possibilities so they can try them out on their own next time.

This cuts down on the number of requests for help from the teacher. Because we want children to become self-sufficient, we fight the urge to arrange for other adults to help in our rooms during writing and reading. Yes, we could probably always use more ears, but we don't want the children to see reading and writing as times when they need more adult help than they do in other subjects. We want them to rely on each other and on themselves. We want them to develop self-discipline. But most of us have never been in classrooms where students worked for hours on end without the teacher addressing the class.

The scene is especially difficult to visualize because the classroom structure is an endoskeleton, analogous to our bodies. Without the bones we have only softness, an amorphous shape. With the bones we have a system in which every part has its function, does it, and relies on the other parts to do theirs. The system works, but pressure or a sharp blow can damage it. Then everyone compensates for a period of time until the structure is again in working order.

References

HANSEN, JANE. 1986. Organizing Student Learning. In *Dynamics of Language Learning: Research in the Language Arts*, ed. by James Squire. Urbana, Ill.: NCTE and ERIC Clearinghouse on Reading and Communication Skills.

HUBBARD, RUTH. 1986. Structure Encourages Independence in Reading and Writing. *Reading Teacher* 40, no. 2 (November).

MAYHER, JOHN, AND BRAUSE, RITA. 1986. Learning Through Teaching: Is Your Classroom Like Your Grandmother's? *Language Arts* 63, no. 6 (October).

NEILSEN, LORRI. 1985. Silent Partners. In *Teachers and Learners*. Durham, N.H.: Writing Process Laboratory, University of New Hampshire.

PERL, SONDRA, AND WILSON, NANCY. 1986. *Through Teachers' Eyes: Portraits of Writing Teachers at Work*. Portsmouth, N.H.: Heinemann.

WATSON, KEN, AND YOUNG, BOB. 1986. Discourse for Learning in the Classroom. *Language Arts* 63, no. 2 (February).

Community |

Seven

The Mast Way teachers became a closer community during the course of the research project. They knew each other before the project, but because they shared their out-of-school interests in the writing they brought to their weekly writing sessions, they became better acquainted. As Phyllis Kinzie, one of the teachers, said after the first semester, "We met away from school. We focused on nonschool topics and we got to know each other as people for the first time."

They felt the power of peer support. Phyllis continued, "You told us we had to support each other. Well, not exactly, but you didn't give us any alternative." The teachers wonder now how much change would have occurred in their teaching if they hadn't written together. The group gave them the courage to take risks, to fail, and to experience the process of learning a new way to teach. They could learn in this climate, and they wanted to create similar networks in their classrooms.

A Supportive Community

Readers and writers support each other.   We begin to create a community when we teach writers and readers to believe in one another. It's often difficult to envision the importance of a network of concerned coworkers when we initiate a reading program. But it's also difficult to imagine how to teach children to support each other until we can support our coworkers. Only then can we learn to support our students. It's embarrassingly hard to learn how to support learning. A writing coordinator told me that his most difficult task is teaching his teachers to approach a child's writing with these thoughts, "I know I'll find something to support." Once we feel confident in our ability to support our students, we can teach them to support each other in both writing and reading.

This may be an even harder task in reading than in writing. As reading teachers, we haven't always seen our role as one of finding out what students have heard in a piece of writing—in the story or book they have read. Instead, we have asked questions to find out whether they found what "experts" thought they should have found. The basic assumption underlying the idea of community, however, is our belief that the student will create meaning that others will find interesting. Something different from everyone else.

We ourselves begin to sense this when we share reading with our own peers. We can get to know each other when we share the books we read. When teachers in my own classes at the University of New Hampshire share books from their personal libraries—mysteries, biographies, detective stories, poetry—they learn about each other. They find out why someone likes a certain book, and this helps them to know that person better. Personal attachments become the hallmark of community. Other components—Time, Choice, Response, and Structure—are sterile without Community.

The Community adds zest to the classroom. It's not a method; it's a life. When I show the videotape from Mast Way on Time and Choice (Hubbard and Whitney 1986), the first response I often get is, "The children look happy." At first that caught me off guard. Happiness had not been our goal when we made the tape, but it comes through in the transactions in the classrooms. This is not to say that a community does not have bad days. We continually experience highs and lows, but we work hard to keep the climate relatively stable.

When one member of the class holds back, we wonder about ourselves and whether there's something we should be doing differently. If we haven't extended an invitation to the children to join a community similar to the one to which we belong, we consider this. Those of us who haven't written and read with our peers probably won't know how to extend an invitation to our children, or know what to create. However, when we experience encouragement, we know our lives become richer than when we stay within ourselves. We look at the class and wonder why the child in question doesn't know that the class is curious about what he reads.

We know that everyone is an interesting person. We start with this assumption: everyone knows something that others will find interesting. Background knowledge, important for comprehension, differs for all. When we as teachers stop thinking of our own knowledge as paramount and recognize that our pupils have also had worthwhile experiences, then we can begin. A community is composed of individuals, each of whom has a unique contribution to make. The supportive community begins with the teacher's belief that each child has something to share.

The teacher tries to find out what that something might be. We're curious, interested. Students sense our genuine respect for them. More importantly, they also learn what it feels like when their friends show interest in them, as the Mast Way teachers learned in their own group. When the teachers met for their second writing session, they all read a draft aloud to a partner and used the support system we demonstrated. They shook with nervousness, but at the end of that session, Pat McLure sighed, "Everyone was so supportive." Trust took hold and grew.

When trust reigns, we can take the risks necessary to try new things, as Eric did one day in fourth grade. Eric had practiced a dramatic oral reading of a section of *Charlotte's Web* for a Scout badge. He asked Phyllis if he could read it to the class. The children heard each other share books every day, but no one had ever read with the pauses and inflections Eric used. When he had finished, the class sat silent and impressed. Phyllis broke the silence with, "Marvelous." Then the class broke into applause.

When the teacher teaches the class to hold the support net securely, children try their wings. Sarla will try to use dialogue for the first time, or Dylan will tell the class how a science fiction story reminded him of a poem the teacher read two months ago. When they make original connections that widen their comprehension, they take risks. The children may wonder what others will think of their unique associations, but if they are afraid to try something new, they can't learn new things.

A Diverse Community

The wider the range of support available to learners, the greater their chances for progress. As teachers, we learn to foster diversity because diverse thinking promotes challenges that push our students' and our own learning. Children who see their entire school as their reading/writing community know that they have many resources available to them. The children I've worked with since 1981 challenged my prior teaching; I can no longer segregate children into top, middle, and bottom reading groups.

We foster diversity. In a classroom where students have diverse skills, abilities, and interests, there are many opportunities for the children to learn from and help each other. As teachers, we teach the children to expect, appreciate, and benefit from differences. They need to know who can generate good titles, who knows how to read which book, and who can help them find information they need.

The children help each other learn, not out of a sense of duty but because they know each other as people. Reading helps this happen.

It did in Phyllis Kinzie's fourth grade. She thought about the teachers' community and wanted to generate more of a community feeling in her class, not because the children didn't already support each other, but because she wanted more of a good thing. She decided to do it via oral reading in large group sessions. It worked.

When I interviewed the fourth graders about reading, John said he learned most about reading in the Big Conference, because he learned about the other kids in the class. He found out what they thought about various books and weighed their comments against his own likes and dislikes. At the same time, because he knew the other students, he could predict whether he might like their book choices. He went beyond the content of someone's comment to consider who made the comment, which helped him interpret their information. When we know a person well, we increase the chance that we will understand both what they say and what we think about it.

Our interpretive community flavors our insights as we read. Children think about who they'll share with—one other person, a small, hand-picked group, or the entire class. They read with these possibilities in mind. When they share, they confirm their guesses about what their friends will think. They also learn that others generate ideas they might not think of.

In the sessions, students often generate challenges. Someone doesn't understand or doesn't agree with the presenter. One December in first grade, Jen shared "Al," a story from a phonetic reader. The children were active in their criticism. "Why would the man hit Al with a mop because he ate a hot dog?" Kim wanted to know. Jen responded with another question, "And why would the man even have a mop in the middle of the desert?" Adrienne tried to handle that one. "Well, maybe he happened to have a mop in his hand, wandered into the desert, and got lost." "You could change that story so it would make sense," Dwayne suggested. "You could have the man get mad at Al for eating his lunch, then go home to get the mop to hit him with."

Collectively, the children pursue an issue. They move away from teacher-centered sessions and raise their own concerns, discussing them back and forth until their understanding has gone beyond what it was a few minutes earlier.

Although we want the community to challenge its members, sometimes this doesn't happen, as Leslie Funkhouser discovered. Because she didn't think one of her second-grade students was being stretched or challenged enough by her peers, she wondered if the student might benefit from response in a third-grade class. After the child shared her writing in a third-grade room, others followed. Children from other classes at Mast Way also began to share beyond their homerooms—not only their own writing but the work of professionals—when the diversity in their own class wasn't broad enough.

Phyllis Kinzie's students read picture books to their own fourth-grade class and talked about how the books meant something different to them now than when they were younger. On succeeding days they were able to appreciate and stretch younger readers who read those books to them.

On another occasion, when Jan Roberts read a Laura Ingalls Wilder book to her third-grade class, the section about making maple sugar reminded her of a story one of her former students had written. She invited the student, Kenny, to read his maple sugar story to her current class. Similarly, Tim, a student from two years before, shared his vast knowledge of Abraham Lincoln through the mouth of a puppet he had made. When teachers remember a student's expertise a year or two later, they evidently value it. And the children now know something new about Kenny and Tim and can use them as resources if they need to.

The teachers also read in other classrooms, from both trade books and their own writing. Marion Stevens, a second-grade teacher known for her ability to read well, read to a third-grade class. Phyllis Kinzie, a fourth-grade teacher known for her knowledge of children's literature, read to a second-grade class. The children value the expertise of their peers, other children in the school, and their own teacher, but they also value that of other teachers. When these teachers share, they want to know what the children think of the books. The children assume that regardless of who reads, anyone who shares will ask the listeners to tell what they heard. Everyone wants to know what everyone else thinks.

Diversity pushes our thinking.   This community feeling that developed among teachers and students at Mast Way contradicts the traditional practices of classroom and/or reading teachers (Heath 1983). More than 90 percent of the primary teachers in this country and approximately 70 percent of the upper-elementary teachers do not believe in the community concept the research teachers developed in their writing classrooms. Instead, they continue to divide students into groups according to achievement level as I did for all of the twelve years I taught in elementary schools. Yet it took only three months in Ellen Blackburn Karelitz's classroom to convince me that there was another way.

Her children didn't meet in top, middle, and bottom groups for writing. I saw how much the children learned when they worked with a diverse group, rather than in a group, where, for example, everyone was a poor reader. We watched the children when they chose others to read with. Poor students elected to spend some of their time with better readers. This Ellen chose to foster rather than squelch. I saw how her understanding of writing influenced the way she taught reading.

Our grouping patterns in reading can support or contradict what we teach in writing. Children who write with good writers consider themselves learners, and this self-concept is reinforced during reading if the children again work with good learners. However, if poor students write with good writers but we relegate them to a low reading group, it takes much longer for them to develop self-confidence, if they ever do. More unfortunately, we give them a mixed message about themselves—and about ourselves.

Reading groups can be heterogeneous, and membership need not be fixed. Some teachers permit groups to remain constant for a period of time, but not too long because responses become ingrown. The teachers in my own graduate-level classes experience this themselves when they meet with one set of peers for an extended period of time. They find that they need fresh input. Again, we have said for years that we should not have permanent groups in reading, but I never knew how to do it differently. Now I know how to do it in writing and can follow the same model in reading. Never again could I support the bottom-middle-high reading group structure that once prevailed in my own classroom, because it cuts into the children as people.

At the end of the Mast Way project, when researcher Tom Romano interviewed Jan Roberts, she commented extensively on grouping. "As we have seen, the heterogeneous groupings break down so many of the barriers that interfere with learning. . . . These barriers prevent children from knowing each other, interacting with each other, learning from each other, and, most importantly, from valuing each other."

Jan continued, "The kids who aren't such good students don't feel bad about themselves. They all feel that they're worthy as students. That to me is important because you get kids who believe they have something worthwhile to say and that they are capable learners, and you get rid of all those interfering feelings that get in the way of their learning, so you're really giving an opportunity to all students."

Jan then commented on her good students. "One of the most important things" she learned was that "the bright kids don't suffer." At Mast Way she sees how book choice lets children expand and stretch themselves way beyond the limits of her former reading program.

In October 1984, when Pat McLure decided to abolish reading groups in her first grade, she noticed instant benefits. She asked Ruth Hubbard to rearrange the names on the pegboard as the children entered the room. The little children gathered in a cluster on the carpet near the pegboard and watched, quietly confused. Finally the two children at the extremes of the class made spontaneous comments. The lowest child in the class, who had not been in a group with anyone, said, "Good. Now I won't have to be alone anymore." The top student said, "I don't think I'll like this. I liked being in a special group."

These children had been in reading groups for less than two months. Research shows that first-grade teachers take on an awesome responsibility when they assign children to groups. The assignments aren't for just one year; they last for many years. When children can feel left out or become elitists in the first month of grade one, it doesn't take much extrapolation to sense the long-term damage a stratified community can have on children's attitude toward others and toward themselves.

Sense of Self Within the Community

Writing and reading by their very nature place the individual in the center—not alone, but in the midst of others. Writing takes nerve, courage. To write with a strong voice draws attention to yourself. The people who read your writing find out who you are. Those of you who don't know me have learned a lot about me in these first seven chapters. It's hard for me to write what I think because I know some people have yet to experience a writing/reading classroom and will doubt what I saw. I have a hard time saying what I think because I know I'll be criticized, but I also know I'm part of a community who supports me. They give me the courage to really tell what I've learned.

My colleague Tom Newkirk says, "Who are you afraid of, Jane?" It's still hard, but my supporters give me energy. So do yours. And our students' supporters give them energy.

We join a community of readers and writers. Christopher learned the value of his friends' energy in February of grade one when his class spontaneously clapped for him. He had a new parrot and read his published book about her to his class. Chris had written every day all year, but he had never before volunteered to share with the class. His teacher, Pat McLure, had not mentioned anything about Chris's not sharing, but everyone knew he never had. When they applauded for Chris, they applauded for the first time all year. They had never clapped for anyone before, but they sensed the significance of this event for Chris—and for the class.

They knew that their community now included everyone in the class, and they celebrated. A real community of writers and readers exists when everyone knows each other as a writer and a reader. The recognition also helped Chris know that he existed. He was no longer a no one. The children wanted to know more about what his parrot Polly ate, drank, and did. Chris had a good time showing them how Polly pecks herself in a mirror, and later he asked Pat McLure if he could add information to his book. She told him she thought authors usually wrote sequels to published books rather than adding pages. The next morning, Christopher wrote *Polly Book 2*. Pat typed it and Chris shared it that afternoon.

In a community, readers and writers want each other to do well. The community helps them realize that they know more than they think they do and gives them the confidence to move ahead more quickly. When words, whether our own written words or our verbal response to someone else's, give us a place in a group, print acquires a new dimension for us. Learning is usually social; we learn very little entirely on our own. Without a community, people have less desire to write or read. We write for ourselves, but, in general, when we write we clarify our thoughts, which influences our interactions with others. Readers don't operate in vacuums either. In a sense, although we read alone—physically—the impact of what we read goes beyond us to affect what we think, say, and do, how we interact with others and, thus, how they perceive us.

Our community values us. When others honor us, our affirmed sense of uniqueness justifies our existence. The writing/reading program fosters individuals (Yolen 1985), which makes it different from the individualized reading programs of past years, in which students each did their own work at their own pace. At that time, we had not yet learned about the social nature of literacy. Only now can we begin to base our teaching on collective influence (Taylor and Strickland 1986).

We can't be literate alone. Words change our thoughts. We go forth to do something in the world, to make our contribution. Others value us and help us to value ourselves. Our literate friends listen, talk, write, read, think, support, and challenge us. This community buzzes.

In a learning community, the teacher spends her time among the students and hears their voices governing their learning. They're in charge. They belong to a group in which everyone works, pursues and brings in outsiders. It happened when Meredith joined Jan Roberts's third-grade class in April 1985. For three days Meredith held back, but on the fourth day she brought a draft to researcher Tom Romano. He writes about what happened.

> She told of four sisters, mom, dad, and many pets. Courtney, Melissa, and I found ourselves in an informal conference group. Meredith handed me the new piece, which I read aloud.
> "So many pets," said Melissa.
> "And so many names," said Courtney.
> "Oh, we had lots more pets than that. We had a rooster named Baron and a horse named Electra and two more cats named Sneakers and Spider. Spider, she died, got eaten by some animal. We couldn't find her face. . . ."

"Oh, gross!" cried Melissa.

"And that's not half the pets we had," continued Meredith. "We had a goat and a pig, too."

The information poured forth from her as Courtney, Melissa and I probed her experience further with questions.

On the next day Meredith met at a table with Chad, Melissa, Aaron, and Matt, her formal conference group. Today they would hold a teacherless conference. Round the table went the sharing until only Meredith hadn't read anything.

"Do you have somethin' you want to read?" asked Matt.

Meredith picked at the contact paper. "Ummm, no, not really."

"You sure?"

"I know," said Melissa, "read that piece about your pets."

Meredith began to protest.

"Oh, wait til you guys hear it," continued Melissa. "She has all kinds of pets."

Meredith didn't move.

"Come on," said Matt. "Don't be shy."

"Well," Meredith said. "I'll have to get it. It's in my desk." She ran from the table, returned, and without so much as a glance at me, began to read aloud.

It's hard to join a new community whether you're a new third-grade girl or a new adult. Liz Turner (who was Liz Turner Sullivan when she wrote the following piece of writing) came to Mast Way from a town down the road. Her arrival as a first-grade teacher the year after the research project ended created within her the same sense of hesitancy that Meredith felt. Liz, as did Meredith, became a member of her new community when she read her writing to her peers. Liz gave her draft to me, along with the forewarning we all give to anything we ever write: Dear Jane, This is a rather free-style piece which has never been cleaned up.

Crisis in confidence, life in a new school, or reflections on open house

On the first day of school I was less nervous than in the past. Possibly it was due to lack of sleep. For the two weeks prior to opening day I had rehearsed the moment over and over again. What I would say to each beautiful child to let them know that I was here to help them learn, help them gain independence, to recognize in themselves what wonderful, intelligent human beings that they are, and most importantly that we together would learn to express our feelings to each other, to respect ourselves as well as our classmates. It was sure to be inspiring.

"Jon, do you want hot lunch every day or milk at snack and lunch?"

"Kris, you gave me sixty cents, do you have a nickel in your back pack?"

"Mrs. Turner Celery, do we have three recesses?"

"Is it time for snack now?"

I felt it slip. Maybe everyone had made a big mistake. I don't belong here. The noise in my classroom was louder than anything I had experienced before. My damn shoes kept slipping on the waxy hall surface.

Why do all the other teachers look so calm?

It was then I realized that my teaching skills, my professional attitude, my philosophical contructs were dependent on geographical location. If only I was ten miles down the road it would all return. "I'm sorry Mr. Merrill, Mr. Lowy, and distinguished colleagues, I thought I was a good teacher but I have found out the truth. If I'm not in Nottingham, New Hampshire, I am unable to count lunch money, my class will be too noisy, and I shake in my boots. Let's just forget it ever happened. I will leave quietly. I'm sure you will have no trouble finding someone who will do a better job."

Wait just a second, Scott is running over to me. He looks happy. "Mrs. Turner Sullivan, I spelled England." There is was—ENLD—in a perfect squiggly scrawl. "You were talking to Andrea so you couldn't help me. I had to do it myself."

I felt the spark. Maybe this class is a little noisy. Danny has spent twenty minutes comparing his pencil to Tom's, but this little nervous boy just spelled England all by himself. Okay, I'll give it a week. Maybe they will let me stay that long.

Monday I woke up at five. It was back—that slipping feeling. For two years I had dreamed of working in a school like Mast Way. I have been so impressed with the thoughts and attitudes of everyone. Liz, I said to myself, you have built this whole thing up. You have got to relax and give yourself some time to settle in. You have so much to learn. It will be great if you get the confidence you seem to think resides in Nottingham and bring it to Mast Way. This is the experience you have wanted. Take it and go.

On Monday things did go better. I was only a dollar ninety short on the lunch money, the kids were a little more quiet, and three butterflies hatched. The kids and I had a nice writing time. At math time the cuisenaire rods worked out well. Everyone was on the right bus. Maybe this will work.

I was still sorting out the day as I opened my front door. I heard a scraping sound. My foot stepped on something squishy. As far as I could see there was garbage: coffee grounds, cigarette butts, and last night's chicken bones on the living room rug, and three days of newspapers shredded everywhere. Newton, my six month old Corgi was jumping up on my leg, so happy to see me. I started to cry. I would have to quit my job because my dog was too lonely at home without me.

I know I take things too seriously. Putting the trash up before I go to school has worked out fine. Even the dog has adjusted. That's why open house was important to me. Life can look pretty rough when you let it. I had really let everything take on mountainous proportions. Noise, lunch money, my dog. Was I offending everyone in the teachers' room with my smoke? I hadn't been so insecure in years. Maybe it was first grade. You know, starting school can be rough. If children can regress during this period, so can teachers and I did.

But the parents saved me. The little girl who I was sure hated me had told her mother that she really liked school. Another parent said that she was thrilled that the kids were learning sign language. A lot of people said positive things to me and I drank it in. I'm sure it's not this concrete, but the parents believe in me. The kids believe in me. Excellence is a state of mind and after one week of nervous confidence questioning I think I'm ready to play the believing game.

References

HANSEN, JANE. 1985. Teachers Share Their Writing. *The Reading Teacher* 38, no. 9 (May).

HEATH, SHIRLEY BRICE. 1983. *Ways with Words*. Cambridge, Mass.: Cambridge University Press.

ROMANO, TOM. 1985. How Did You Get That Way? In *Teachers and Learners*. Durham, N.H.: Writing Process Laboratory, University of New Hampshire.

TAYLOR, DENNY, AND STRICKLAND, DOROTHY S. 1986. Family Literacy: Myths and Magic. In *The Pursuit of Literacy*, ed. by Michael R. Sampson. Dubuque, Iowa: Kendall/Hunt.

WEINSTEIN, RHONA. 1986. Teacher Expectancy. In *The Contexts of Classroom Literacy*, ed. by Taffy Raphael. New York: Longman.

YOLEN, JANE. 1985. The Story Between. *Language Arts* 62, no. 6 (October).

The Warp: Listening | Eight

The weaver carefully threads the first set of threads—the warp—onto the loom. The warp gives the fabric its strength. Similarly, a writing/reading program begins with listening, and listening holds the program together.

Leslie Funkhouser, a second-grade teacher at Mast Way School, says that the most common question she receives from observers is, "How do you hold back?" Traditionally, we have pictured the students as the listeners and the teacher as the person to whom the children listened, but now we see ourselves as the number one listener. This role reversal hits us unexpectedly and catches us unprepared.

We spend a lot of time developing our own listening skills as we begin to examine our teaching. We find this basic skill a prerequisite if learning is to happen among our students and between them and us. The children must know that we hear what they say in order to believe in themselves, a hallmark of an independent learner.

This chapter is, in a sense, a condensation of the five previous chapters, using listening as the lens through which to reexamine Time, Choice, Response, Structure, and Community. Listening and Talking hold these components together (I will discuss talking in the next chapter). We share listening and talking with our students when we no longer put our knowledge on a pedestal above theirs. Our students' knowledge counts, and we make time to find out what they know.

Time to Listen

We struggle to find time to listen. The success of our search for time to listen rests on the firmness of our belief in the worth of what students know, because their current understanding determines what they can learn next. When the implications of this reality hit us, we talk less, listen more, find out what students know, and increase the impact of our teaching.

We listen to what the children say, write, and read. Listening to what children say sets the stage for us to understand their writing and reading.

We build in time to listen to what our students say. When we take time to listen, we not only hear words, we also hear a child's tone of voice. Plus, facial expression and body language contribute to a message. When Megan doesn't look at us, the solution is not, "Look at me!" Instead, we hold back, lower our voice, and try to offer reassurance. "I used to get extremely angry at my friends when I was in fourth grade." Then we wait. If Megan talks more, we wait again, and then ask one slow question, such as, "What do you think you'll do next?"

When we're quiet, the reluctant speaker, whether upset or shy, can talk. We see sureness or hesitancy at different points in the tale, and these clue us in to significant happenings and/or information the child doesn't understand. With our acquired information we can respond. Listening isn't a quiet activity. It includes response because, otherwise, Megan doesn't know if her teacher has listened. When we acknowledge our students' words, they know that they have an audience and rise to the occasion. They're on stage.

Their voices become strong as a result of our focused listening. (Welty 1984 writes about voice also.) We give them the courage to begin and the nerve to continue sharing their out-of-school knowledge about roosters or the view from the back window of their apartment. They know that we are not listening just to find out how little they know. We assume that they know something we don't know, and we want to find out what it is. When we get a glimpse of it, we want to learn more, and we ask questions.

Our interest in what the students know pervades our teaching. Our attitude toward them as people determines our student-teacher relationship. Gradually, we learn more and more about each student. As they see our interest in each of them, they value each other and themselves more. When the overall feeling in a classroom starts to become "We all know worthwhile things," students become curious about each other's knowledge. Questions confirm for the possessor of knowledge the fact that someone else values what they know and thus values them. The general tone in the classroom becomes one of wonderment. Students can move out as learners.

Our questions, and the questions of classmates, may be those a student realizes he is curious about, and he may seek answers. However, when Mark tells us about his roosters, our questions may not be about something of interest to him, and he may not choose to pursue them. Regardless, our interest in our students helps keep them involved.

Whether or not they pursue the exact questions we ponder, students investigate their own knowledge. Children who collect coins want to learn more. A child who hardly knows what a bald eagle is decides to study them after his teacher introduces endangered species. Children can tell us and each other what they are learning, and they can write about it.

We build in time to listen to their writing. Writers who read their work aloud put themselves on the line. By sharing his work, Mark says, "Listen. Here's something I know." He hears his own voice, and the audience hears his voice. Children sense each other's emerging confidence and bolster it.

In her response to Mark's writing, Suzanne said, "I could tell you liked the part where you talked to your grandma because you smiled when you read it." If Suzanne hadn't seen Mark read, she wouldn't have been so sure of how to respond. The eye-to-eye contact between writer and audience helps both the author and the other children. Mark learns to hear himself in his writing and realizes he must write loudly and clearly if his listeners are to hear him. The listeners learn to use these same listening skills when they read.

We build in time to listen to children's responses to what they read. The practice children get in listening to authors read helps them "hear" the voice of nonpresent authors whose work they read. Listening thus plays a part in reading comprehension.

We provide time for readers to find their own voice in the writing of others. Students know that their voice may be different from that of the writer. When their friends share drafts, they hear them explain their intentions, which frequently differ from the way they might work with the draft. Subsequently, when these writers read, they listen for the author's voice and look for places where their own point of view may differ from the author's.

Children also need time to listen to the voices of other readers who respond to a book. Since the writing/reading classroom is premised on inviting each other's interpretations, the children come to a discussion to hear each other. As they listen, their personal response to a book becomes richer, a chorus of voices. The children begin in their own minds to consider the options other readers may entertain so that they come to a discussion with answers to questions they have anticipated. Active listening propels readers to listen to many voices while not letting any one be drowned out.

Children need time to contemplate the alternatives they hear. We see them look out the window when they read. They are learning to listen to themselves.

Listen for Choices

We teach children to consider options in various situations, but here I will focus on book choice. Most children, like those of us who read, list books they hope to get to soon. They share books daily and know of several titles their friends have enjoyed. But a few of them have trouble finding a book. We provide as large a collection of books as possible, but a child like Joshua has to know how to find something he can handle in a bookshelf that's bigger than he is.

He needs help with strategies or he'll become anxious. We ask, "What would you like to find?"

He stumps us when he mumbles, "I don't know."

We don't want him to become dependent on us so we ask, "Who could you get to help you?"

He shrugs.

We think of two children who know lots of books and suggest, "Go get either Jeannine or Chad."

Joshua shuffles away and returns with Chad, who has performed this service before. Chad assumes some authority. "I'll choose three and you choose one of those." Brad picks *Wake Up, Jeremiah* (Ronald Himler), *No Bath Tonight* (Jane Yolen) and *The Very Busy Spider* (Eric Carle).

Joshua perks up. "Will you read them to me? Then I'll decide."

The teacher walks away but later, she approaches Josh. "This morning you couldn't find a book. What did you do?" She listens while he recollects how he got his reading process started that morning. Then she asks, "What can you do if you have trouble again some day?" We pursue a situation until we can listen to a child tell us what he is learning. Josh knows he learned something today about the process of selecting a book. Other children who have problems finding books may find these questions helpful: "What good book did you hear recently?" or "Where does Chad get ideas for books?" The child can answer the second question because we not only talk about book choices in individual conferences, the children listen to each other's reasons for selections in both small groups and Big Conferences.

We listen to children's answers to the question "Why did you choose your book?" and learn whether they need help. If Joshua's answer is always, "I heard it at the listening center," it may be time to suggest a new source for him. Children's progress depends to a large degree on their ability to choose appropriate books. We need to know if their awareness of options is widening to include books read by friends, teacher, and family, or composed by favorite authors or representative of several genres.

Listening Is Response

Listening is an active process. Good listeners don't have poker faces. We show involvement. We get tired. It's hard to be always on our toes with at least one specific, receptive comment in support of a reader's thoughts. We're sensitive to what the students are on the verge of saying, think along with them, and choose a question about something we sense is important to them. Listeners carry the responsibility of response.

We respond verbally, but a critical aspect of listening is our nonverbal response. When we watch someone we can tell whether they are listening. Similarly, we want our students to know we are listening to them. At least four behaviors (Cooper 1977) help us become consciously aware of our listening skills.

Listeners use eye contact. The first element for many of us to focus on when we listen is eye contact with the student. Sometimes we purposely glance around the room to keep tabs on the class while a student talks to us. We have trained ourselves to give our students the impression that we aren't listening. Loss of eye contact tells a speaker that the listener wishes he would stop talking.

Often we can hear every word children say, even if we don't look at them, but we miss their facial and body expressions. Further, they sense that something else is more important, because our attention at least appears to be elsewhere. If we value every nuance of the child's behavior, we must maintain eye contact when the student talks, or shares writing or reading.

When we start to think about eye contact, some of us find out that it isn't comfortable for us. For one thing, we worry that we will stare and make the student uncomfortable. Since the purpose of eye contact is to elicit information, we don't want to make children uneasy. We learn to rest our eyes naturally on the child because those who are talking will say more if their listener's eyes meet theirs.

Eye contact tests our consistency. All writing is important—a child's draft, a child's finished work, and books written by professionals. When writing is shared, we listen. Sometimes, the discrepancies between our response to various kinds of writing send conflicting messages to our students. When we let children draw while we read to them, for example, we convey that reading is less important in the reading program than the individual writing conference. If we stop to ask a child to tell us about his writing, we don't draw a picture of our dog while he talks to us. We watch him as speaker, writer, and reader.

Ellen Blackburn Karelitz instituted the Author's Chair as the place where either she or a child read to the class, giving importance to this role regardless of who played it. If two children and the teacher read to the class each day, and the children respond each time, they become quite skilled at the focused listening that response requires.

When children play both roles, reader and listener, they understand the role of listener better. They know what kind of behavior they appreciate from their listeners.

Listeners' faces wear expressions.   Our countenance should reflect the tone of the student who is speaking to us, whether it is concerned or confident. We needn't show the extremes a child might express, but if a child is worried, we don't grin thinking that a smile will make the child feel better. A smile as a response to a problem leads the student to think we aren't listening.

Listeners plan their body posture.   Body posture shows our empathy with the speaker. I learned a new term when I started to become aware of the importance of listening: arms akimbo. The fastest way to stop talk is to put your hands on your hips. Some of us stand arms akimbo unintentionally. We need to realize the message we send to someone talking to us. Hands across our chest is another negative sign. The most receptive body posture is leaning forward. This has been the most difficult for me to learn. It's so easy for me to lean back in my soft swivel chair when students come to my office. I have to make a conscious effort to lean forward so that my outward stance tells my students I am intent on what they are saying.

Listeners wait.   When the speaker appears to be finished, we wait. We want to learn as much as possible and if we pause, the speaker will often tell us more. But if we jump right in, he must stop. I don't sit and count seconds, and my interruption skills are terrific, but we wait. The other person knows we are more interested in what she has to say next than in what's on our own mind.

Listening behaviors account for most of the activity in conferences, whether one-on-one, small-group or whole-class. When Ellen Blackburn Karelitz confers with a child or a group, she listens most of the time and lets the child or children talk. When Ellen teaches teachers in the New Hampshire Writing Program, she suggests that they tape their response sessions when they return to their classrooms in the fall. One of Ellen's students was Janet Aliapoulios, a first-grade teacher in Winnetka, Illinois, who taped her conferences and heard herself talking less. But "It's hard to be quiet," she says. The conference is an occasion for the child to talk and for the teacher and classmates to listen, whether the child talks about her own draft or a professional's book.

Reading is sharing. When we enter the Mast Way classrooms, the children want to tell us about the books they're reading. Even very young children come running. "I can read another book. Wanna hear it?" These children know that when they get excited about a book, someone will respond to their enthusiasm.

The Structure for Listening

The structure of the conferences permits listening. Listeners have a format in their heads that they use when they respond, and this determines their focus in a response session. Sometimes we fear structure because we think it may ritualize interactions and result in sessions in which children have no sense of commitment or caring. However, the format of the conferences and classroom strengthens students' ability to respond.

The structure of the conferences. When we started our project at Mast Way, we worried about the questions the children asked each other: "Where did you get your topic?" "What's your favorite part?" "I liked your title." "What bothers you about Yolen's book?" "What will you read next?" "Your description was good." "Who can help you?" The children had learned these generic questions, which could apply to any piece of writing, and asked them as a matter of routine. The children didn't even have to listen to a reader in order to ask these questions, and we noticed that they didn't even listen to the answer. The inquiries were false, not based on a sense of wanting to know. We called them pro forma questions and sought to eradicate them.

Teachers and children need a basic structure, but it must bend to fit the child and the piece of writing. When researchers first developed conferences, the notion of teaching via response was new, and we used these questions as a crutch. Now it is time to refine response. In order to do this we need to look at the origin of the generic questions.

They emanated from a two-part response format we want to preserve: affirm and extend. In one version of this, the child who shares initiates the response by telling the group what he thinks is good about the writing he shared. After the group responds to his comment, other group members offer their affirmations. Then the child tells the group what bothers him in the writing, and they respond to this concern. The child's concern may be a big enough topic of discussion to complete the session, or other children may raise a question or two.

In either case, the comments and inquiries are specific. When Jaime read *Leo the Late Bloomer* (Robert Kraus) to her second-grade class in September, one of the other children said, "My favorite part was when Leo's father started to watch TV and let Leo alone." This specific response can only be made by a real listener, someone who heard the story and thought about it. Listeners are thinkers.

The same child also wondered about something. "Do you think if Leo's father had not left him alone he might not have ever bloomed?" This child thought *bloom* meant "being allowed to just be yourself," and ended up answering his own question (Funkhouser 1986), "I think everyone blooms. It might just have taken him a little longer." His question was specific to the piece of writing shared, represented a genuine concern, and showed a listener's mind at work.

The general structure determines specific responses. Jaime did not know exactly what Andy or anyone else would say, but she knew they would find something of value in the piece of writing she chose to share. When they asked questions, she knew they were interested in her book. The predictability of the structure allowed Jaime to take the risk necessary to share, and because the format is firm, the children met Jaime's expectations. She'll dare to take another risk.

The structure of the classroom. The physical arrangement of the classroom affects listening. When Jaime read, her class clustered close to her on a swatch of carpet, bordered on three sides by bookcases, in the classroom library. Many of the Mast Way classes came together for their share sessions either on a carpet or in a circle of chairs. Proximity promotes interaction.

The seating pattern reflects the value we place on different kinds of writing or various types of response sessions. A similar arrangement for all listening promotes the mind-set we need to respond to all writing with grace and interest. Identical formats—whether a teacher shares a professional's book, a child shares a draft, a teacher shares a draft, or a child shares a professional's writing—show our students that we value all writers and readers equally. If, on the other hand, children sit in a cluster on the carpet for some sessions, in a circle on the carpet for others, in a circle of chairs at other times, and in rows of desks for still other sessions, they assume that there is a reason for the difference. The organization of the group encourages or inhibits listening, and facilitates or counters interaction.

A Community of Listeners

I recently visited the sophomore English classroom of Marla Hamilton in Hudson, New Hampshire. She worried about my visit because this was only the fourth day of the course. Most of the students had never been in a writing course where the initial response to their writing was always positive. But she needn't have worried. During the first three days, she had taught the students to listen for strengths in a piece of writing by reading them drafts by her previous semester's students. On this day they brought their own writing for peer response. Ms. Hamilton asked who would volunteer to read their previous night's journal entry to the class, and six volunteered, two of them boys.

Next, the class met in small groups to read drafts of their first piece of writing. I sat with one group while Marla moved among the others. Everyone read and responded. They didn't need us. These students knew that their friends had no freedom about how to respond. They must support each other. This gave them the nerve to read their writing aloud.

They wanted to find out what their friends liked in their writing. They will continue to try to write well, and much of the impetus will come from the listening and subsequent response of their peers. Everyone receives ideas for their writing as they share their early drafts, final drafts, and the final drafts of professionals. Thus, they also promote each other's reading and support each other's learning. (See Kantor 1984 for another high school classroom.)

The atmosphere in the classrooms I visit never ceases to amaze me and the teachers. The students become skillful in their ability to hear each other's contributions when they share what they read. Somehow, we fear that students will stab each other, but that very rarely happens. What often occurs instead is that the structure we establish for listening during writing and reading begins to spread throughout the day. The students become more sure of their positions with each other and can count on their friends to keep their antennae sensitive to what they each do well. (See Bruffee 1983 for more information on the collaborative nature of learning.)

The research project ended the spring of 1985, and in September Ellen Blanchard had a new class of third and fourth graders. She compared notes on her new students with a friend at another school. The other teacher said her fourth graders weren't good listeners. Ellen said, "I can tell one of the things all the Mast Way teachers stress is listening. On the first day, my students knew how to listen and respond to each other."

References

BRUFFEE, KENNETH A. 1983. Writing and Reading as Collaborative or Social Acts. In *The Writer's Mind*, ed. by Janice N. Hays, Phyllis A. Roth, Jon R. Ramsey, and Robert D. Foulke. Urbana, Ill.: National Council of Teachers of English.

COOPER, JAMES. Gen. ed. 1977. *Classroom Teaching Skills*. Lexington, Mass.: D.C. Heath and Company.

HANSEN, JANE. In press. Listen to Learn. In *Ideas and Insights: Teaching the English Language Arts K–6*, ed. by Dorothy Watson and Ruie Pritchard. Urbana, Ill.: National Council of Teachers of English.

KANTOR, KENNETH J. 1984. Classroom Contexts and the Development of Writing Intuitions: An Ethnographic Case Study. *New Directions in Composition Research*, ed. by Richard Beach and Lillian S. Bridwell. New York: Guilford.

WELTY, EUDORA. 1984. *One Writer's Beginnings*. Cambridge, Mass.: Harvard University Press.

The Woof: Talking | Nine

Eventually I figured out the obvious. Daniel couldn't teach himself to read. Neither could Melissa, nor Jason, nor Jeremy. Their teacher couldn't always teach them either because she was usually with other students. They had to teach each other.

Ellen Blackburn Karelitz taught them how to give help, and when you have a room full of six-year-old teachers, you have talking.

This contrasted sharply with what I was used to, regardless of whether I taught first, second, third, or fifth grade. When I had a reading group, the rest of the class worked—quietly. Better yet, they worked silently. I don't think it ever occurred to me that my students would learn more about reading if I taught them to talk to each other.

Oral language has invaded each preceding chapter, but here I will highlight its importance. Children spend more time on-task when we encourage talking. They respond to each other and to their book choices. They help each other within the structure of their work time and when we hear their voices we know a community can exist.

Time to Talk

Listening and talking, the warp and the woof, are not two sides of the same coin. They intertwine. People talk if someone listens and responds to them. People prefer to listen to strong, interesting voices, not monotones. Students' diverse voices get writing and reading started because we need to learn who each child is, and talking keeps them moving forward when everyone knows how to respond. Listening and talking are the basic languages of learning and teaching.

Children enter school with oral language as their mode of expression. They need time to tell us the things they want us to know, happenings they want to share. The more they share the more they have to tell us. We hear them buzz around us, but we get nervous. We don't know how to channel the noise, so we insist that it must cease, even though a long-standing maxim in education has been: start where the child is. We do not know how to handle any other option than to refuse to let our students do what they can do.

Willes (1985) studied teacher-child interactions and learned that we do not give children time to talk because we fear discipline problems. During the first few weeks of school, teachers turn children into pupils by teaching them to be quiet, not to initiate conversations, and to respond briefly when the teacher speaks to them. Our management concerns don't permit children to use talk as a way to learn—a way to figure things out.

Decisions in schools from kindergarten through high school are based on control. Students, we fear, will become disorderly if we let them talk. In order to relieve our anxiety we must first believe that children will learn if they talk and then find ways to teach them to talk in a productive manner.

Talking is a way to learn.   Babies learn about oral language by noticing connections between voices and actions. Talk brings results, so they try it. Toddlers not only experiment with words, their language shows us the concepts they are starting to comprehend. One day a toddler labeled a fingernail clipping a moon (Nelson, Rescorla and Gruendel 1978), which was his way of saying, "I just noticed something. I think this clipping has the same shape as the moon you showed me last night." The child discovered this comparison, and the conversation he started with the word *moon* not only gave his parent information, but also a chance to tell the child that his new understanding was correct. The parent had an opportunity to extend the child's knowledge. If, on the other hand, this child had been told to remain quiet, we not only wouldn't know as much as we do about what he knows, but we would prevent the child from using language to test his hypothesis.

Lewis Thomas (1983) writes, "Language is what childhood is for." Children may not form perfect constructions when they speak, but they learn more when they construct their own knowledge than when they listen to us construct ours. They do learn when they listen to us, but they need to put their hunches together in their own words and test them out on someone do they find out what they understand. Often, others can't figure out what the child is trying to say, so the child tries again. Children practice and practice, but this practice isn't repetition. Their utterances change as they try and try again. Children don't learn to talk by repeating drills over and over again. They gradually get better as they talk our ears off.

However, even though children have mastered our language system (Menyuk 1980) by the time they enter school, they need time to practice, because there is still much they want to learn about their world. Because they have used talking as one of their primary modes of learning, we need to build on the process they've spent years developing. They can continue to use language to learn as most of us do.

In our daily lives, we hear ourselves say, "I was confused, but now that I've explained it to you I've figured it out better." We experience the benefits of talking, yet we often bar our students from this way of learning. When oral language is an available mode of learning, our students can learn more than if we discourage their use of this channel.

We teach children to use talking in writing and reading.   We can decide to let our pupils interact, rather than concentrating our energy on diminishing the value of talking. Ellen Blackburn Karelitz abandoned the term "Silent Reading" because her budding readers needed to work together in order to make as much progress as possible. When children made new discoveries, they needed to test them out with someone else; when they were stumped, they needed to get help in order to move ahead.

Whether we want children to receive help with their reading depends on our definition of reading. If we expect readers to compose meaning, then they must be able to find out what the words are and clarify the parts that confuse them. If we give readers the responsibility of coming to discussions with responses to their books, then they must compose interpretations of their books beforehand. The teacher doesn't call groups in order to check students' comprehension. The students meet to share their reading, test their compositions against those of others, learn from others, and walk away enriched. The preparation for the sharing, and the sharing itself, require unquiet time, time to think out loud.

Talking About Choices

We have always intuitively known the importance of book choice; because it was so important, we did it. We chose the books and stories our students read because we knew their learning depended to a great extent on whether they had an appropriate book in front of their minds. We thought they couldn't handle this decision themselves and we were right. Often, they can't. Because choice is complicated, we can't simply turn it over to the children. But we can teach them how to choose. We start by finding out what they know about book choice; they, in turn, frequently ask this question of each other in conferences, "Why did you choose *Babe, the Gallant Pig* [Dick King-Smith]?"

Why did you choose *Babe, the Gallant Pig*?   Questions about why they chose their books start them thinking about various reasons for reading and expose them to the purposes different people set for themselves. Children's answers to book choice questions vary with their age and with the book they've chosen. They often mention the author, "I chose it because I like Dick King-Smith. I liked *Magnus Powermouse.* Or, "A gallant pig has to be funny and I like books with humor." Younger children often give these answers about their books, "I like Dr. Seuss." "I chose it because Jason read it and he could help me." "I chose it because Arden read it to us and I liked it." "I chose it because I heard it lots of times and knew I would be able to read part of it already." "I liked the pictures." All readers sometimes say, "I just picked it off the shelf." These reasons go through their minds on subsequent days when they peruse books.

By talking, they increase the number of books they become familiar with and can choose from when they read. They hear about authors, types of books, and books about particular kinds of information. Talking about books is one way to rehearse for reading.

How did you learn to read *Make Way for Ducklings* (Robert McCloskey)?   We ask and the children ask each other questions about how they learned to read their books. Also, "Did you have any problems? Show me where you had trouble." Children share with each other the strategies they use to become better readers. They can try plans they have not used to facilitate their progress. They talk about reading, the act of reading.

The children know that reading is not always easy, and they acknowledge their frustrations, a necessary part of learning. If we can't say, "I don't get it," we can't get our confusion clarified. Unfortunately, in schools students are often afraid to ask questions. We need to rethink the notion of learning and encourage inquiry (Papert 1980).

If we are in the process of learning something, we are on our way. We know some things, we are learning others, and more is to come. Learning is movement along a primary path that has many secondary paths to entice the curious explorer, the one who truly wants to see the world, the student and teacher who don't want to miss anything. But choice also means that we recognize when it's best to remain on the main trail. Children need to ask questions about how to go about learning. If we encourage their questions, we support them as learners. They talk about their options and pool everyone's collective wisdom, which includes our knowledge. Choice requires lots of talking to help children see its importance and realize what to consider.

In reading and writing, instruction takes place during response, and in many cases the response is oral. We teach children how to talk about reading. (We can teach them how to talk during math, etc., but that's someone else's book!) Our fear of noise can fade if we structure the children's responses. They not only learn how to seek help and respond, but when they do, they realize that they learn more than when they must leave their concerns unresolved. At other times, they don't seek help but rather, want to share their excitement.

The children initiate response sessions.   Regardless of the children's reason for wanting a response, they initiate the response sessions. They want to show off their creations, the messages they compose. This sharing and their friends' response keep their interest high. They thrive on the questions their friends ask. The reading/writing program would fall apart without these conferences.

Teachers organize response sessions in many ways, but, in general, they provide for both spontaneous and scheduled sessions. Spontaneity is helpful because if the teacher hears a child read something, or use an interesting strategy, the teacher may want to share this with the class. The system allows for these unpredictable moments because the teacher needs opportunities to teach the other children what readers do. Similarly, if a child has an expected problem or joy, the child can have an audience.

In whole-class conferences, the teacher empowers the students to conduct the sessions and plays the role of group member. For the occasions when children have signed up, each signature declares: "I have read something I want to share. You will build on what I see as its merits and, as a group, we will use my reading as a springboard for some original thinking. Please come. Let's talk books."

In October, Barry, a child in Pat McLure's first grade, shared *Tales of Oliver Pig*, by Jean VanLeeuwen, in which Grandmother Pig comes to visit, and little Oliver Pig gets his monster books and toy elephant to put in Grandmother's room (Hubbard 1985). Barry requested comments and questions about his book, and Chris asked, "Why do you suppose he got monster books and a toy elephant for an *adult*?"

"Maybe he was being sneaky," Barry suggested. "She wouldn't really care about that stuff, but Oliver could sneak right in with her and cuddle up and she'd read him the book."

"I don't think so," Roger stated. "Oliver's a *nice* pig. I think he gave her his favorite monster books to read; then he thought if she was scared, she could hug his elephant."

Children pursue a line of thought.   The children attributed deeper motives to Oliver's actions than their teacher had considered; they can provide substantive interpretations of books. When we give them the responsibility of response, they know they must generate comments and questions; we teach them to build upon each other's contributions, rather than permitting each child to offer his or her own idiosyncratic response. When they stay with one line of thought, fewer notions about a book will enter a session, but the notions they do discuss will provoke more thinking. It's new for us to teach children to respond to each other in a reading discussion, but when we teach them to extend each other's contributions, our teaching reflects what we know about learning (Wells 1986).

Typically, learners don't hear something new and, presto, understand it. We comprehend a new concept best if we construct our own model of it. As learners, when we respond orally, rather than only by listening, we increase the possibility that we will understand something new. The same is true of our students. When we listen to what our students understand from what they read, we hear what they might need and interact with them to fill in gaps and provide appropriate new information. When teachers listen to tapes of conferences, they hear differences between the kinds of comments and questions offered by themselves and the children. But the main difference between the talk of the teachers and the children lies in the quantity, rather than the quality of each. We must let them talk if they are to pursue a line of thought.

Susan Sowers documented the talk pattern in Ellen Blackburn Karelitz's classroom, and the pattern was the opposite of the norm. Normally, the talk pattern in classrooms is: Teacher asks a display question (a question to which the teacher knows the answer—not a genuine question), child delivers a short answer, and teacher evaluates ("Yes," "No," "You're close"). Teachers talk twice as much as students, and since we know that there are twenty-five pupils per teacher, each child talks precious little. However, Ellen's children talked twice as much as she did.

At the reading table, for example, they initiated talk about their books rather than answering a teacher's preplanned questions. Ellen does ask questions, but she piggybacks her questions on comments the children offer. She follows her own rules. When we let students bring what they are learning to each other for questions, they become more involved in their peers' challenges than in our fake questions. One major criticism of schools (Goodlad 1984) is that students are not involved, although this need not be the situation as often as it has been.

We feel our head shift gears when we begin to value the knowledge of our students. We want to find out what they have gained from their reading, untainted by us. We come to a large or small group to listen to a child open the conference. When the first child finishes what he has to say about his book the teacher continues to listen. She doesn't say a word. She waits for another child to respond to the reader. When it is the children's responsibility to initiate sharing and response, they know the teacher considers their response to what they read worthwhile. More importantly, when it's their responsibility to respond to the reader, they have to listen.

We worry that children will not listen; that they will daydream, and worse yet, that they will poke each other and goof around. We worry about control. However, we have never tried a response approach to teaching children to run sessions. When I taught small reading groups, if someone had suggested that I teach a child to lead the group, I would have pictured the child coming to the group with a list of questions and asking them, one by one. The group would listen to the "teacher." They not only wouldn't respond to each other, because the "teacher" would initiate all the talk, but it would be the "teacher's" knowledge they learned to honor, not each other's. If the knowledge of the group isn't important, children have no reason to listen to each other.

The dominant mode of teaching in schools in this country conveys to students that their knowledge is not important enough to share, that we revere our own knowledge and transmit it, even though we know that this is not the way to accomplish the best learning. Children can't learn how to read by listening to a lecture on the reading process, nor can they explore the various meanings of a book by only answering one person's questions about it, especially if the questions have set answers that prevent discovery of new connections. When we use the transmission model to teach, our students must control their impulses to think; if they think, they'll miss something we believe is more important than their thoughts.

However, when the Mast Way students congregate together, they come with different expectations. They know that the speaker will want a response, and they think about what they'll say. Regardless of the specifics, they know they'll support the speaker's learning process. They may challenge the speaker, but they do so because they realize that the speaker expects to hear from the diversity within the group. When students know they have a supportive audience in front of them, they talk.

They speak with conviction. I hear it in their voices, just as I hear the strength in my own voice when I serve as a consultant and have a supportive audience before me. What a tremendous difference there is between those occasions when I know the audience is critical of what I have learned about reading and another situation where I know the teachers are excited about what their children can do. If heads shake back and forth and foreheads wrinkle, I speak hesitantly, but I can almost "dance off the stage" when I see heads nod up and down and faces smile.

Similarly, children do not fear the sound of their own voices when they know that their teacher and their classmates value their spoken thoughts. They can use these same strong voices when they write. But if they cannot speak in strong voices, they may use timid, flat words when they write and may not offer the response they really feel to their reading. We teach them to exercise their strong voices when they read by speaking in strong voices ourselves and letting the students know what we think about many issues. In this way we show the children that it's good to speak up.

Talking Permits Work

During reading, children spend more time reading than in groups. They need lots of productive time to read in order to have something to share. Basically, children need three kinds of help in order to read their books: help with book choice, words, or comprehension. I have already considered book choice; here I will look at ways to provide a structure that will allow children to receive help with words and comprehension.

Children talk about words they don't know.　If children have trouble with words, they either read with someone else, choose a book at the listening center, or ask friends for help with individual words. Reading with someone else occurred naturally in Ellen Blackburn Karelitz's class. Children went to other children who had authored books or who had read the books of professionals to the class. They deliberately chose those titles because they knew who could help them if they needed it. A teacher may set aside certain places in the classroom where children can read together, limiting the number of children who can be together at one time to three if necessary.

Some children choose to read alone but need occasional help. They need to go to someone and their teachers permit movement. Also, teachers spend some of this work time moving among the children and devote part of our time to helping them with words and conducting comprehension conferences. Children approach us and each other with questions like, "What's a louse? I have to know because I want to read this to the class and Robby will probably ask me what a louse is."

Children talk about content.　Children have questions about meaning as well as about words. When Matthew read Judith Viorst's *Alexander and the Terrible, Horrible, No Good, Very Bad Day*, the references to Australia confused him so he asked Julie because she had read it to the class and he assumed she understood it. Julie knew Australia was far away but she couldn't satisfy Matthew's curiosity when he brought her a globe. They had a problem and decided to solve it by going to the library.

On some occasions, children go to other children just because they like something rather than because they have a question. "Hey, listen to this," Mark says as he flashes Roald Dahl's *Witches* in my face. "It's gross." I respond to him in a brief manner, "What's so gross?" He reads to me, we both groan, and he returns to his book. Later I ask him to share the way I responded in order to teach him how to respond to others.

We foster children's talk about the books they love. They become more involved in the books they have chosen than they ever were in our purple mimeographed worksheets. Children learn more about the value of reading when they share a good book with a friend than when they draw circles around words or fill in blanks. When they talk, they keep each other's enthusiasm high.

Friends Talk

Children who talk to a variety of people have better developed oral language than children who talk to only a few people. Here also, the writing/reading program resembles young children's experiences when they learn to talk. Because explaining our knowledge to many others involves a greater risk than sharing it with a few, it provides a greater challenge to our oral competence. In order to ensure that everyone understands us, we refine our language as much as we can.

We talk differently to different people.   Sometimes after children have shared a book in a conference with the teacher, they feel spurred to share it with a small group. One day, Maryann wanted to share with the class because in the small group, "the children asked lots of questions." They were interested, and she was eager to hear even more questions. She not only wanted and felt their support, but as she shared the book three times, she explained it better each time. Different audiences provided additional experiences. More importantly, Maryann explained her book differently to her friends than she did to her teacher.

Reading and writing may be schoolwork, but children like to interact, and when their mingling gives a positive cast to their work, their accomplishments become celebrations. They want their own place in the world, but they don't want it at the expense of others. Rather than fearing each other's accomplishments they talk about each other's contributions and rejoice in what each does well. These expressions of delight demonstrate oral language in one of its most valued uses.

We use oral language to support each other.   When Gary shares a book because "It's my first chapter book" his classmates realize the significance of Gary's session. They root for him and cheer him on. This recognition from friends makes a student's progress more real for him. This is especially true when Gary knows his friends know what they're talking about. They are readers.

When the important people in our lives are readers, we tend to read. When our community talks books, we talk books. We want to be part of our group, and our ability to support others and explain our own stance secures our place in that community.

References

GOODLAD, JOHN. 1984. *A Place Called School.* New York: McGraw-Hill.

HUBBARD, RUTH. 1985. Reading Aloud: Comments or Questions. *Teachers and Learners.* Durham, N.H.: Writing Process Laboratory, University of New Hampshire.

MENYUK, PAULA. 1980. What Young Children Know About Language. In *Discovering Language with Children,* ed. by Gay Su Dinnell. Urbana, Ill.: National Council of Teachers of English.

NELSON, KATHERINE; RESCORLA, L.; GRUENDEL, J.; AND BENEDICT, H. 1978. Early Lexicons: What Do They Mean? *Child Development* 49.

PAPERT, SEYMOUR. 1980. *Mindstorms.* New York: Basic Books.

THOMAS, LEWIS. 1983. *Late Night Thoughts on Listening to Mahler's Ninth Symphony.* New York: Viking.

WELLS, GORDON. 1986. *The Meaning Makers: Children Learning Language and Using Language to Learn.* Portsmouth, N.H.: Heinemann.

WILLES, MARY J. 1983. *Children into Pupils.* London: Routledge & Kegan Paul.

Evaluation | Ten

Evaluation is the stickiest topic in this book. In the fall of 1986, Mary-Ellen MacMillan, Donald Graves, Brenda Miller, Peg Murray, Ruth Hubbard, and I began a three-year research project at the Stratham Memorial School in Stratham, New Hampshire, because we fear that traditional assessment procedures can scare many people away from attending to the processes of writing and reading. Pressure to raise scores may never diminish, but we do need to show what students can do beyond blackening in someone else's correct answer.

As one of my first tasks in the project, I interviewed children to find out about their powers of self-evaluation. Four of the questions I asked each of them were:

- What's something new you've learned to do in writing?
- What would you like to learn so you can become a better writer?
- What's something new you've learned to do in reading?
- What would you like to learn so you can become a better reader?

Karey, a first-grade girl, in regard to what she's recently learned in writing said, "I think."

I asked her to explain and she said, "I think about what to write about. I look around the room and think about what each person has written. Andrea, Vanessa, and Sarah have all written about rainbows so I decided to, but mine's different. One day Carolyn wrote: 'I SAW A WATER FOUNTAIN. IT WAS PRETTY.' I decided to write about a water fountain I saw, and I wrote what Carolyn wrote but then I did the rest myself."

Next, Karey wants to learn more sounds. She had tried to read one of her drafts from the beginning of the year to me and couldn't read some of it. "I wrote this a long time ago," she apologized. She wants to learn more sounds so she can read her writing in the future.

Chris, a fourth-grade boy, brought his most recent piece of writing, and I asked him to read it to me. "No. You have to read it yourself." I did and when I finished, before I could say a word, he jumped in: "Now you know why you had to read it yourself. The ending is gross." His writing was about an overnight at his friend's house when Chris ate too much greasy popcorn and the draft ends, "I threw up." Chris knows his friend will think it's great.

What has he recently learned? "To write good endings," of course.

I wondered what he wants to learn next and he surprised me. "I want to write more good endings. This was my first one. I have a hard time knowing when to stop. I have to learn to leave out unnecessary information. Then I'll get to the ending faster and the ending will be better." I'm not convinced Chris' strategy will always work, but he knows what he wants to learn.

None of the children had trouble evaluating their writing. Nor their reading. Karey said she'd just learned to read a book, *Rhymes and Tales*, the first preprimer in the Holt basal. Next, she wants to learn to read a library book.

Chris' new learning was quite different from Karey's. "I can get into a book." When I asked for an example, he explained an experiment he did when he read a book about a blind boy. Chris had tried to get himself a drink of water with his eyes shut but he "messed up."

Chris wants to learn to "read faster. I have to read more."

These children often talk about what they do when they write and are beginning to talk about what they do when they read. When their processes are familiar to them, this awareness helps them try the new options they hear about from friends and teacher. Their own evaluation of their work is the most important aspect of evaluation, because when students know what they do well and choose what they want to work on for growth, their own progress is their goal. When they work for themselves more than for the teacher, we see an upward surge in their attitudes toward reading. Since the root word of *evaluation* is *value*, the evaluation scheme should reflect whether students value the process of reading itself.

How Does the Group Do?

Traditionally, the question that overrides all others when we assess reading is "What are the standardized test scores?" We give top priority to product assessment even though for ten years we have given lip service to the importance of the reading process. (Suhor 1985 writes about test validity.) Assessment itself needs to be evaluated (Mayher and Brause 1986), but before we look at alternative directions, let's consider writers' reading scores.

Teachers and administrators in Texas, Wisconsin, New Hampshire, Maine, Connecticut, and other states have gathered positive evidence. In Connecticut, writing coordinator Jack Kirby has evidence from California Tests of Basic Skills' scores. Teachers in one school tried writing and, as Jack phrased it, "The scores went way up. The school board was pleased."

Here are the scores Jack's school board liked—the National Curve Equivalents of the Total Language portion of the test. I have reported the numbers accurately, but I have attributed them at random to grade levels because some increases are not as high as others, and I do not want to cause any teachers to suffer.

- Grade 1   Fall 1984   58
           Fall 1985   72
- Grade 2   Fall 1984   72
           Fall 1985   71
- Grade 3   Fall 1984   53
           Fall 1985   82
- Grade 4   Fall 1984   57
           Fall 1985   66
- Grade 5   Fall 1984   62
           Fall 1985   59

Three of the five grade levels made good gains, which reflected the teachers' varying commitments to writing; some wanted to teach it and some did it only because they had to. The increases do not even reflect a change in reading instruction, only in writing instruction.

Mast Way Elementary School teachers not only taught writing but also changed their reading instruction. I never looked at the Stanford Achievement Test scores from Mast Way because the teachers were exploring new ways to teach reading, and I feared that they would be afraid to take risks and try unknown procedures if I scrutinized test results. During the first year, the teachers refined their writing instruction, and during the second year, they experimented with their reading environments. By the end of the second year they were just starting to feel good about this enormous change in their belief system. Although it would be reasonable to expect the Mast Way scores to go down because the teachers, in effect, were novices, this didn't happen.

The SAT has two main sections within reading: comprehension and skills. According to John Lowy, the Mast Way scores on the skills subtests of the Stanford went up at the end of year two, and he was excited about the promise in these scores. The skills subtests had bothered him for fifteen years, ever since he had come to Mast Way. He had urged the teachers to try more than one skills-management system, but nothing worked. During the second year of the project, however, many of the teachers quit teaching skills either in isolation or according to a predetermined hierarchy. Instead, they tried to teach them in the context of the children's work when the need arose, and this proved to be a safe direction for continued experimentation.

The Mast Way comprehension scores had always been OK, but the Chapter I reading students were weak in comprehension as well as in the skills areas. Millie Woodward, the Chapter I teacher, changed her teaching a great deal during the second year of the project, and even with all her experimentation, plus that of the classroom teachers, the Chapter I students grew. (Chapter 18 is about Millie.)

When I interviewed Millie at the end of the project, she said that some of the children no longer needed Chapter I help. Her students' scores reflect their classroom program as well as their supplemental work, but writing can help students even if they only write with their reading teacher.

Paula Fleming (1986) saw an increase in the test scores of her remedial readers when she used writing in their reading program. Her goal was to show one year's growth on the *Diagnostic Reading Scales*, an individually administered reading test. She studied a group of eight second graders and a group of eight fourth graders. Their average growth after eight months of instruction was:

- Second grade: Oral reading   16   months
                        Silent reading 32.7 months
- Fourth grade: Oral reading   19.7 months
                        Silent reading 13.7 months

Paula met with each group for four one-hour sessions each week. For forty to sixty minutes of that weekly time allotment, Paula read to her students and for the remainder of their time with her, they wrote and conferred. These meetings were in addition to students' daily reading groups with their classroom teacher. Paula provides scores only for her referred students, but classroom teachers have similar evidence.

Nancie Atwell's (1986b) eighth graders read, write, and respond regularly, and their average reading scores are now at the seventy-second percentile, up from the fifty-fourth percentile. Similarly, Joe Biver's upper-elementary students in Athens, Wisconsin, write frequently, and even though his section contains the students who have problems, their reading scores at the end of a year of writing are as high as the scores in the other sections. This can also be the picture for classes with even more extreme problems.

Robert Bahruth's class of students from migrant families in Texas improved when he changed their program (Hayes and Bahruth 1985). His twenty-two students, ages ten through sixteen, knew little English and had limited reading abilities. Some were nonreaders. He focused on ways to strengthen their self-concepts, read to them daily, and wrote back and forth with them in class. In April, on the Informal Reading Inventory administered by the Chapter I department, his twenty-two students showed marked improvement of:

- One grade level: one child
- Two plus grade levels: seven children
- Three plus grade levels: thirteen children
- Four plus grade levels: one child

Hayes and Bahruth end their chapter on their students' achievement with this thought: "These scores should in no way obscure the tremendous progress the children made. Our children now know they can learn; they have learned how to learn. . . ." This reflection brings me back to my focus for this chapter, students' evaluation of their own reading accomplishments and progress. Instead of focusing on what we think the group can do, we need to turn joys and concerns back to the student, so that each one can express what he can do and hopes to do.

What Do I Do When I Read?

Students like those in Robert Bahruth's class, who have learned how to learn, know something about their learning process, and as their teachers imply, that knowledge may be more important than their scores. We attend to procedural knowledge when we ask, "What do I do?" This is a new question for assessing what students know, and when we ask a new question, we need a new test (Harste 1985), or at least an additional piece in our evaluation pie. Reading can draw on writing for a possible entry point into a more comprehensive way of looking at evaluation.

"What do I do when I write?" begins the student's evaluation when we teach writing with an emphasis on process. We regularly talk about what we do. Children ask each other how they choose topics and titles, and where they learned so much about fishing. Because the students have the language to talk about what they do when they write, they can also use this language for reading.

"What do I do when I read?" becomes a logical question if you're in a classroom where the act of learning takes priority. But this question has not been a part of reading instruction. When I ask my university students to monitor their reading process, they say they've never thought about what they do when they read. Yet we may get insights into what to teach our students to do when *they* read if we know what we do when *we* read. Regardless of readers' ages, as we talk about what we do, we realize that we sometimes read better than at other times.

What can I do well when I read? In order to find out what they do well, students need to choose books they can learn to read. In Ellen Blackburn Karelitz's classroom we watched the children's choices and noticed that they included books at all levels—easy, medium, and hard. The children read favorites over and over again until they could read them like pros; they read easy books to gel their skills. They kept challenging themselves with difficult books, which they'd try off and on for months until the day came when they could read them. Mostly, the children read from books they could almost read, those they could learn with only a few tries. When Leslie Funkhouser started to let her second graders choose their reading books, she showed them how to classify books into the above three categories (see chapter 4).

Now, many of the first, second, and third graders at Mast Way write *E M H*, or *E M CH*, at the top of their written response to their books. Sometimes they circle more than one letter because a book has some parts that fit into more than one category. A page with a small amount of print may be Easy while a longer page may be Hard. Also, sometimes a book may be Medium to read, but Hard, or a CHallenge, to write about.

We also watched the children monitor themselves in another way. Ellen Blackburn Karelitz explained to her students what the letters on the spines of the Holt basal readers meant. The basals sat on the book shelf, available for selection at all times, and each child chose them at some time during the year, some children often. We observed as a child picked level D, read it, and then tried book E. E was too hard so she reshelved it, read several other books, and tried E again a few weeks later. When a basal was right, a child sometimes read the entire book.

When Daniel discovered that he could read the first hard-cover book in the series, he read it from cover to cover in two days. At the end of the year, when Ellen needed to record reading levels in the school records, most of the children knew their level, and she met with the others. In a few minutes she and a child could determine each child's instructional level.

These students know what they can do, but they don't think only of themselves when they think of reading class. Reading is a time to share books or parts of books and to talk about books. Students can explain why they intend to share a book or why not, what they will tell if they tell about a book, and why they want to share certain parts. Todd liked the beginning of chapter 10 in *Kavlik the Wolf Dog*, by Walt Morey, and read, "Here he stopped and stood, nose lifted, as if he quested the breeze." Todd liked the picture this sentence created, the sound of it, and the new word *quested*. Opportunities to share help keep Todd's interest keen, develop his ability to evaluate writing, and help him see himself in relation to other readers.

Students seek out certain people when they have a particular book to share. Sometimes they want to share with others who have read the book, or if the book is about hunting, for example, they may want to share with someone who has hunted. Again, we can draw parallels to ourselves. I share different kinds of books with different friends and am amused by the books some people, who don't know me well, recommend to me. Similarly, I know some people never get around to reading books I recommend to them. It's difficult to get to know each other as readers, but these children receive practice at an early age.

Part of the children's responsibility during reading in these classrooms is to respond to other readers. Students can explain why it's easier with some authors or certain kinds of books or why it's harder in large groups, small groups, or with one friend. They sense when a reader is sharing something that's especially exciting or particularly difficult to read or explain, and they provide appropriate support.

Phyllis Kinzie's students used to amaze me with their ability to shift their response approaches from student to student and situation to situation. She and I would invariably twist with nervousness when a child who wasn't a terrific reader started to share, but the class leaned forward, took the challenge, and responded with great care. It was as if they shouted, "I've been through this. It's tough. You helped me. I'll help you." They are able to explain why the group clapped, laughed, or asked very few questions. Our ability to respond to other readers helps strengthen the ties we have with our learning community.

Probably the number one thing we do when we read is learn. We learn content from professional authors, friends, and teachers. We also learn what they do when they write and read. We learn about them as people, we learn about ourselves from them, and we value all these kinds of learning. Our students keep appropriate records of what they have learned about content, responding, sharing, or book choices as Pat McLure's first graders do for the books they read:

Book, Author	Read	Shared	Written About
Can I Keep Him? Steven Kellogg	x		x
Three Kittens Mirra Ginsberg	x	x	
No Bath Tonight Jane Yolen	x		

This record system can be varied to satisfy any age level through adulthood and any degree of detail. Students can date entries and classify each book with an *E* or *M*, or *E, M, CH*. They can keep track of books they choose, their reason for choosing a book, and whether they finish it or not. They can record with whom they shared and what part they shared if they didn't share an entire book. They can record significant responses from others and their own responses to others. There may be some records teachers want and others the student has options about; but both keep their records as simple as possible and record information on the spot, not later, because later may never arrive. Sometimes teachers record information beyond what students record, like Tom Romano's note about third-grader Chad's entry for *Save the Raccoon:*

> This was an easy-to-read book that Chad heard in a small group. Some days later, he picked out the book and engaged in the longest session of silent reading I've yet to observe him in.

Romano's note bears some similarity to the summary he wrote of Chad's reading at the end of the first semester:

> Chad knows when the language of a book is difficult for him, but he will stick with the book because the subject matter interests him. He will play around with a book for weeks. He likes being read to and likes reading a story that's been read to him.

Summaries, semester records, and grades for marking periods may take extra time, but we record evaluations regularly. We write during conferences and periodically interview children to learn how they perceive themselves. We help them see their progress. One chart some teachers use to record progress is a three-column chart written across the entire inside of each child's writing folder:

Things I can do well	Things I'm working on	Things I plan to learn
I can ask questions in conferences	I'm learning how to piggyback comments on other students' comments	I want to compare books to other books by the same author
I can read riddle books	I'm reading articles in sports magazines	I want to read a biography of a hockey player
I can find root words	I'm learning the meaning of suffixes and prefixes	I want to learn lots of prefixes and suffixes and use tons of them in one humorous poem

Often the items on the chart shift to the left as students become more facile at some things and derive new plans. The types of entries for the chart are endless—whatever is important to teacher and child.

Another way for students to see their progress is to look at past work. In January, Jan Roberts, Chad's third-grade teacher, showed him his first reading journal entry from September and his latest one. He could see his progress. In his case, he had begun to write more and his content improved. His knowledge of what he has learned about response to reading helps him become an involved reader. The various kinds of information discussed throughout this section tell more about students than scores from worksheets or tests, which give only a partial picture. When we give grades, we want them to reflect not only scores but also students' process knowledge in terms of such questions as: How do I respond to others? What kind of comments do I make? What kinds of questions do I ask?

Most important is the student's own evaluation of what he does when he reads. I remember vividly the shock in the voices of my students the first year I taught in the New Hampshire Summer Writing Program: "We get grades for this course?" To them, grades didn't make sense. Throughout the course, they had evaluated their own work, and yet it was all going to culminate in a grade given by someone else. The students had received no grades throughout the course, as none of my students do in any courses I teach, but the system requires a grade for university records. "What values would the grade reflect?" was my students' concern.

I tried a version of Nancie Atwell's conferences (1986a) as a way to center the evaluation on the students' views of what they knew. On the last day, they met with me in groups of three. Each person shared the main thing they had hoped to learn in the course, the main thing they did learn, and the one thing they intended to do in the fall because of the course. Each of the fifteen students had different answers for each of the three questions, but, in general, the individual students knew their own contribution to the group, knew what they valued in each of the others, and saw themselves as learners. Students who can work with others and who have plans for the future can continue forward.

What would I like to do next?   Learners are people who want to move ahead. As third-grade teacher Jan Roberts says, "We have always tested to find out who the good students are, but we also need to know who the good learners are."

Good learners not only know what they can do now, but they have plans for what to learn next. Our task as teachers is to help our students set realistic goals. When they have plans, we can help them accomplish those plans. We know what to teach. Second-grade teacher Leslie Funkhouser says teaching with response at the center of reading rests on the teacher's ability to trust her students to tell her what they want to learn. We can respond to someone who initiates. We establish the community of learners and support those learners' efforts. Our students' constant evaluation of what they can and can't do enables us to help.

A student may want to locate Ungava Bay after reading Jan Andrews's *Very Last First Time*, want to find another book by John Gardiner after reading *Stone Fox*, want help with a word in an I Can Read book, or wonder what to write in response to Cynthia Rylant's *A Blue-Eyed Daisy*. The student may raise her questions alone with us, in a small group, or in a whole-class session. We may teach, help the student figure out who to ask for help instead of us, or ignore the student because we know she can find help elsewhere. Often, this is our best teaching technique.

We can't be their primary resource or they will think they can learn only when we are present, which will curb their progress considerably. As they evaluate their progress they share how they learned what they know, who helped them, and how they might get help with what they want to do next. Phyllis Kinzie periodically asked her fourth-grade students to go through their writing folders and choose a good piece of writing, write about why it was good, who helped them with it, how the person helped, what they wanted to learn during the next few weeks, and how they'd go about learning it.

I have several quotations in my notes from conferences with students that refer to the plans they'd set for themselves. Todd decided he wanted to learn how to keep a log and started one for his swimming. Gradually his log became more explicit as "we," for example, became a list of five boys' names. Students take their plans seriously because we take them seriously.

Students may want to learn how to read a certain book, sound out vowels, learn about rhyming words, acquire the nerve to read to the class, think of comments in a small group, write down how they feel about a book, or ask questions in the Big Conference. The list is longer than the number of students in the class; they surprise us with what they want to know, which is why we ask them. We can't predict what each of them wants to learn.

How Do I Feel About Reading?

At Mast Way, the students first liked to write and the teachers looked to their writing instruction for guidance when they taught reading. A teacher's own definition of a good writer frames her instruction and assessment in writing. Jan Roberts began her description of a good writer with: "A good third-grade writer first of all is somebody who feels good about herself and likes to write."

How about a good reader? Jan said a good reader is similar to a good writer: "Feeling good about oneself as a reader. That's really important." To underscore her belief, Jan doesn't deal extensively with phonics during reading time, the 8:45–9:30 time slot each morning. If she requires her students to do worksheets and practice phonics during reading, those activities will not only take time away from books, but she fears her students will learn to dislike reading and she doesn't want that to happen. Jan, and many of us, think of people we label "readers" and what they do when we set up our reading program.

I could think of my own reading pattern this week. I have just finished *Excellent Women* by Barbara Pym and liked it, but it wasn't wonderful. I'm in the middle of two books but can't seem to stay with either. However, a friend recommended *West with the Wind* by Beryl Markham, and I can't put it down. It's a great book for me, and as I read it I share it, note parts I want to share with others, and think about who I'll recommend it to. I am constantly looking for a special book, as other readers do, and when we value this we build it into our reading program.

Children learn the importance of a good book, and they learn that it's not always easy to find a great book. But the better their choices, the more interested they become and the more effort they may put into their reading. They want a good book because then they will stick with it, insist on figuring it out, and improve. Sometimes readers try several titles before they find one they really like, and reading is that search.

Students can keep a list of all the books they read, star the special ones, and explain what distinguishes these from the others. In addition, students can talk about why a book was only "good" and not great, but still worth recommending to a friend. It helps us to know ourselves as readers when we can be explicit about what we like to read, but this knowledge mainly helps ensure that we do like to read. Students who don't like to read will probably not become independent readers.

There are many hallmarks of independent readers and we want information about students in regard to each behavior. Independent readers like to read, read beyond reading class, consider themselves readers, are considered readers by others, try a variety of books, read a variety of books, know how to pursue a reading task, know what they can do, know what they cannot do, know what their specific areas of interest are, know how to use the library, do use the library, and support others so they can consider themselves readers. Most importantly, they read.

The more students read, the better readers they often become. Nancie Atwell's students (1986b) read a lot and their scores have improved. In previous years, 21 percent of them scored in the bottom quartile, but last year only 2 percent fell into that lowest quartile. In June, 92 percent of her students read at home for pleasure, and on the average they each owned ninety-eight books, up from fifty-four in September. Students who are part of a culture of readers are more likely to become readers than if reading isn't the thing to do in their classrooms.

Reading can be fun for both students and teachers, but many teachers tell me they get bored teaching reading. This can change when teachers and students read and share books they like. In evaluating their instruction, teachers consider many things, and one is whether the students like to read.

Whether or not they do may be very complicated, but for our new research project we decided that we want the students to enjoy reading. If we teach them what they want to learn, we think they will be more likely to want to read. In order for them to tell us what they need, they must be aware of what options lie ahead. Our task is to find out what their plans are and help them generate options along the way. They must learn to monitor their journey. To this end, the question for our project is: How can children's ability to self-evaluate their own reading and writing be described?

References

ATWELL, NANCIE. 1986a. Making the Grade: Evaluating Writing in Conference. In *Understanding Writing: Ways of Observing, Learning & Teaching*, ed. by Thomas Newkirk and Nancie Atwell. Portsmouth, N.H.: Heinemann.

———. 1986b. Making Time. In *To Compose: Teaching Writing in the High School*, ed. by Thomas Newkirk. Portsmouth, N.H.: Heinemann.

FLEMING, PAULA. 1986. The Write Way to Read. In *Understanding Writing: Ways of Observing, Learning & Teaching*, ed. by Thomas Newkirk and Nancie Atwell. Portsmouth, N.H.: Heinemann.

HARSTE, JEROME. 1985. Portrait of a New Paradigm: Reading Comprehension Research. In *Landscapes: A State-of-the-Art Assessment of Reading Comprehension Research, 1974–1984*, ed. by Avon Crismore. Bloomington, Ind.: University of Indiana.

HAYES, CURTIS W., AND BAHRUTH, ROBERT. 1985. Querer Es Poder. In *Breaking Ground: Teachers Relate Reading and Writing in the Elementary School*, ed. by Jane Hansen, Thomas Newkirk, and Donald Graves. Portsmouth, N.H.: Heinemann.

MAYHER, JOHN S., AND BRAUSE, RITA S. 1986. Learning Through Teaching: Is Testing Crippling Integrated Language Education? *Language Arts* 63, no. 4 (April).

SUHOR, CHARLES. 1985. Objective Tests and Writing Samples: How Do They Affect Instruction in Composition? *Phi Delta Kappan* (May).

"Grumpy. /g/ /g/ /g/ I think that's a g."

Charles writes a g.

"Grumpy. /gr/ /gr/ There's an r."

Charles adds an r.

"My dad was grumpy. Grumpy. Grumpy."

Charles adds a p.

"Grumpy. /pe/ /eee/ It ends with an e."

Charles adds the final touch. His word is: grpe.

"My dad was grumpy. The . . ." Charles continues his writing. He's sounding out words, the words he needs, to say what he wants to say. Without invented spelling, he wouldn't be able to rely on himself. He couldn't say, "I can write."

Because his teacher doesn't spell words for her students, they sound them out. If their teacher started to spell words for them, they would besiege her with requests, and she wouldn't be able to focus her time on meaning. With the undaunted spirits that most young children bring to school, they write about *sgrlls* and *flayrs* in the *mdo* (squirrels and flowers in the meadow), which keeps their emphasis on the meaning, where we want it for reading. Invented spelling keeps the focus on the content and off the mechanics.

Phonics is a servant. It serves the message. In our reading/writing program young children learn the purpose of phonics when they write . . . and when they read.

Invented spelling focuses the teacher's and the child's emphasis on the meaning of a book, helps children develop the expertise they need with sound-symbol relationships, and permits children to take initiative in their own learning.

Invented Spelling Places the Emphasis on Meaning

Don Graves and I began our visits to Ellen Blackburn Karelitz's classroom in September 1981. That November I gave a talk about the research project at the conference of the National Council of Teachers of English in Boston (Hansen 1983). One thing had struck me more than anything else during those first two months. The children insisted that what they read made sense. They gradually built up their phonics skills via invented spelling, but Ellen used most of her time with them to keep their attention on the meaning of print. She responded to the children's efforts to put messages on paper.

Respond to the child's need.   When I was a Chapter I reading teacher, many of my students stumbled along, reading words that made no sense in the context of the story without appearing to notice the discrepancies. Yet this seldom happened with Ellen's fledglings. They took Easy-to-Read books and struggled, but they reread until something made sense, just as they did when they wrote.

During writing, they didn't write strings of nonsense. They carefully placed words in sequences and assumed that all authors did likewise. These little writers insisted that print, wherever they saw it, make sense. Ellen's children knew the essence of print. They had to create meaning when they wrote and when they read. Their desire to compose pushed them forward. No one told them it would be easy and it wasn't. They thought writing and reading were hard work, but their teacher supported their efforts. She helped them hear the sounds of letters and learn to write the letters they wanted. I also learned to help.

When I paused beside Matt, he read his writing to me and told me about his cute gerbil. As I left he resumed his writing. He had written only a K for *cute* and wanted to know what other letter there was. This was a big question, because Matt usually wrote only initial sounds. I asked him to say *cute* and on the third repetition he heard the /t/. I smiled and moved on. I can remember the day when a frown, rather than a smile, would have appeared on my face if I had seen Matt's writing.

I would have labeled KT an "error" as if that's the way he would always spell *cute*, rather than looking at it as an accomplishment because he can hear both beginning and ending sounds. Susan Sowers (1986) compares what we see in children's writing to what we see in their drawing.

No one worries when a child's first drawing of a person is a head propped up on two stick legs. As the errors become more sophisticated—two stick arms protruding from the head where the ears should be—no one fears this schema will become a habit though it may be repeated a hundred times. Although deficient by many measures, the drawings are not interpreted as signs of visual, cognitive, or fine motor problems. They are greeted as a display of intelligence and emerging proficiency.

When we focus on the process of learning rather than only the product, we see what our students can do—Matt can hear both initial and final sounds. But we have a hard time shifting from product-oriented selves to process-oriented selves.

If I spell children's words, I take their attention off the process of creating meaning and focus it on instant perfection. They stop sounding out words; they no longer need phonics. On the other hand, if I don't spell words, the children come to realize that sounds are a tool they must acquire. Teachers who have taken the risk and given invented spelling a full chance usually testify to their children's growth, and research backs what these teachers see.

Nathan, Temple, and Burris (1982) documented the patterns children use as their spelling evolves. Matt used to hear only initial sounds, but now he has begun to hear final sounds. He is moving along a progression his teacher fosters. Through her teaching, he will gradually hear a medial vowel, learn to represent /k/ with a C, and understand the final e. We watch for the opportunity to stretch Matt's ability to hear sounds, and I sense it the day he dwells on the /o/ after he has written an L to begin the word *lot*. I know he will hear the final /t/ and sense his confusion about this other sound he now hears. He doesn't appear to want to write the T yet. I ask Daniel to bring his book, *The Sun*, read it to Matt, and point out the o in *hot*. As Matt writes an O, I walk away.

Respond to the child's message.   Matt will gradually hear medial sounds but, mainly, when we think back on Matt, we think of WHAT he's writing about. This was the first time he'd had a pet, and he liked to watch his gerbil chew. When we pause beside Matt, he knows we have stopped to hear about his pet's latest antics. We must keep our thoughts primarily on content if we want to emphasize meaning. (Lindfors 1985 draws the necessary parallel to language development with our emphasis on meaning.)

When children believe they have something to say and know the class wants to hear it, they write many words every day. They need to know phonics because they want to write ". . . a LOT of cardboard," not only, "He chews cardboard." Phonics lets them put down their messages, including words such as *despicable* and *marvelous*, in the fall of first grade. But phonics isn't just for children. It also permits us to write nonstop. When we don't know a word, we give it our best shot, as the children do, so we can get on with the task at hand. Because phonics is a system of generalizations with exceptions, rather than a set of rules, it bugs us throughout our lives. Invented spelling, then, is a technique of fifty-year-old as well as five-year-old writers.

Writers don't interrupt their flow of thought to look up the spelling of a word in a dictionary. They don't even interrupt themselves to look up a specific detail. They leave a blank to fill in later because they want to get the entire puzzle spread out before them. If we spell words for our writers, we contradict what we know about writing, and divert their focus away from meaning, the focus they need for reading.

Invented Spelling Provides Phonics Practice

Florence Damon, the kindergarten teacher at Mast Way, decided to find out how many sounds her children could learn if she discontinued the "grunt and groan" lessons she had used for years. She helped her students with sounds only when they were in the process of writing and reading. If a child was stumped, she provided what he needed at that time. For example, Keith might want the word *garage* but not know what to write for /g/. This would be an occasion for her to teach the letter g. However, Florence may not be there when Keith wants to write *garage*.

The children write daily.   When they have a spelling problem, the children ask the others at the writing table and use the letter cards on the table. If no one can help, they can go elsewhere, to another child or to a book. More often, they draw a line and proceed to the next sound. They write every day and don't need all the letters today. They have 180 days this year to practice using sounds to generate meaning. Gradually the gap between what's on their pages and standardized print narrows. However, for most of us the gap never disappears but this does not mean we cannot be terrific writers and readers. Florence Damon's students possess the number one characteristic of a writer: they have things to say. The daily opportunity to write something to read to the class prompts them to learn their sounds in a way that is more important to them than ditto sheets.

Florence's children knew more sounds by the end of the year than did her students in former years, when she taught group lessons with worksheets. They learned them gradually, as they needed them. Learning had a purpose. The same focus on need carries through into reading.

The children hypothesize and approximate.   Children learn to read books they choose, and when they learn to choose books that are not too difficult, they can gradually learn the words they don't know. This is the method of learning they used when they learned to talk; they listened to a barrage of language and picked out the words and messages they needed. We let them continue to use this method to acquire written language.

They read from familiar books. Gradually, they read more and more words, until one day they can read the entire book. Sometimes they skip words as they skip sounds or letters in writing. At other times they use sounds they know from their writing, and when they want to, they ask for help. Since they read every day, there are lots of words and sounds they don't know. There would be no point in trying to learn many sounds in one day—the child wouldn't remember them all anyway—but a few specific lessons may help.

We can bring children together for skill sessions. Because we spend time with them when they write and read, we know what phonetic generalizations to teach. If I were to have a class lesson on /ch/, I would do it because I had seen that some children needed it. My teaching always follows a philosophy of response, response to what my students need. This guideline runs counter to that represented by the hulking, gray cabinet Janet vonReyn (1985) found in the corner of her kindergarten classroom. It contained the dittoes and workbooks of the teachers from whom she inherited her room, experienced teachers. Janet was a first-year teacher. The wisdom in the metal safe nagged at her, and although she finally succumbed to its presence in January, by March she knew she had to close its doors.

The worksheets and workbooks represented a way of teaching that ignored what her children needed. Typically, readiness workbooks place several children in the position of studying all the sounds, one at a time, whether they need them or not. Not only do these workbooks miss rather than hit the needs of many children, they defy the child's need to gradually figure out his world. Worksheets demand accuracy. We score them for correctness, which implies that a child is wrong if he is still in the process of learning something. Worksheets reward learned behavior rather than the behavior of learning. We need to think about phonics activities in terms of what children do with language.

They use language in a context. For the first two weeks of first grade, Daniel drew disjointed pictures of objects that were not related to each other. During those several days, he learned, because he heard other children tell about the escapades behind their pictures, to draw a story. He didn't call it drawing. He said he was writing. If Daniel had spent time labeling isolated pictures on worksheets, it might have retarded his concept of what it means to write. Instead, he had to think of what to put on blank paper. Since reading is the act of creating meaningful messages, and worksheets would have taken this responsibility out of Daniel's hands, dittoes might have inhibited his growth as a reader.

By the middle of September, Daniel had written his first complete story, "I C M" and read, "I climbed mountains." Daniel can already work with real writing, the kind that creates a message. In the context of a complete text, he can gradually learn his sounds. Worksheets of isolated words would require less of him than he can already do by himself. If teachers put me in a corner and said they think it would help Daniel to spend some extra time learning to hear final consonants, I'd have to admit that this may sound sensible. However, I would give a great big caution. We don't want isolated lessons to diminish the time the children have to figure out meaningful texts.

Extra lessons can help.   Extra lessons can help, but they should be very brief: five minutes of exposure to /ch/, with examples from both the writing and the reading of children who know /ch/. I'd conduct the skill sessions during a time of day labeled Phonics, or Skills, or whatever, even though I realize some teachers would have these lessons as part of writing or reading, because then it might be more obvious to the children how the skill is related to their work. I can follow their line of argument, but I'd be careful about creating a system for these lessons either at the beginning or end of each writing or reading class. Somehow, this might place undue emphasis on skills and distort the children's concept of what reading is all about. Regardless of when I had the lesson, I can't think of a reason for a child doing a /ch/ worksheet during writing or reading class.

Some teachers would like to continue using a few worksheets, but these should be completed at a time of day when they don't take away from time to read and write. I urge teachers to try letting children learn phonics while they read and to discontinue phonics worksheets and workbooks. Most teachers will find that invented spelling gives a tremendous amount of constant practice, which is more meaningful than worksheets. If I wanted to provide extra practice during writing or reading class, I'd capitalize on situations like the following.

One day when I stopped next to Adelle, she was practicing *Little Bear Comes Home* (Else Minarik), the book she had signed up to read to the class the next day. She was on this page:

"We can picnic here," said Mother Bear.
"It is nice here, by the river."
"Let's go for a swim," said Father Bear.

I listened to her read successfully until the word *swim*. She looked at me, and I said, "What do you think?"

Finally she said, " 'Surprise' is too big and I don't think it sounds right anyway."

I learned two things. Adelle realizes that the beginning sound and context will not work for her in this instance. I have worked with Adelle enough to know that she applies the /w/ sound for *w* and hypothesize that the problem could be the short *i*. I flip back through the pages she's read to look for a short *i* word. I find *did*, Adelle reads the sentence, and I ask for the sound of the *i*.

Children can write and read.   Children can read their own spellings better than complete spellings, and they can read their own written compositions better than oral compositions recorded by their teacher. As Ellen Blackburn Karelitz explains, "It has to do with control. The child remains in control of his writing if he writes it himself." If someone spells *have*, he can't read it but he can read *hv*. If someone records his oral message, many words are beyond his reading. He's no longer in control. Researcher Ann-Marie Klein learned this in Pat McLure's first-grade classroom at Mast Way.

Andy, one of Pat McLure's children, compared what happens when he reads his own writing and when he reads something some-one else wrote from his dictation. "My own writing is easier to read. I have to spell the words. I have to write them and that helps me put it in my mind what I just wrote." At first, Andy and other children may not realize the benefits of the extra work writing requires, but in time, they learn to rely on themselves.

They learn that writing and reading are things they can do at any time, in any place. In order to write they need paper and pencil, but they do not need another person. If you can do it yourself, you are more likely to do so than if you can only write when an expert is nearby. This is why I left so quickly earlier, when Matt asked me to help with *cute*. As soon as I could confirm what he knew, I left so he wouldn't become dependent on me. He knows I think he can write without me and he does. Reading is similar.

When the children's strategy is to hypothesize and speculate, they create their own message and move ahead. Invented spelling gives children and teachers a mind-set toward learning that may be labeled "Invented Reading." The children don't need someone else to constantly confirm their correctness; they know if they're creating a message or not. A book is something they can enjoy wherever, whenever.

Children can explain what they do.   We regularly ask the children how they have figured out something.

"You paused for quite a while on that word. How did you figure it out?"

"You read *saw* for *was*, but you went back and read it again. How did you know you had to go back?"

"Yesterday you drew a line for g, and today you put a g on the blank. How did you learn what it was?"

The more we ask children to explain what they do when they read, the more aware they become of their strategies. They provide more thorough answers and explain their processes to their friends. Common questions the children ask each other are, "How did you learn to read that book?" and, "Where did you have trouble?" When

Adelle read the Little Bear Book to the class, one child asked her, "What words were hard?"

She answered, "*Swim*. It has a sound I didn't know. Mrs. Hansen and me found the sound on another page. It's /i/." Adelle knows the phonics lesson was relevant, but explanations like hers do not come overnight. It takes time for children to make the connections.

Initially, they say, "I sounded it out," whenever we ask them how they figured out a new word, even if we know they figured it out from the context or through a rhyming pattern, asked another child, or found it in their writing. Somehow "sounding it out" is a phrase they learn from the world beyond the classroom and we need to work hard to broaden their repertoire. I do think children need to learn phonics, but it is only one of the ways, and often the most inefficient way, to figure out words in a book. Children not only need to become aware of how they really did figure out a word, but if they did "sound it out," they need to explain what they did more specifically.

Eventually, when we ask a child how she figured out a word, she thinks back over the process she has just used and explains, "I read ahead and then I knew what it had to be." The more children can explain what they do the more independent they can become. If they have problems, they can go through their repertoire and decide on a probable strategy. Then they can say, "I figured it out myself." This brings me to the primary reason for invented spelling, which isn't phonics or an emphasis on meaning. Children who spell their own words can say, "I did it myself."

They can feel this sense of accomplishment if we hold back. Sometimes it's difficult to believe students will learn if we don't direct every move, but their self-confidence can grow, as remedial reading teacher Joey Menzies found out. She taught in the Northwest Territories of Canada, and one of her third-grade students resisted a long time when she refused to spell for him. He sat and stared in defiance. Gradually, he drew pictures of his bike and of ramps, conferred with the group about his bike experiences, and watched Joey and the others write. He finally surrendered. Joey writes about his change in attitude:

> He was working with limited phonetic skills but he continued to persevere with his piece about bikes until he'd added enough information to satisfy himself. During the editing I introduced him to a dictionary. He knew he could only use it on completion of a piece of writing. His teacher informed me that for the first time his attendance was perfect. He was very proud when he brought back his first published book to be placed in the class library. Within a few weeks he and I had developed a relationship of mutual respect.
>
> His teacher, Rose Goudeau, had offered me her support in the beginning when he had rebelled against spelling words on his own. He had difficulty adjusting to being placed in the position of being an

independent learner. She informed me that he had worked with two remedial teachers who had given him all the information he needed to complete ditto work successfully. He had experienced frustration in working independent of me. When his teacher asked him what he'd learned with me she was amazed at his response (and so was I). He responded right away listing various skills. He had learned what he knew.

References

HANSEN, JANE. 1983. The Writer as Meaning-Maker. In *Teaching All the Children to Write*, ed. by J. L. Collins. Albany, N.Y.: New York Council of Teachers of English.

LINDFORS, JUDITH WELLS. 1985. Understanding the Development of Language Structure. In *Observing the Language Learner*, ed. by Angela Jaggar and M. Trika Smith-Burke. Newark, Del.: International Reading Association; Urbana, Ill.: National Council of Teachers of English.

SOWERS, SUSAN. 1986. Six Questions Teachers Ask About Invented Spelling. In *Understanding Writing: Ways of Observing, Learning & Teaching*, ed. by Thomas Newkirk and Nancie Atwell. Portsmouth, N.H.: Heinemann.

TEMPLE, CHARLES A.; NATHAN, RUTH G.; AND BURRIS, NANCY A. 1982. *The Beginnings of Writing*. Boston, Mass.: Allyn and Bacon.

VON REYN, JANET. Learning Together: A Teacher's First Year Teaching Reading and Writing. In *Breaking Ground: Teachers Relate Reading and Writing in the Elementary School*, ed. by Jane Hansen, Thomas Newkirk, and Donald Graves. Portsmouth, N.H.: Heinemann.

Much confusion exists about skills instruction within a response-centered classroom. Whenever I give a talk or conduct a workshop, one of the first questions someone asks me is, "How do you teach skills?" The answer isn't simple.

The skills issue is at the core of the process/product dichotomy (Walshe 1984). Research on the writing process began because writing teachers emphasized mechanics more than meaning. Reading teachers also receive criticism for focusing too much on skills. However, when teachers decide to focus on meaning, they still teach mechanics, because skills help meaning. If writers' skills are poor, readers will have a hard time constructing a message. Similarly, if readers' skills are shaky, those readers will have trouble. So, we do teach skills. There are three principles teachers keep in mind when they work with their students on skills.

1. They teach autonomy. Their students learn not to rely on the teacher but rather, to become independent learners. The teachers structure their classrooms so the students can get help when they need it. The students learn when and from whom to ask for help.
2. They teach what the students need. These teachers spend time with their students when the students are in the process of reading and writing. They listen while the students try to solve their problems. Then, based upon what they see and hear a student try to do, they teach a skill the student needs and can handle in order to move ahead.
3. They make good use of their time. They may have thirty students and maybe a list of ninety skills to teach. That's twenty-

seven hundred encounters. Impossible. When a student needs help, the teacher selects the skill most crucial to the text at hand, but she doesn't teach the skill to only one child. Others take part. However, if there is another child who already knows the skill the writer needs, that child teaches. Several children teach and learn a skill on any one day. The teacher teaches the skills the other children in the classroom can't teach.

There is no standard list of skills to teach for either reading or writing, but many teachers have either their own mental lists, the list in the basal reader or language arts text, the school's curriculum guide, or an accountability system. Regardless, skills are a necessary part of any program. Of the many skills on various lists, general categories for study skills, usage, punctuation, phonics, spelling, and context clues are common. My main goal is to show how response-centered teachers teach skills.

Context Clues

Two kindergarten children sit on a pillow in the classroom library and look at *The Very Hungry Caterpillar* by Eric Carle, the book their teacher read to them after recess. Other children work on various kinds of activities around the room while their teacher makes her rounds. As she approaches the library, Anna announces, "We can read this!" Their teacher, who has read the book to the class at least five times, responds, "Will you read some to me?"

As they start to read, two nearby children come to listen. Before long, the readers get stuck on the word *after*. Anna, one of the listeners, helps, "Just keep going. You'll get it."

The readers read on, " '(and) ———— that he felt much better.' " One of the readers exclaims, "I know what that part is," and goes back and reads, " 'and after that he felt much better.' "

After two more sentences, the teacher continues her rounds, but before she leaves she has a skills conference. "You really like that book, don't you. Why?"

"The food makes me hungry."

"Me too. I noticed back here (teacher points to *after*) you didn't know this word at first. Tell me how you figured it out."

"I think you helped us that way one time. Anna helped."

"Yes, she told you to read ahead and that worked."

The ability to use context clues is the most helpful reading skill. In general, readers use context clues to figure out words more than they use any other skill. Readers who are writers are used to pushing onward. When they write, they put down their message as it comes and move ahead. They have something in mind and they want to get it down. They don't just string out words. They know words follow words for a reason.

Writers attack reading in a similar fashion if we keep the focus on meaning (Galda 1984). Young children need many familiar books to read so they can try to construct the meaning themselves. They begin to read the way they begin to write. They jump in fearlessly. Older children also need to use context skills as their first line of attack when they meet an unknown word.

Spelling

Writers don't often produce final products the first time they try a piece of writing. They struggle through their message from beginning to end in order to find out what information they have to work with. Then, they go back and work on smaller and smaller chunks until they get down to the one-word level. The main thing students learn about spelling is *when* to check their words. They have to learn when spelling counts.

If writers think they should spell correctly on early drafts, they interfere with the main goal of their own writing: to produce an interesting message. The following examples illustrate the difference between how Scott wrote about his grandma and what he might have written if he had worried about spelling on his first draft.

> Won da me and my fathr and mothr want to my grandmas to viset hr becus she jest came awt ov the hospdl. She had a ne operashun becus hr ne crdlig is bad. Wal we wr thar we toct with ech othr my gramu told us thot hr ne is betr

> Me and my dad and mom saw my grandma. She had a bad leg. It is good now.

Writing teachers judge the first sample as the better piece of writing and, because they want their students to compose interesting material, they do not tell them to spell correctly on their first drafts. Students who worry about spelling too early tend to use familiar words and compose dull pieces of writing.

Further, if students think the spelling in every piece of writing must be corrected, they interfere with their own progress, because the time they spend fixing the spelling on a dead-end piece of writing would be better spent on a piece of writing that may turn out to be significant. It is important for writers to write, and writing is composing. The writing teacher wants her students to spend a significant portion of their writing time composing. When they are composing —putting words together—they are also practicing their spelling.

However, when a writer decides to bring a piece of writing to final copy, it's time to think about spelling. Whenever possible, the child solves her own problems on her road to becoming an independent learner, so she is in charge of her misspelled text. For very young or inexperienced writers, adults carry most or all of the responsibility for spelling, but when a child can take spelling responsibilities as a positive challenge, she begins to take over.

Ultimately, she circles each word she thinks is spelled incorrectly. Then she finds out how to spell those words. She uses any method other than asking the teacher. Next the child goes to a classmate, and the classmate draws other circles around words whose spelling he wonders about. The writer now checks those words.

At this time, the writer is ready to go to the teacher, who checks the spelling list in the writer's folder to see if the child has attended to the words she misspelled on previous texts. Then the teacher goes through the entire text as quickly as possible. If the teacher finds misspellings, she indicates them with a general mark such as, "There's a word for you to check somewhere in these two lines." The teacher does this with maybe two words and corrects the rest herself. The child adds a couple of words to her spelling list. She chooses the words in consultation with the teacher from the various words she misspelled and now, finally, the teacher may teach a skill.

Christy has added *with* and *they* to her list. The sight word *they* does not involve a skill, but *with* can provide a skill lesson. The teacher teaches *with* in whichever way makes sense to the child. Christy may have written *with* as *yith* or *with* as *weth* or *with* as *wif*. In Christy's case, she spelled *with* as *wif*. Her teacher recently heard her read *with* with a *th*, so she thinks Christy can learn to spell *with* with a *th* instead of an *f*. In three minutes her teacher dictates *bath*, *moth* and *path*. As Christy writes each word, the three other children at the table (we teach skills lessons with other children present) may choose to write them also.

This lesson is not a test situation. With each word, everyone talks about how to spell it, helps one another spell it right, and comments on the *th* sound.

Christy goes off to find the two or three misspelled words in the sections her teacher marked, and then she will check for punctuation.

Her teacher goes to another section of the room to help someone else at a different cluster of desks.

Eric asks her, "How do you spell *lean*?" Eric is just learning how to listen for sound-symbol correspondences and, therefore, needs to spell his own words. If someone tells him how to spell a word, he won't have to learn phonics. So when Eric asks how to spell *lean*, his teacher answers, "What do you mean?"

"I lean over when I jump."

"Oh, yes, you do, don't you? Say *lean*."

"*Lean*."

"Yes. Say it again and listen to the way it starts."

"*Lean*. /l-l-l/ *L*?"

"How do you make an *L*?"

Eric doesn't respond.

The teacher asks, "Who could help you?"

"Denise."

Eric is right in the middle of composing, but he goes to Denise. Young children often demand help with spelling while they are composing initial drafts because their command of phonics is so limited, they can't even get their ideas down. They get help from others when they need it.

Phonics

Phonics competence varies from the limited knowledge of novices immersed in invented spelling to that of more advanced readers like Johanna, who sits in her second-grade classroom in April. She is reading a Shel Silverstein poem and stops at the word *thigh*. She knows it's a body part because it's part of a series of other body parts, but she can't even guess what it might be. Because context won't work (Petty, Petty & Becking 1984) her teacher waits for Johanna to tackle the word phonetically. Her teacher must hear how Johanna will attack the word in order to know how to help. Johanna finally begins: /t/. Johanna pauses and tries again: /t/.

Her teacher writes *thigh*—/t/ in her notes. She thinks she remembers a *th* problem on a recent day with Johanna, so she glances up her page of notes. Yes, she labeled "Thursday: Tuesday" and also, she said, "/t/ . . . /t/," when she came to *thistle* in one of her books.

Johanna wants to read the Shel Silverstein poem and looks to her teacher, who says, "Please get your math book." With Johanna's math book in front of them, her teacher continues, "Find three words that have the letters *th*."

Johanna instantly spots *math* and says, "Oh, it's /th/. It starts with /th/."

"Yes. Find two more examples, Johanna."

In a couple more minutes they go back to the poem, and Johanna can label her thigh for the first time, "A *thigh*? What a weird word."

They laugh together and Johanna reads the poem.

The situation might have been different. Johanna might have said /th/, when she saw *thigh*. She might have paused and said /th/ again. This time her teacher could teach the sound for *igh*. A nearby child could jump in, "It looks like *high*." A second child, "And it's in *night*." A third child, "It's *thigh*. I should know. Mine are stiff from hiking yesterday."

The children have found patterns many times, and the teacher watches as they spontaneously start a list of *igh* words.

The teacher leaves them and looks for another child who needs her.

Punctuation

This time the teacher stops at Joshua. He is polishing a piece about getting ready for a football game.

Going to a football game

One dull Sunday morning I got up & went to the breakfast table. Mom Pop & my little sister Jessica were already therre. Good morning I said. Good morning my father said back. How would you like to go to a Foot Ball game? Would I? I said I'd love too. What time should we leave? About 2:00 what will give us unough time to get ready. I had never been to a Foot Ball game before!

Part II

It was almost 2:00. I can't wait I cant wait. I kept on saying. My Dad said he had some good news & he had some bad news. I want to hear the good news first I said. O.K. . . .

Joshua draws boxes around the places he thinks need different punctuation. A friend also checks the punctuation. His teacher begins the conference by looking at Joshua's list of "Things I Can Do" in his folder.

Things I can do

1. I put capital letters on names of towns.
2. I put capital letters on names of teams.
3. I put capital letters on names of people.
4. I put periods after Mr. and Mrs.
5. I put a period at the end of a story.
6. I put a dash in a score like 23–26.

She scans Joshua's work and finds he has attended to these skills.

Then she studies the boxes Joshua has made on his paper. Three of his boxes follow quotes because he thinks he needs commas at those places. He has no quotation marks. "Yes, Joshua, you did pause here when you read. Also, this is where your Dad talked. What did he say?"

Joshua moves his finger back up the page and reads, "How would you like to go to a football game?"

His teacher explains, "You need to put quotation marks around his words. Let's find some in your book."

Joshua opens Marjorie Sharmat's *Nate the Great*, they find quotation marks, he inserts them and then finds another spot in his writing where someone talks.

His teacher comments, "Yes, now it's clearer to me because I can see exactly what your dad said."

He goes off to find the rest of the places where he needs quotation marks. (For an interesting, funny essay on punctuation, see Thomas 1979.)

His teacher goes to another set of desks.

Usage

Now we are in a fifth-grade classroom, and Marcel has decided to publish his piece about when the police stopped him on his dirt bike. He thinks it is flawless. No edits necessary.

His teacher begins by checking through Marcel's "Things I Can Do" list.

Things I can do

1. I capitalize names, towns, and states.
2. I put periods after abbreviations.
3. I use *were* with plurals.
4. I use commas inside quotation marks.

She notices that Marcel has forgotten a comma inside one set of quotation marks and says, "You and David found almost everything, but check number four again."

Marcel finds the spot, inserts a comma, and his teacher begins a careful edit. She notices one usage error and doesn't think this correction will bother Marcel: "Me and my friend went to the sand dunes."

They open his C. S. Lewis book and look for three similar constructions. This takes two minutes and two of Marcel's nearby friends help.

Marcel records "My friend and I" on his list of "Things I Can Do," dates the entry, corrects the phrase in his writing, and chooses to rewrite the entire story himself rather than have a typist type it for publication.

The decision about whether a usage pattern should be corrected is often difficult, because usage in writing often reflects oral language patterns. We cannot expect a child to write several usage patterns he does not use when he talks (Fisher 1980). A young child cannot imitate adult language patterns he does not yet use, and the confidence of bigger children is shaken if their writing is overcorrected. For young children, if usage is corrected with too much precision, they can't read the corrected piece.

Study Skills

Sam approaches his teacher. He is reading a book about some boys on an adventure and found a section in which the boys watched some otters. He didn't know for sure what an otter was and there was no picture. His teacher started to tell Sam about the otters at her cabin but bit her tongue. She'd better let Sam try on his own first. Then she'd add her tale. "How can you find out, Sam?"

Without an answer, Sam goes off to the library where he corners the librarian. "Ms. Taft, help me find out about otters."

Wise Ms. Taft calmly responds, "What are two places you could look, Sam?"

Sam stops short. He likes film loops; maybe he can find one on otters. If not, he can always look in an encyclopedia.

The adults return Sam's question to him because they want him to be able to say at the end, "I did it myself." They help him find options when he has a question, but he chooses the process he will use to find his own answer to his own question.

Sam does not find a film loop. He finds a picture in an encyclopedia that he shares with both Ms. Taft and an older boy from another class who happens to be in the library. This boy wonders if otters are like beavers because he has written a report on beavers. They both disappear around the stacks to find a book about animals. The older boy helps Sam read two paragraphs in a section about otters, "Otters have webbed feet like ducks." Sam decides instantly he has to read this to his class.

He practices and practices these two paragraphs and shows off his study skills two days later when he reads to his class. They talk about otters. His teacher relates her story about the otters who slide on the icy riverbanks at her cabin in the wintertime. Finally, one of the students asks Sam, "How did you find those paragraphs?"

"Well, Mark's big brother was in the library and showed me this, the index. Here (pause while Sam flips pages) is the word *otter* and three page numbers. Sometime when you need some information, I'll show you how it works."

His teacher dates "Knows how to use an index" on Sam's skills list. She also writes, "Otters. Learned from older student in library. Will teach 'Index' to others."

This cycle goes on. Children need help and their teachers help them become independent. Their teachers give specific assistance in situations when the children can't move ahead. They all remember to attend to mechanics only when these enhance a meaningful, interesting text. Students learn to think about skills as they read and write.

References

FISHER, CAROL. 1980. Grammar in the Language Arts Program. In *Discovering Language with Children*, ed. by Gay Su Pinnell. Urbana, Ill.: National Council of Teachers of English.

GALDA, LEE. 1984. The Relations Between Reading and Writing in Young Children. In *New Directions in Composition Research*, ed. by Richard Beach and Lillian S. Bridwell. New York: Guilford Press.

PETTY, WALTER T.; PETTY, DOROTHY C.; AND BECKING, MARJORIE F., EDS. 1984. *Experiences in Language: Tools and Techniques for Language Arts Methods*. 4th ed. Boston: Allyn and Bacon.

THOMAS, LEWIS. 1979. *The Medusa and the Snail*. New York: Viking.

WALSHE, R. D. 1984. Teaching Writing: Attend to "Skills" as Part of "Process." In *Children and Learning*, ed. by Walter McVitty. Portsmouth, N.H.: Heinemann.

I have a collection of readers, the oldest of which is 180 years old. Comprehension questions, called "exercises," first appear in my 1879 *McGuffey's Fourth Eclectic Reader*. A scan of the questions reveals the strong moral character of the stories. Some representative titles are: "Perseverance"; "Try, Try Again"; "Where There Is a Will There Is a Way"; "True Manliness"; "Waste Not, Want Not"; and "Emulation." Passage 50, "The Right Way" by Frank R. Stockton, has this typical question within its set: "Would it have been right for Andrew to have told an untruth even to help Jenny out of trouble?" This question reinforces the intended message of the selection and, in a sense, is not a real question. It is a dictum. It ensures that the reader will get the intended message from the story.

Not until recently did we realize that reading class is not an occasion for indoctrination. Prior knowledge research in reading implies that we should teach each reader to recognize what she knows and build on it. Each reader will inevitably start and end at different places. Research on writing reinforces the idiosyncratic nature of responses to text.

During writing, students celebrate, challenge, and defend their own work and the work of the other writers in their community. They work with their writing in ways similar to those real authors use. They think of themselves as writers, feel bonds with writers beyond their classrooms, treat other writers the way they treat each other, and appreciate and question the work of professionals.

When their teachers, including myself, realized that writing is an author's opportunity to speak in a strong voice, we decided to let the children's voices be heard during Reading. As an audience, they cheered and protested. What the children did as writers challenged our former reading instruction head on.

Teaching based on response is at odds with the historical and present stance represented by basals. But if we believe in what we do when we teach writing, we question traditional reading instruction. The five key elements of a writing/reading program—Time, Choice, Response, Structure, Community—caused me to see basals in a new light.

Time

This section complements previous information about the amount of time students spend with books. We use all our convictions to find more time for students to read in our already-full schedules. We must discontinue something in order to find time to read real books.

Students across the country often read an average of one story a week, and spend their remaining time during reading class on workbooks, worksheets, games, projects, and sometimes math. For these students, that one story is a basal story, and when assignments for five days center on it, its importance is critical. (See Goodman 1986 for more information on basals.) As students get older they may spend as much as six weeks on one story, because traditionally, we have wanted to stress each part to be sure that they totally understood it. We wanted students to get the meaning we thought the author intended, and we devoted time in a reading program to that goal. The decision-maker was the teacher, who decided what a story meant. Time to ensure that students understood a story was often more important than time to read.

However, when we teach reading from the same philosophical perspective as writing, we use time differently. The students spend most of their time reading books. Comprehension is inherent, and students share their books daily. However, this use of time is not focused on getting across the message the teacher thinks the author intended, because the authors in the class know this is not the way writing works. They know that various classmates respond differently to the texts they create when they write. They spend their time in comprehension discussions contrasting and comparing their varied insights into what they read. They come together to learn from each other as well as from the teacher and the author.

They do not discuss everything they read. They mustn't. If they have to share everything, this somehow implies that reading for oneself is not valuable. Within the daily period called Reading, students read books for themselves and books they decide to share.

They have time to read because their teachers abandoned language arts texts for English and workbooks for reading. Some continued to use reading worksheets, but their students seldom used them during Reading time. They could be used during Worksheet time, or Study Skills time, or whatever the teacher decided to call it, but not during reading because they would take away from time to read.

As adults, when we think of someone we know whom we would label a Reader, we think of the person as one who spends a lot of Time reading. The person may be busy but finds time to read. I repeatedly find teachers who picture a reader as a person with a book in hand. Recently, I conducted a session for teachers in Peterborough, New Hampshire, and asked each of the participants to write the name of a person they knew who is a reader, list three characteristics of that person as a reader, and from the list of three, circle that reader's most salient trait. I then chose ten people at random and wrote their reader's most outstanding behavior on the overhead projector.

1. Reads a lot (books).
2. Shares books I would like.
3. In discussions of all kinds, supports herself (reads books, magazines, newspapers).
4. Reads research on teaching.
5. Reads constantly (books, magazines, news).
6. Reads to grandchildren often (books).
7. Likes to read (books, magazines, news).
8. Thinks (reads books, magazines, news, and music).
9. Shares books with others.
10. Reads every night (books, magazines, news).

No one's reader did anything similar to worksheet activities. They all read books, newspapers, or magazines. As teachers, our own definition of "A Reader" conflicts with what we often have our students do in school. Basal programs coopt the time of day called Reading for activities we don't associate with readers, but this need not be so.

Students can read complete pieces of writing during reading. They can read stories from their basal, library books, newspapers, magazines, their own writing, or that of classmates and other writers in their school. All these types of reading can include prose and poetry, fiction and nonfiction, and narrative or content area information. Students need immersion in print besides their basals to satisfy their appetite and interests during reading class.

From writing research we learn that even with the best writing teacher in the world, a student must write frequently or the instruction will fall on blank paper. Similarly, when we place "Read" at the top of students' list of Things To Do, we acknowledge the necessity of practice; more importantly, when we say, "It's time for reading," we mean, "It's time to read."

Choice

I told the teachers in Peterborough that one characteristic of a reader wasn't on their list, although I hadn't predicted that it would be. It's so basic we don't even think to say it. But it was true of all ten readers:

1. The person chooses her own books.
2. The person chooses her own books.
3. The person decides what she will read.
4. The person selects articles.
5. The person selects the books, magazines, news she'll read.
6. She and the grandchildren choose the books.
7. He chooses his books, magazines, and newspapers.
8. He chooses his books, magazines, newspapers, and music.
9. She chooses her books.
10. She decides what she'll read each night.

These readers all choose their reading materials. "A Reader" is a person who decides what to read. However, it's difficult to envision choice in relation to the notion of basals, because in the past we have always assigned stories. However, teachers can include Choice in reading, even if they decide to keep basals in their classroom.

Choice involves a monumental change. In writing, topic choice was difficult for us to try, but once we have taught children how to choose topics, we can't imagine a writing class in which we determine the majority of the writing. Children would cease to view themselves as writers if we told them they could no longer choose their own topics.

Similarly, children take off when we teach them how to choose books. In grade five, a girl who chose her books throughout grade four explained in an interview, "If you couldn't choose your own books, reading could be pretty boring." Children become interested. They like to read, and we sense this in only a few weeks' time.

This does not mean we have to hide the basals in closets. The children can use the basals as anthologies. They find stories they like and read those. Ellen Blackburn Karelitz's grade-one children particularly liked a song from a basal, "Mr. Rabbit, Mr. Rabbit" and a story in which a grumpy man yelled, "Stop that noise!" Several children read that story to the class from the Author's Chair.

When a few children find a story they all like, they can meet to share it in a small group. Children will often decide to read what their friends read, whether it's a story or a book. Ellen Blanchard's third- and fourth-grade students post the title of a basal story they like. When a few others read the story, they meet to share it, regardless of their grade level or reading level. Choice need not eliminate sessions in which readers compare insights on something they've all read.

There is no need to continue to assign reading. Years ago, there were not the hundreds of choices now available; and sometimes there was only the text. Choosing books should no longer be an issue in schoolrooms. We started assigning reading when we didn't have many books and when we wanted to control comprehension. Now that we do have books and know enough about reading and writing to expect diversity when reading is shared, we can move books out of supplementary, recreational reading into the center of the reading program.

Response Sessions

The essence of the difference between writing instruction and basal reading instruction lies in the word *response*. Basal programs, when used as the manuals suggest, reject the belief that children learn best when adults respond to what they know. This is a harsh statement, but when we understand writing instruction, we can no longer use basals as they are intended. We cannot operate under two philosophies (Blackburn 1984). Either we give up on writing or we use basals differently (or we don't use basals at all). The notion of response forces us to bring our teaching together to give us a consistent approach when we teach our students.

I was a classroom teacher in the late sixties and early seventies. When my students came to a discussion, I focused on the final product: their proper answers to my questions. My students went through the process of figuring out the story on their own as they read it silently, while I met with another group. When they came to their group session, I checked their comprehension. My goal was not that my students respond to what they read; they were not responsible for composing a personally meaningful message to share with their peers in order to receive response from them. (See Aiken 1984 for an essay on the importance of children's insights.)

In the classrooms described in this book, some of the children meet to discuss stories from basals, and both teacher and students come to these discussions equally prepared. They may be ready to share a part of the story they liked, and they may all come with a question, something the story made them think of that they'd like the group to discuss. Students respond to each other's comments, and they don't always agree.

Jan Roberts wanted her students to focus on the main idea. The following discussion transpired one day when she met with some of them to discuss a story about the magician Harry Houdini (Hubbard 1984). Jerry began, "I think the most important thing was that the teacher cared—really cared—about his student."

Denise: "Nope, I don't think so. I felt more like the teacher is better and wants to prove it."

"My answer's completely different," Joan announced. "I thought the author was reminding us how dangerous the sea is—that you have to think about that when you're swimming."

"I think the author wanted us to know that you can be whatever you want," Matt added.

After a discussion of these differing views, Jan Roberts spoke, but not as teacher-leader. She did not offer students the "correct" interpretation. "You know, I had a different idea. I thought it was more about Houdini as a person."

Matt smiled, "So yours is the fifth idea."

"Yes."

The discussion continued with divergent answers, Jan offering her own viewpoint but as a "fifth idea." In the past, her discussions followed the more typical basal system pattern, but now that her students have written for several months, making choices and considering options in their writing, she has revised the way she teaches reading. When Jan Roberts reflected back on the discussion she said, "Last year I would have pushed and pushed until they came around to my answer."

Later, as the students talked about many of the details in the story, another characteristic of writing discussions emerged. Denise commented, "I'd like to ask the author where he got all that detail."

Jerry nodded, "Maybe he read magic books."

"What else might he have read?" Jan Roberts asked.

"Encyclopedias."

"And some biographies."

"Maybe a movie," Matt added. He thought a moment, then jumped up, "OR . . . I know!! He could've gone right to Houdini's family. Maybe they could tell him stories, or he could ask them questions. Maybe they even kept records he could use."

Jerry was on the same track, "Or old newspapers?" His face fell. "But they'd be thrown out. . . ."

"Well," Jan told them, "he could've. You can go to the library to see old newspapers. They store them on microfiche."

The children talked about the story as a piece of writing. They are writers, and getting information for their own writing is something they think a lot about. Details give writing its credibility. Even Pat McLure's first-grade children notice them. They question facts and "rewrite" what they read.

In December, Tara suggested some changes for *Caps for Sale* (Hubbard 1986). "You know, if I had written that, I would've made it different. First of all, I'd change the monkeys to owls 'cause there's no monkeys in New Hampshire. The owl could be sitting up in the tree and when he looked for his caps he could say, 'Who took my caps?' and the owls could all say 'Whooo . . . Whooo. . . . ' Then they could fly right down and bite his nose!"

Jill agreed that would make it a better story and suggested another change. "I'd have him carry the caps in a pack instead of on his head, too. Wouldn't that make more sense?" Little did Jill know, another published version of this old tale does portray the peddler with the caps in a pack.

My point is not whether Tara's or Jill's rendition would be any better. But as young writers, when they discuss a piece of published writing, they know it's a final draft—a draft—something to monkey around with. After they have published their own work, they talk about how they would change it if they had another chance. Writers know about the nonpermanent nature of print, and now, because their teacher has set up a similar structure and philosophy with their reading, they have learned to approach the writing of professionals the same way they approach their own writing.

These children determine the path of their discussions. In typical basal programs, the teacher does not set self-direction as a goal when she meets with students. This is a major difference from writing, where a major goal in any kind of conference is to teach the writers to respond to and assess their own work. These children continue to assess writing, whether it's a trade book such as *Caps for Sale*, or a basal.

They can meet for their discussion with or without their teacher. This is important. If we must always be present, we give students the impression that we are the only authority. Even though we can add information to a session that will stretch the children, we must leave them alone at times, because they must learn to value each other's knowledge—and their own. We teach them how to respond so they can do it when we aren't present. We teach independence in both writing and reading. If we can't trust students to meet without us, then we have some teaching to do. We may need structure.

Structure

It bothers me when teachers say that basal-centered classrooms are more structured than those based on response. On the contrary, if children spend a lot of time reading and sharing books they have chosen, the classroom must be highly organized or it will be a mess. The structure is tight but in a different way than the basal classroom.

In a response-based philosophy the teacher not only sets up the routine, she teaches the children to use it. This is probably what I found most difficult to understand and what many teachers find difficult to learn. Initially, when a few children meet to share their books, or a common book or story, the teacher establishes a structure. Every teacher's format will be different, but each teacher decides on a routine and initially adheres to it like Super Glue. If the system calls for children to read aloud a part that "works," then they practice this format until they can do it without the teacher. The teacher listens to herself and gradually eliminates her part. If she hears herself saying, "Who's next?" she must transfer turn-taking to the group.

She may say, "Fred, when a few children have responded to the part you read, you tell the group, 'Thanks,' and then there will be only two people left. Beth and Anthony, you will decide who is next." The teacher keeps mum when Fred's turn expires. Absolutely mum. The children can eventually take over the group. Sometimes by the end of only one session the teacher can shift group management from herself to the students.

This new notion of structure is based on the concept of self-discipline, rather than on the usual external structure kept in place by the presence of the teacher at each group meeting. It involves trust on the part of the teacher, both that she can teach children to manage their own interactions and that the content of their discussions will be challenging even without an adult present.

In thinking of classroom management during reading we have always seen ourselves as the leader of each group and the children as working alone for the majority of the time. When we weren't there, we kept students apart. For the most part, we let children interact only when we were present, and even then we channeled interactions so that our students provided answers to our questions rather than acting as independent readers.

Years ago, my students worked on the assignments I gave them without talking to others. I didn't want them to ask for help because my emphasis was on the product—the worksheet—and if they got help I wouldn't know how much each of them knew. They worked alone, depended on me to correct their work and tell them if they did it right, and relied on me to get them started with some new work the next day. Their entire work cycle—getting started on something new, learning along the way, and evaluating their growth—rested in my hands. (See Anderson 1984 for insights into worksheets.) If they did learn, they couldn't take the credit, and if they failed, they weren't responsible for that either. I taught them to depend on me, even though I labeled their work time "Independent Work Time."

Reading/writing teachers have a different definition of independence. They think it means "to grow away from the teacher." They value the contributions of all the authors during writing and of all those same authors, the readers, during reading. They teach children to turn to each other. Their children's thoughts during work time differ from those of my former students, who kept wondering, "Am I doing this right? Well, I'll find out tomorrow." The Mast Way children get up and get help rather than working in a confused state. They don't rely on the teacher because they aren't doing an assignment for her. They are doing a task they have decided to do, and a classmate can often respond to their quest. They are reading a book and want help with it.

The test of a well-structured classroom is whether the children can read books, get help from others, and share books in small and large groups with and without the teacher. They benefit from her support, but she has taught them to learn from each other. She teaches them a structure to follow and then she can focus on content, which gets lost without disciplined organization. When the structure becomes routine, content reigns. The information the children want to learn stands in the spotlight. They can learn, pursue ideas, be excited. Children who are reading, helping, and sharing may not be quiet, but they will usually be on-task. At the same time, the teacher gains energy from her students' enthusiasm and is amazed by their insights. She supports and stimulates their interests. As a member of their community of learners, she can often challenge them beyond where they extend each other.

Community

The notion of community is also foreign to reading instruction centered on basals. Typically, a basal program contains achievement-level groups, which draw lines to separate the larger group into castes.

In a typical primary classroom the teacher divides the children into groups, and in many upper-elementary classrooms, the teachers teach the class as a whole. Often, the class is tracked. When the school or the teacher sets up groups based on achievement levels, the children begin to label themselves as good, average, and unsatisfactory regardless of the labels the teacher uses. Each stratum works separately from the others. If the entire class is one track, the children are physically separated from people of other levels.

Although we are very accustomed to this type of grouping in reading, it weakens a writing community. Writing teachers question the benefits of a system that insists on a bottom, middle, and top. We have never used leveled groups in writing, and we don't need them in reading.

In reading/writing classrooms, teachers do not divide their students into ability groups because they realize that writers learn much from each other. Students know about one another as writers and feel close to each other. In time, teachers realize that as long as they continue to divide their classes into reading groups, the children cannot become a community of readers because they do not know each other as readers. Groups split the community. So these teachers abolish reading groups and teach the children to support each other.

As in writing, where children meet to respond to one child's work, in reading they meet to respond to a book one child has read. In writing they were usually interested in the topic and wanted to learn more from the writer. In much the same way, they were usually interested in the book being shared and wanted to learn more from the reader. As the year progressed, several children would read the same book, other titles by the same author, or books that were somehow similar. The reading groups became sessions to compare, contrast, and share stories.

They met to talk about books and got to know each other as readers. When children share reading and writing, they not only can tell where another child lives, how many brothers and sisters that child has, what kind of pets the child loves, what she does for recreation, and where her family goes for vacation, they can also tell what books the child has read. Children who know each other as readers and writers have more channels of information open through which to understand and appreciate each other.

I don't think it's possible to create a Community of Readers if traditional reading groups are the basis of reading instruction. It's even more difficult to create a Community of Readers within a fifth grade, for example, if we track children. We must be careful not to erect walls to keep our students away from each other (Shannon 1985).

The notion of community is powerful. It warrants a book by itself. The recent spate of studies on effective schools presents evidence against grouping and tracking. We have no evidence to justify placing poor readers into groups by themselves. No one has shown that this results in their becoming better readers than if they worked with good readers.

As far as the good readers are concerned, if we look at the product, their scores, they may also become better readers if they work with good rather than poor readers. No one, however, has yet done a study of what happens when good readers work both in their own classrooms and also in other classrooms where some students are better than they are. The few students who are at the top in their school need to be tested on their ability to function as community members as well as how they perform on standard tests. Our society depends on them to help others.

The ultimate decision for a teacher is, "If I want to keep the basal in my room, HOW do I use it?" This teacher then asks:

"Will I give my students Time to read other selections?"

"Will I let my students Choose which stories in the basal they want to read as well as which books, magazines, and newspapers?"

"Will I let my students Respond to what they read?"

"Will I set up a Structure within which I teach my students to seek help from each other while they are in the process of reading and to conduct their own groups?"

"Will I establish a Community in which my students know what their classmates know as readers, respect them for what they know, and want each other to do well?"

References

AIKEN, JOAN. 1984. On Imagination. *Horn Book* 60, no. 6 (Nov./Dec.).

ANDERSON, LINDA. 1984. The Environment of Instruction: The Function of Seatwork in a Commercially Developed Curriculum. In *Comprehension Instruction: Perspectives and Suggestions*, ed. by Gerald G. Duffy, Laura R. Roehler, and Jana Mason. New York: Longman.

BLACKBURN, ELLEN. 1984. Common Ground: Developing Relationships Between Reading and Writing. *Language Arts* 61, no. 4 (April).

GOODMAN, KENNETH. 1986. Basal Readers: A Call for Action. *Language Arts* 63, no. 4 (April).

HUBBARD, RUTH. 1984. The Fifth Idea. In *Children Who Write When They Read*. Durham, N.H.: Writing Process Laboratory, University of New Hampshire.

———. 1985. Reading Their Way. In *Teachers and Learners*. Durham, N.H.: Writing Process Laboratory, University of New Hampshire.

SHANNON, PATRICK. 1985. Reading Instruction and Social Class. *Language Arts* 62, no. 6 (October).

Here are samples of Matt's written work, responses to books he chose throughout third grade. He read a variety of books, and his reflections give me insight into him as a person. He's a reader I'd like to know.

Oct 1 1985

Matthew
Clifford's Good Deeds
By Norman BriDWell

this Book is
about Clifford
Doing Good Deeds.
Clifford is all-
ways skrouing
up   it is so
funy   one of
Clifford's Good
Deed were Clifford
was holeDing a Branch
Doun wen a kitten
was on the Branch
By mostack Clifford
Let the Branch
Go and the Kitin
whent flying Like
a Rocket

Date   November
21,

**DisNEy's
WONDerfl World of
KNOWLeDGe**

Tom Thumb is about
a cupel that whant
a ciled and this
Littel Mogition
Named Merlen. and the
cupel ask Merlen for
a baby and Merlen says
as small as your hosbes
Thumb and they say yes
and so they Get a baby
as small as his thumb
and they have so many
prolbes Because eveything
is so Big and the stuf
can sQuish the baby

the New Kid on the Block
Poems by Jack Prelutsky

this Book is about Funny Poems
that Rhyme and that kids Like
and understand. I chouse this
Book becouse I Like Poems
my Best Poem I Like Best is
Homework! Oh Homework!
I will Read it to the class

1-30-86

the Easy BaseBall Book

This Book tells you some Reminders
about BaseBall. and it tells you about
some moves about BaseBall to Like
How to Hit How to throw and stof
Like that.

How to Pich a Ball

Raise your Hand with the Ball in it.
Put your weight on your Back Foot
and trow

How to Hit

Keep your Back Foot in Place
steP with your Front Foot strate
at the Picker and then swing

I chose this Book Because
I Like BaseBall

the main Idea is to Play Better
BaseBall iF you Play Bad

Submarines at war   3/18/86   mAtt

German submarines are called u-Boats.
u-Boats Fought Long Battles with ships of
Britain and the USA in Both World Wars.
u-Boats tried to sink ships carrying
supplies across the ocean.
u-Boats worked togather in wolf Packs.
u-Boats sank 2,828 ships During
World War two.!
        the End
u-Boat means under water Boat
        By Robert van toL

How to Eat fried worms   matt   5/7/86

DeaR tHomAs RockWELL
I ReaLy Like How to Eat Fried
worms the Book.
my Faverite Chapter is the
First worm when Billy
was Nervous about Eating
the worms. But Latter
on in the Book around the
11th worm He was used to
Eating the worms and at the
end. He keped on Eating the
worm after the Bet was all over
Why Did you use the word
Basted. [bastard]
I Did not understand the Part
when the Book kepted on
saying Fish Fish Fish Fish
it was weird.
chapter nine the plotters
I Did not understand that chapter.
this is one of the Best
most interresting. Book I ever
Read. and it Has Good sespenci. and
it makes you not Put the Book
Down

Matt's teacher, Jan Roberts, teaches her students to compose written, as well as oral, responses to what they read. Their responses to the writing of professionals rest on the same principles as their responses to one another's writing: they come from the children themselves. The children respond to the book rather than to a teacher's questions. Their written work springs from a goal very different from the one I had for seat work when I taught.

In 1979, I would have given these two purposes for written work: 1) My students must work quietly alone, because I need to teach reading groups; 2) I will correct their work later to find out how well they comprehend and know their skills. While I still think it's important for students to not interrupt us when we are with other students, and I want information about their comprehension and skill proficiency, I now see these goals encompassed by other issues.

Matt's work illustrates at least two other important aspects of children's written work at Mast Way. When children think of reading as writing, rather than something from which teachers generate questions, they respond to what they read and share their responses. These will be the subjects of the next two sections of this chapter. They mesh with the philosophy of the writing program, whose center is Response. Written work, similar to oral sessions, gives students the responsibility of responding to what they read.

Students Write Responses to What They Read

As teachers, we can't know what's important to children. When we think back to their writing, they choose to include different information than we would. When a child writes that the most significant event in the football game he attended with his dad was the three hot dogs he ate, we don't insist that he include who won the game. Likewise, when children read, their books are important to them in different ways than they are to us or to other students. We learn this when we read their work.

We train ourselves to stop looking for what's wrong and start looking with curiosity to find out why a book was meaningful to a child (Simpson 1986). Readers' responses can take many forms and this variety provides a challenge for us to encourage when we change from worksheets, which take initiative away from our students, to blank paper, which places responsibility for initiating a response on the reader.

Readers' written responses take many forms. The children read many kinds of books just as they write in many genres during writing class. Their most important writing is the writing they do when they generate their own compositions, as the authors of the books they read do. When they are authors, they gain their greatest insights into the reading process, but the writing part of the reading program provides a place for children to think on paper about what they read.

Matt, whose work appeared at the beginning of this chapter, wrote responses to twenty-two books during third grade. He didn't write something about every book he read; that might make his written work a drag, and part of response is learning which books merit response. Students decide which books to respond to and what form the response will take. The response may include why the child chose the book, what surprised the child, what the child learned, the child's analysis of the writing, things the child wondered about, something the child didn't understand, something the child wants to share with others, or how the child thinks other children in the class would respond to the book. Students highlight different types of information, depending on what kind of book they have read and the quality and quantity of their experiences with written response.

In the fall the children often wrote about a book without putting themselves into it. Later they put themselves into their response more frequently, as these two first-grade examples show.

Name Kate
Title olD DEVIL WiNd
Author By Bill MaRtiN J.R.

IN Tas [this] soRe [story]
IT GOS ON. aND
oN AND oN.

Name JessIca
Title THe vERy HunGry cATERPILLAr

I NOTisT
TheaT waN The
caTeRPiLLAr was A
BuTERFLy He HaD All The
caLas TaT E Eat.
[colors—with a New Hampshire accent—that he ate]

Jessica writes about what she noticed in the book and assumes that others will not have noticed the same thing. Several children chose to read this popular book, but Jessica asserts her independence. Her teacher fosters risk-taking, so that from the beginning of her career as a reader, Jessica knows others encourage her to lose herself in books. She does not read to find out what others want to know. She looks for her own way to respond and, thus, writes about what she noticed. (Rosenblatt 1978 writes about the personal nature of response.)

The teachers say that children's first move away from retelling often comes after they share orally. One teacher said, "I read *Bunnicula* to the class, we discussed it, and some of them read it. They wrote a reaction rather than a retelling." They knew everyone had heard this story, so they didn't retell it.

When students write a slightly new type of response, their written work can be shared so others may consider this approach. Some children seem to be particularly adept at creating new forms for their journal entries. Jeremy organized his written work into a format of his own.

Name   Jeremy B   **Date**   4/17/86
Title   Ira sleeps over
Author   Bernard Waber

At the biging [beginning] of the story
Ira spees [sleeps] at a farenis [friend's] house.
tay [They] did a lot soff. [stuff] in the mittle
of the story tay go to sleep and
tall gost storys. At the end
of the story tay both get
there tatty bears.

Name   Jeremy B   **Date**   4/24/86
Title   a book about Christopher Columbus
Author   Ruth Belov Gross

in the beginning of the
story Christopher
Columbus desres [discovers] America.
in the middle of the story
he mets Indians. At the
end of the story Christopher
Columbus gose back to
Italy.

Jeremy's written work sounds like him and not like any other person. He and the other children not only show their comprehension when they write about their books, but their responses display the vital role prior knowledge plays in reading. Our background not only influences what we learn but, more importantly, our differences give us our reading voices.

The teachers help children value themselves and develop confidence in what they hear in books. Traditionally, children did their written work for their teacher, but independent readers grow in classrooms where teachers strive to recognize the potential in each child and help him find the path he will travel. They help the students see possible new ways to respond, to stretch themselves as readers.

Teachers encourage a variety of written responses.   It's one thing to notice the variety in a child's responses, but we take another step when we value this range of response. (Torbe 1983 writes about various ways to respond to literature.) At first we value written work that shows a full, clear summary of everything that happened in a book because we can tell that the child understood the story. However, this kind of writing can be perfunctory, dry, dull, and boring to read—as well as to write. Gradually, we encourage children to put their feelings into their responses and write with a focus: "What's the one thing I want to write about this book?" Children choose the direction for their written work in much the same way they move away from bed-to-bed stories in their writing.

This, however, takes time, not only for our students, but also for us. When we write, we too have a hard time choosing one thing to say. Like our students, we want to tell All About Running instead of The Race in Exeter. As we realize the importance of selection in our writing, we carry this understanding over when we respond to a book and look for specific details to support what we think. However, it's difficult to listen to the children's written work through the same ears we use when we listen to the writing they author.

We want to check children's comprehension. Jan Roberts's evolution in her attitude toward written response provides an example of how difficult it is to let children's written work fit in with the overall reading/writing program. Jan began the 1984–85 year by allowing student choice in reading but requiring the children to write about each book they chose. She designed a nine-part format for them to follow when they wrote a response to a book. As the year progressed, however, she gradually took away the format because it constrained the children's responses. Not only did all the children respond in the same way as one another, they responded similarly to all kinds of books, and any one child's responses to several books showed no highs and lows in the child as a person or as a reader. The form did what forms do. It made everyone look alike.

At the end of the year Jan studied the responses her students wrote. She decided that the form had gotten in the way of her students' reading. It impeded the amount and variety of books they read. Some of them chose short books so they would have time to complete the tedious task of writing answers for the form. Others began responding as a routine. Instead of stimulating thinking, the form numbed it.

Jan started the next school year with no format. The children wrote. This is hard when we have not done it before and fear open-ended tasks, but writing puts children in a position to compose entire thoughts, which demands more from them than answering worksheets or filling in forms. As one third-grade boy explained it, "You have to put it together in your head first. . . ." The children create, or "put together," their own written work.

Jan kept exploring written response during the 1985–86 school year and told the faculty about a breakthrough that came when she kept a journal on an adult fiction book. She analyzed her own response pattern and shared her process with her students. For example, she learned that she didn't want to compose a written response every day. Since then, she has not required her students to produce daily written work in reading. When she told this to her fellow teachers, principal, librarian, two visitors from Australia, and me at a meeting in the spring of 1986, one of the teachers wanted to know how often she did require them to write.

Jan said she has no requirements. The other teacher asked, "But what if someone hasn't written a response for two weeks?" "Then I'd talk to that child." Jan can handle exceptions because she knows her children as readers; she lives among them when they read. "I hear them talk about their books in the meantime," even if they haven't written a response. Jan Roberts's main concern is that her students do respond, and if, for a while, a student responds orally, she weighs that in her overall picture of the student. She wants her students to respond in a way that helps them love books, and constantly adjusts her teaching with this goal in mind. This is not to say that Jan would not encourage that child to write. She held the reins in her classroom for years and she knows she still does. When she thinks it's necessary, she'll nudge, often in a session with a child in which she and the child create options and the child chooses a move.

Jan saw two options for herself emerge when she kept her reading journal, and these became choices for her students. At first, she felt compelled to write frequently but found that this sometimes interrupted her. When she talked about it with her students, some of them had never tried to write as they went through a book, while others had never waited until they finished. Now they consider both strategies or a combination.

Just as the children learn when their teacher shares options with them, the teachers learn from each other when they share, as the Mast Way teachers did when they talked about how they each dealt with written work. The teachers vary in the quantity of responses they require. Some require a written response each day at the end of reading. In this case, the children choose what to respond to in the books they have read from that day. Other teachers require a written response every other day. Some base the number of responses on the material the children have read rather than on the calendar. They may have their children write a response for each book or every other book. They may require a response to each chapter or to every set of three chapters. The main consideration is that the amount of time children spend on their written responses does not overshadow the time they spend reading.

This was an issue for Leslie Funkhouser, who worried for more than a year about what people would think if they came into her room during reading and her students weren't "working." It took her a long time to feel comfortable with the notion that reading a book was legitimate "work" for students in reading class. Now, the children in her class read more books than they write about and they write their responses during a time of day set aside for that task. During reading, they read and share orally.

Each week in Pat McLure's first grade, the children choose one book they think is of medium difficulty and work on learning to read that book for the week, although throughout the week they also read other books. They share their chosen book with Pat some time during the week and it's the one they write about. Older students, however, may not need to reread a book for a week in order to perfect it.

Ellen Blanchard's third- and fourth-grade students write after they have read five books. They may write in the various ways I have already discussed, design a book jacket showing the best scenes and write a short version of the story on the front and back flaps, write about experiences they have had that are similar to those in the book, or create a new character for the book and explain why they would add this character and how he/she would change the story.

For example, one boy added a girl character to John Fitzgerald's *The Great Brain.* This book takes place in a private boys' school in the 1800s, and the addition of a girl completely changed the book. The girl was really smart, so smart she outwitted the Great Brain at all his schemes for making money and selling chocolate bars. Finally, he went into business with her.

The child who wrote this is verbal; has considerable difficulty writing and dictated it into a tape recorder, but it took a great deal of original thought. The children continue to take their written work seriously, remain involved in it, if they have lots of choices and variety. Otherwise, the work becomes work. Sometimes several of Ellen's children study one theme.

Once, several children from both third and fourth grade, and from all reading levels, read friendship books. Then each child selected one of the books and wrote a response to one common question they generated, "How did the characters in my book show their friendship?" Later, they used their written responses for a discussion to compare the books. At another time, several children read fairy tales they had chosen, and for each two fairy tales, wrote: How They Are the Same, How They Are Different, and What I Liked About These Stories. At other times they may compare and contrast different books by one author. These last few examples may sound less open-ended than some I have mentioned earlier, but they are quite different from the seat work these same teachers used to assign. The students will all write something different because they have read different books.

On other occasions, groups of students may read an assigned book. Margaret Kolbjornsen, a fifth-grade teacher, changed the written work for her students on these occasions. She says, "I'm the traditional teacher here, but these worksheet questions are new for me." They show how Margaret teaches her students to view their reading as writing and to provide their own response, as Jean and Jennie did to a story called "Wild Heart."

1. I think the author does an especially good job . . .
   Jennie's answer: . . . of describing when La Bruja has the baby because it has detail.
   Jean's answer: . . . in describing the day going away and the night coming like describing the colors and looks and how the ground felt.
2. Give your reasons for your choice using some quotes from the story.
   Jennie's answer: "She heard its tiny breathing and felt its warmth,

and she was flooded with rich desires to love and tend the little creature dropped in the thicket."

Jean's answer: I chose this quote because it seems so pretty and that I'm right there and watching it all. "Dawn came with a glow of pink and gold. Below that, there was a thick white mist among the grass."

These questions of Margaret's and others, such as, "Tell about a time in your life when you had the same feeling as one of the characters," give students a chance to provide a response of their own. This is one difference between the written work these teachers are now trying and the assignments they used to give. Not only do the students work with a different mindset than in former days, but the teachers read their students' work with new expectations. They read to discover, find out, learn what their students heard in their books. They expect to be surprised by what they see on their students' papers.

Readers Share Their Written Work

In November 1985 I conducted a workshop for teachers in Edmonton, Alberta. In the workshop we each wrote a response to a reading we had chosen from four pieces of adult literature (short stories, poems and essays) and then met in groups. Each person in a group had chosen the same reading. In the groups, we read our written responses to each other and orally responded to them. After our discussion, we each wrote a response to a person in the group. Of the various comments about the workshop, the teachers liked reading what another person in the group wrote to them.

I learned this workshop format from the teachers at Mast Way. Some of them follow a similar procedure with their students. I have also learned that this way of using written work is quite different for teachers, and until we experience it ourselves we don't feel its potential value for our students. In general, the notion of responding to peers' written work is new to us.

Readers receive response to their written work.   Regardless of how teachers and children write their responses, response to their written work is important. This kind of writing, like their regular writing, is written by writers who say what they think is true and want to know what others think of what they think. The way the teacher responds to their written work follows the tone they establish during oral response to reading and the children's regular writing.

The teacher reads to learn about a child's reflections. The children don't try to second-guess the teacher, and the teacher, in turn, doesn't read their journal entries to find out if they have understood a story. She also keeps a journal and reads some of the same books her students read, but her responses are her own. She doesn't write what she thinks goes through a child's mind because she learns more about herself when she responds in her own way. Similarly, she doesn't want her students to write what they think goes through her mind. (Fulwiler 1986 writes about the value of journals.) They respond on their own and she supports what they hear in their books.

The focus in reading is consistent with that in writing: what the child knows. We don't highlight errors with red either in writing or in reading. This doesn't mean that we never find something we disagree with, but it does mean we don't correct errors. When we read something that sounds questionable, we ask about it, as we do with other kinds of writing. Sometimes we put our request in writing, sometimes we ask in individual reading conferences, and sometimes we ask within a small or large group setting. Children can receive response to their work from classmates and their teacher in all these ways.

One way some teachers respond to their students' writing is by letter. Nancie Atwell (1985) writes about her correspondence with her middle-school students. Other teachers use similar letters. When Helene Coutoure, fifth-grade intern at the Oyster River Elementary School in Durham, New Hampshire, began a letter-writing system with some of her students, Sarah's interest in reading jumped instantly. In her first letter to Helene she wrote, "thank-you for picking me. . . . I think you should do this with some other kids because I had fun reading the book then telling you about it and writing this letter to you." Regardless of the format, children can see benefits from their written work when it is no longer only an assignment.

One day in Phyllis Kinzie's fourth grade I met with a small group, and the "notes" they took during reading became a topic for discussion. The term "notes" was the label Phyllis used for her students' responses to what they read. As they read they noted parts that struck them in any number of ways: maybe they learned a fact, maybe something in the book triggered a connection, or maybe they liked the sound of a part. The latter type of note came to Darren's mind during our discussion.

I shared a piece of my writing and lamented that it sounded boring in one section because I couldn't think of a more interesting way to phrase what I wanted to say. Darren suggested, "Maybe if you read through your reading notes you'd find a nice quote that would help you." Darren knows that his own written work can help him as a learner and that the ultimate response to his work is his own opportunity to use something he recorded. He often writes his responses with that in mind. When both teachers and children do the same work, everyone sees himself, herself, and each other as a learner as well as a teacher.

Readers respond to others' written work. Students will think of many ways to share their written responses. They may prefer to have others write to them before they respond orally because it helps them clarify what their book meant to them. They may even write a response to the response. When others respond to them, they learn what a book meant to someone else and this helps them clarify their own interpretation. It also requires that they consider those other people when they explain the book. They know what they will have to defend or teach.

The children's written responses are one way for them to show others what they know about a field of study. In November, when Chad read what he had written about a coyote book to the entire class, researcher Tom Romano saw Chad stand up as he fielded the questions and comments. He had started to feel like an authority. It was obvious he liked the position he had placed himself in. He knew more about coyotes than anyone in the room. Sometimes children have their audience in mind when they write their responses to their books.

Jason, a second grader in Leslie Funkhouser's class, knew he would read his journal entry to some friends when he wrote this on March 25:

> **OLiver's lucky day.**
> **by P. Mcbrier.**
>
> This book is about a
> boy. His name is
> Oliver. He starts a
> pet care bisnis. He put's
> up sum siyns. Iyl read you
> his motow. He sed.
> > Im good with dogs.
> > Im good with cats.
> > Iyl evin babey sit your
> [page 2]
> rats. lots of kids at school
> teys him bekos he starts
> his own pet car bisnis.

Jason liked the part about the motto, chose it to share, and pictured himself reading to his friends when he wrote, "I'll read you his motto." Jason has several opportunities to share his reading log. He shares a reading journal once a week with a small group. Also, during reading they may share with a friend just as they share with their teacher when she circulates among them before the small group for that day meets. Finally, three children sign up to share something with the class each day, and one of their options is to share a reading log. Nicole shared with the class one day after she had shared in her small group.

When Nicole read the following journal entry, she and her classmates shared thoughts with each other and stretched their thinking. Her teacher, Leslie Funkhouser, wrote about Nicole's share sessions (1985):

Nicole began sharing her journal for that day [with a group of her second-grade classmates].

"I read the book *First Grade Takes a Test* by Miriam Cohen. It is about this first grade class where all the kids take a test and only Anna Maria passes the test. She's sent to a special class a few days later because she's so smart. My favorite part in the story is when it tells about George who read the question on the test that said:

"RABBITS EAT
___ lettuce
___ dog food
___ sandwiches

"and George raised his hand and said: 'Rabbits have to eat carrots or their teeth will get too long and stick into them.' The teacher nodded and smiled but she put her finger to her lips. So George carefully drew in a carrot so the test people would know. Comments and questions?"

Hands shot up.

"Where did you get this book, Nicole?"

"Why do you think only Anna Maria got the answers right?"

"Do you think the other kids were really dumb?"

"I think George's answer was good because rabbits do need carrots for sharp teeth."

"That's like the tests we did last year."

"Do you think Anna Maria was really the smartest kid in the whole class?"

Later in the morning, Nicole brought her journal proudly to our whole-class sharing session.

"I have a good journal today," she beamed. "The small group had a lot of questions. Can I share it with everyone, Miss Funkhouser?"

Again, she read, finishing with, "I have more to write about this." The discussion which followed was equally as thought-provoking as the earlier one with the smaller group.

"If you were the author of this book, would you change anything?" asked Heather.

Nicole paused, her chin resting in her hands.

"Yes. I'd make George the one to go to the special class because he really was thinking and knew the most information."

References

ATWELL, NANCIE. 1985. Writing and Reading from the Inside Out. In *Breaking Ground: Teachers Relate Reading and Writing in the Elementary School*, ed. by Jane Hansen, Thomas Newkirk, and Donald Graves. Portsmouth, N.H.: Heinemann.

FULWILER, TOBY. 1986. Journals Across the Disciplines. In *To Compose: Teaching Writing in the High School*, ed. by Thomas Newkirk. Portsmouth, N.H.: Heinemann.

FUNKHOUSER, LESLIE. 1985. Who's the Smartest? In *Teachers and Learners*. Durham, N.H.: Writing Process Laboratory, University of New Hampshire.

ROSENBLATT, LOUISE. 1978. *The Reader, the Text, the Poem.* Carbondale, Ill.: Southern Illinois University Press.

SIMPSON, MARY K. 1986. A Teacher's Gift: Oral Reading and the Reading Response Journal. *Journal of Reading* 30, no. 1 (October).

TORBE, MIKE. 1983. Writing About Reading. In *Fforum: Essays on Theory and Practice in the Teaching of Writing,* ed. by Patricia L. Stock. Upper Montclair, N.J.: Boynton/Cook.

Phyllis Kinzie shared Byrd Baylor's poem *The Desert Is Theirs* with her fourth-grade students during their study of deserts. Part of it goes like this:

> This is no place
> for anyone
> who wants
> soft hills
> and meadows
> and everything
> green
> green
> green . . .

> This is for hawks
> that like only
> the loneliest canyons
> and lizards
> that run
> in the hottest sand
> and
> coyotes
> that choose
> the rockiest trails.

> It's for them.

> And for
> birds
> that nest
> in cactus

and sing out over
a thousand thorns
because
they're where
they want to be.

It's for them.

the desert has
its own kind of time
(that doesn't need clocks).
That's
the kind of time
snakes go by
and rains go by
and rocks go by
and Desert People
go by too.

That's why
every desert thing
knows
when the time comes
to celebrate.

Suddenly . . .
All together.
It happens.

Cactus blooms
yellow and pink and purple.
The Papagos begin
their ceremonies
to pull down
rain.
Every plant joins in.
Even the dry earth
makes a sound of joy
when the rain touches.
Hawks call across the canyons.
Children laugh for nothing.
Coyotes dance in the moonlight.

Where else
would
Desert People
want to be?

The children responded. Todd heard about the yellow and pink
cactus blossoms. "And purple," added Alison.

Jenn remembered that everything and everyone celebrates rain.
Matt piggybacked with, "Hawks get so excited they yell across canyons."

John continued, "The children stay up all night."

Phyllis Kinzie asked, "Let's see how many things you learned about deserts from this poem." The list goes on and on.

These children learn content from poetry, fiction, songs, auto-biography, historical fiction, biography, newspapers, magazines, ed-itorials, essays, media, interviews, other students' books, and nonfiction literature. They use textbooks as reference books—sparsely—to look up the specific details they want, but the bulk of the reading they do in their content areas is from real books, a change consistent with the shift to real books for reading in most Mast Way classrooms. The kinds of books they read for content come from the same categories as those they read in reading class.

They respond to this writing by focusing on the information, as they do when they share their own writing. They come to a writing conference to find out what a classmate wrote about, to learn from the author, and they open professionals' books for similar reasons —to find out what the author knows.

Read to Learn

Writing gives content areas a chance to be center stage because con-tent area writing and reading begin when children start to write and read. However, this hasn't come across clearly in what I, and others, have written about our New Hampshire research. Occasionally a teacher somewhere asks me, "How do we make the transition from process writing in the primary grades to content writing in the upper grades?"

I fear that my disappointment in my ability to communicate shouts out from my face. I don't know what kinds of answers I mumble, but the real answer is, "There is no transition. Primary children receive response to the content of their writing while they are in the process of writing. The same is true for upper-grade stu-dents." I see at least two aspects of content learning throughout the grades: 1) When writers write, they concentrate on their information; 2) when they read they respond to another writer's knowledge. Thus, writing, reading, and content learning all move along, side by side.

Writers write with information. The notion of reading for infor-mation begins with our first responsibility in the writing program: We convince our students that they do know something, and that, therefore, they can write. We shift away from an emphasis on me-chanics to a primary concern for content, because if a piece of writing has no information, help with language or correct spelling and punc-tuation will not make it a best-seller. Writers must have something to say.

If I have nothing to say, I can't write. Content is the heart of writing, the essence of what we read. The most striking thing I learned during my first three months in Ellen Blackburn Karelitz's first-grade class was the impact of her focus on content. When they wrote, the children scattered letters among their pictures, but they didn't pick those letters from the sky. Their letters represented the sounds they heard in the information they wanted to share. They struggled to get print to make sense. This process carried them into reading.

Print had to make sense. They knew those marks were someone's attempt to tell them something, and they wanted to find out what it was. They read to learn. This drove their desire to learn to read. When I studied reading in graduate school, I learned that children first learn to read and then read to learn, but these little children turned that notion of reading upside down. They were writers, and writers write information. Thus, when they read, they read for an author's information. This insistence on meaning helped them learn to read.

At the end of the 1982–83 school year, I analyzed the transcripts from sessions in which children shared a professional's book with the class and looked for the children's search for information. I discovered two shifts during the year. At the beginning, the children asked readers about their reading process. "How did you learn to read this book?" was a typical question. They shared the strategies they used to figure out words. It was because they knew there was content that they knew whether a word made sense. If it didn't make sense, they knew they weren't reading it right. They monitored themselves without our having to say, "Now, does that make sense?" Later, I noticed a different focus in their conferences.

The majority of their responses dealt with language. They had gone beyond the expectation that print makes sense; they also wanted it to be interesting. Language highlighted information. It was as if their assumption that print produces a message was so basic, they had to unscramble the marks on the page, delight in them, and then, finally, the message itself became their topic of discussion.

This shift came in the spring. Throughout the year, the children had talked about the content of every book, but they spent most of their time trying to find out how the reader was able to read the words or sharing the fun of the language. As more of them acquired strategies about what to do when they got stuck, they asked fewer process questions and more content questions. Regardless of whether they shared *Little Bear* or a nonfiction book, they looked for what they learned.

Writers write to learn.   Sometimes they learned about mother bear's love, and at other times they learned the size of a brontosaurus, but they could always learn something from a piece of writing. Writing is writing, and in a way, there is no such thing as content area writing. When we write a poem we first learn what it's about, then we figure out how we want to say it, and if we like what we have composed, then worry about the mechanics. Similarly, if we are in the midst of learning about blood circulation, we may write about it in a poem or in another genre, but we still have to work with what we know until we decide what information to include and how to relay it, and eventually polish it, as Jacob did in Margaret Kolbjornsen's fifth-grade class:

A day at cell school
by Jacob Michaels

Character list

Chub: white blood cell
Carrier: red blood cell
Clot: platelet
Ms. Hearty: teacher
Mr. Stomach: principal

> One day Ms. Hearty said to her class. "Today we'll tell Mr. Stomach what we want to be when we grow up. Chub, you go first."
> "I want to be a policeman and kill those nasty germs."
> Carrier said, "I want to be a mailman and bring food and oxygen to all the other cells with my friend Blood."
> "I want to be a repairman and fix up all the cuts," said Clot.
> Then Ms. Hearty said, "Very good. Class dismissed."

Jacob's play contains lots of information. The process of writing it helped him understand circulation because he had to decide which information from the class unit he wanted to include and how he wanted to convey it. (Levine 1985 writes about writing in science.) He learns, also, on occasions when he writes personal narratives, but the children don't write narratives as often as many people think.

Newkirk (in preparation) categorized all writing from grades one, two, and three at Mast Way school and the Oyster River Elementary School in Durham, New Hampshire, and found that more than half of it was nonnarrative. Their informational writing led them to read much content, also. They read to find out something. Whether they wanted to know about colonists or how a mystery would be solved, they read to learn. The children came to understand this because it's consistent with what they did when they wrote. They wrote to clarify, to learn about what they knew as Jacob did about the circulatory system. However, they not only learned about content because they wrote, but they clarified their notions about content when they responded to writing.

Writers respond to information. The response system encourages learning from all types of writing. (See Evans 1984 for writing in math.) Response to any print can be structured using some variation of the all-class writing conference that the fourth graders held for Byrd Baylor's poem. When a little child shares in kindergarten:

the other children want to know who is jumping, where, and how high. They come to learn, in this case more from the writer than the writing itself, and they ask questions about the content of the writing. The response system places these young readers in the position of viewing a piece of print as something from which they will learn—if they ask questions. This represents another switch for us.

Not only have we traditionally thought of children as question-answerers, we have also defined "question" differently than the children do. They ask "real" questions, queries about something they don't know, whereas we have not done this. Instead, we have used questions to "check comprehension." From the first day of writing, children ask questions to learn. When we let them pursue their interests we find ourselves in the midst of a major change in the way we promote learning. We begin to ask real questions, questions to which we don't know the answers, and we teach the children to follow our lead. Often their inquisitiveness leads them on a search for new content and we encourage their searches.

Fourth-grader Eric Harter wrote a narrative about Eclipse, his Border collie, and when his classmates asked him questions about the breed that he couldn't answer, he became interested and researched Border collies. He learned about their roles as cowherders and their sense of smell. When he continued to write, he worried about how to interweave his new information into his narrative and keep it interesting. Here is part of Eric's final draft:

> . . . I'm very proud to have a border collie because they herd sheep or cows. Usually they herd sheep, but Eclipse is so big he has to be a cowherder. In England we saw border collies herding sheep. All the shepherd has to do is train the dog to listen to different kinds of whistles for everything he wants the border collie to do. My father thinks we might get some ducks so that Eclipse will have something to herd.
>
> Border collies have a very good sense of smell and eyesight. Sometimes Eclipse stands in the yard with his nose up when a breeze goes by. The only problem is fall and spring are mating seasons for animals. On a breezy night Eclipse usually takes off. . . .

Eric's learning strategies are purposeful: 1) He shares what he knows; 2) He adds specific information to his text; 3) He decides what format to use to present his information. He mentally sorts through possible avenues to explore and chooses which information he wants to try to include. Thus, writers have at least three strategies they can use when they develop their writing topics. At other times students' interest in new content begins with reading.

Children often choose content area books during reading and write responses to the choices they find particularly interesting. A child may not highlight the same points that we would, but that is also true of adults when two or more of us read a book. Different people find value in different parts of what they are learning. We try to foster this in our students.

When children write about the content books they have chosen, we know they learn, as this third-grade boy shows us:

Lion Cubs Growing Up in the Wild December 9, 1985 This book is about lion cubs. This book says that after it rains lions drink water from the rain and that lions live only in afica and small parts of india. When lion cubs are born their mother puts them in a hiding place. Sometimes the mother lion moves her cubs to other hiding places. When lion cubs are born they have spots, and when they grow up they loose the spots. Sometimes the mother lion leaves her cubs in a hiding place and goes of to hunt. When lion cubs are by themselfs they be very quiet. If lion cubs are noisy animals might eat them.

When this child shares his content area writing, in this case written work in his reading journal, the other children tell him what they have learned, and if their interest is piqued, they ask questions. He appreciates hearing what they have learned from him. Usually, he knows more than what he wrote about, so he can answer many of their questions. Or he may read more and then choose to write more. The response system sets the tone for learning, since everyone in the classroom is always wondering about something.

Kathy Matthews (1985) creates this kind of environment in her pre-first-grade class.

> The most important thing I do is create a climate of trust and acceptance. When one's ideas are respected it's easier to share and answer questions. This means, of course, that as a teacher I must be willing to accept information and logic that, by most standards, are inaccurate. Just as I view invented spelling as a developmental process that does not diminish the quality of the content, so too, I emphasize the thinking, not whether the content is accurate.
>
> It is far more important that Jon chose to speculate in writing about the changes in his jar of three green beans than that he justified the liquid in the bottom as "water 'cause it was cold and snow [mold] got on the beans and now it's spring and it's warmer and the snow's meltin'."

Jon's writing shows his learning, his way of trying to figure out new content in what could be called his science journal or his writing journal or his thinking journal or whatever. Kathy Matthews creates an environment full of problems to puzzle over. Other teachers use different ways to suggest explorations.

When Leslie Funkhouser introduced "Endangered Species" to her second grade, half the class chose an animal and researched it during reading and writing. In this classroom the children also had several animals—ducks, fish, turtles, and chameleons—and some children spent part of writing class watching them carefully to record their habits. Similarly, when Pat McLure brought an incubator into her first-grade classroom, her children became excited, and many chose to read and write about chicks. It's ideal when we don't have to require topics, because students often learn more when they pursue something they've decided to learn about. But sometimes we must have our entire class study one unit.

Students can pursue their own interests within class topics, as Cora Five's fifth-grade students (1985), Susan Benedict's second-grade children (1985), and Jan Roberts's third-graders did when they studied American history (1985). As part of their study of colonial New England, the third graders went to York, Maine, to visit restored buildings. Each child took notes during the trip and later wrote about it. Chad wrote about the bus ride in "On the Way to York, Maine"; Aaron described the entire trip in minute detail; Sarah wrote about the old school house and Brent about the gundalow boat, his favorite item. Justin wove his experience into this piece of fiction.

Ship Ahoy

The ship is coming in! All of the townspeople
were gathered around the John Hancock Wharf and
warehouse to see the first European ship come in.
Ho, the ship is coming in,
I'm sure, I don't have the
slightest doubt it isn't docking here!

I'll be ashamed of everyone
if it doesn't come in,
Oh, the ship is coming in! (tune of last line: "Glory, Glory Alleluia")

The children enjoyed Justin's share session, complete with his glorious last line, and they displayed copies of their own writing in the Resource Center and in their classroom. Students from all grade levels read their writing, shared the content, and questioned the authors. Learning took place when the various Mast Way students and teachers read and shared, but the experience didn't end there.

Incoming third graders preview curriculum topics by reading the written legacy of the previous year's class. The students' writing provides continuity from one year to the next and is an important part of what they read in content areas. When they read past Mast Way authors, they may or may not be able to respond to the author in person, but they do learn from each other and talk about the way their fellow students write. Also, they keep what they expect in their own writing in mind when they use professionals' writing for content study.

Learn from Well-Written Content

Teachers let their students use poetry, fiction, and a myriad of other sources of information for their learning. They don't think of content area reading as textbook reading. Textbooks may be used as references like any reference books, but the main source of information is children's literature. Nonfiction and all other types of literature override a textbook for content learning, just as they displace the basal reader for reading instruction. Being able to respond to all kinds of texts and contexts helps children learn from what they read.

I was surprised in Ellen Blackburn Karelitz's class one day when Misty read her published book about her grandfather to the class, and one child asked, "Was all of this true?"

"Everything but the part about the funeral. In the book, I said I went, but I didn't get to go."

When children expand from accounts of their lives into fiction, they learn firsthand the role of information in fiction. They know that fiction is based on fact and they often look for the "real" parts. Teachers help them learn to use fiction as part of their content area diet when they highlight the presence of information in fiction.

In December, when Jan Roberts read *Greyling* to her third-grade class, she asked the children what they had learned. Melissa answered, "The moss around the house." Other children elaborated about how the moss keeps the house cool in summer and warm in winter—a form of insulation. Such discussions reinforce the children's knowledge that information is available from many kinds of books and helps them find facts on their own.

The children in Ellen Blanchard's third- and fourth-grade class sometimes use this form:

> Name of book:
> Author:
> Type of book (circle one): fiction
> nonfiction
>
> Six new facts I learned:
> 1.
> 2.
> 3.
> 4.
> 5.
> 6.

What did you like about this information book?

The children use these sheets when they meet in groups to share the different books they have each read. They may not acquire information in every encounter with print, but they realize that they can learn content from many sources and can write, themselves, in all the ways professional writers do.

Russell Freedman (1986), author of children's nonfiction, writes about the qualities of good content area writing, especially the frequent use of illustrations and photographs in nonfiction. Shortly after reading his article, Jean Garland, the librarian in Bartlett, New Hampshire, introduced me to *Large as Life*, written by Joanna Cole and illustrated by Kenneth Lilly. This two-part series includes one book about nighttime animals and another about daytime animals. Detailed, colorful paintings supplement the text. The author does not expect her text to stand alone, since both sources of information— illustrations and print—are necessary for the message. This common feature gives us one possibility to suggest when we work with our students on the many ways to put together their information.

Phyllis Kinzie conducts lessons on leads. One day, for her turn in the all-class conference, she shared four leads on the same topic; one from a nonfiction trade book, one from a poem, one from an encyclopedia article, and one from a magazine article. The children compared them, shared leads on succeeding days, and worked on their own leads when they wrote about their topics of study.

Jack Wilde, fifth-grade teacher in Hanover, New Hampshire, begins his class's animal unit by reading fiction about animals to them for days before they begin their study. They talk about what worked in a piece of writing and what they learned from such books as Jean Craighead George's *The Wounded Wolf*. Then each student chooses an animal and writes fifty questions about it.

They categorize their questions, collect data, and use the Cornell note-taking system on their cards. They write one note per line and categorize it in the margin. They share their notes with a partner. Jack continues to read to them from well-written material, such as Randall Jarrell's *The Bat-Poet*. They talk about which pieces of writing they feel drawn to as readers and what makes writing interesting.

They write their reports in many forms—a series of letters, an interview, a diary (of a polar bear), a poem, a narrative, a journal (of a mountain lion's adventures), or a Who Am I? They work with a partner as they develop their final drafts and manipulate their information. One student moved the parts of her poem around for one-and-a-half weeks before she was satisfied. They have to solve lots of problems and deal with information in more challenging ways than in traditional reports.

Brian wrestled with the problem of how to convey the dolphin's intelligence and finally wrote this report:

Harold (A Dolphin Tale)
by Brian Ogden

My Younger Years

My mother knew as my wildly splashing tail emerged that this was the birth of an unusual dolphin. She took most careful care of me, especially being sure that my dad or any other male dolphin did not bite me. . . . I could not breathe without sticking my entire head out of the water. As I grew older, I grew rapidly gaining 18–20 pounds a day just by drinking my mother's milk! I looked like my dad a bottle-nosed dolphin. I was longer and plumper than the common dolphin my markings were not as striking. My back was black, almost a purple gray, with my coloring fading to white on my stomach. I soon developed an appetite for cuttlefish, squid, and other small fish. However, I must admit that the first fish I ate gave me a terrible stomachache. By wanting more food it brought me to farther distances away from my mother an therefore they geginning of my adventures.

At the age of 4½ (most dolphins stay with their mothers for only 3 months) I decided to leave my mother and explore the world. When I first set out I thought it was going to be a nice peaceful swim. I was wrong. . . .

My Years in Captivity

I soon became acquainted with my trainer. Every day we had some kind of routine. I had to wait for the best dolphin to do his full turn, jump high out of the water, then I would use up all my strength to swim on my back. I was the best at that. For some strange reason each time I did a trick my trainer gave me a fish or two. He sometimes sneaked a couple extra fish to me. I had no objections to his behavior. I realized how much easier life was without having to struggle for food, but I also missed my friends in the ocean and the adventures.

I often heard my trainer talking about how intelligent he thought I was. He thought the games I played with the other animals in the tank were very interesting. I could even solve problems like getting a fish to eat out from under a small rock. I got the fish out by killing a scorpion fish (It is armed with many poisonous spines.) and prodded the fish and it came out. The thought it was remarkable that I could solve so many problems and insisted to his friend that I had a great mental capacity. When they laughed at him he got mad and said that a dolphin's brain was about the same size as a human's. . . .

My Golden Years

I was afraid that I had lost my instincts. As I plunged the full 70 feet my lungs compressed. I hadn't gone so deep in years. It felt great. I stayed down for about 15 minutes. This was the most refreshing dive I had in years. Soon I sighted a school of dolphins, some were bottle-nosed, others spotted. As they approached me I sent out my 'greetings' communications signal and they clicked to me 'Would you like to join our group?" (Dolphins are always friendly to other species of dolphins.) . . .

I decided to join another group of about 50 dolphins heading for warmer waters (South). I wanted to live out my life with these dolphins, hopefully having an adventure or two.

Brian's report shows that content area study can bring good writing and reading together. Students read good literature and, in turn, write it. They use perfunctory texts and references only to locate facts, not as sources for ideas about how to write well. Our basic decision to let our students use their knowledge about writing in content areas produces a tension between the obligation we feel to teach certain facts and the necessity of choice for students in order to maximize the chance they will be interested enough to work as hard as they must to produce high quality work. Some courses of study include many facts, but we now realize that facts are less important than we thought in previous decades.

Harste (1985) says that there is a move away from teaching specific content because of the knowledge explosion. There is too much information for us to teach it all. Students start early at developing areas of expertise and acquire information about many other areas when their classmates share their knowledge with them. The emphasis is on the process of learning, not on the product and not on whether the entire class has covered the same body of information throughout the year. While this is ideal, we may need a more realistic approach.

When we pursue a required unit with required facts, we tell the students what to read and what they have to know. Although they must all learn it, they spend the majority of their time pursuing a personal interest within the unit, and we do likewise. Sometimes, however, even this can cause us anxiety.

Fifth-grade teachers know they have to send their students to middle school with report-writing skills but dread dull reports. Luckily, many middle school teachers now recognize good writing and don't want their students to write reports that sound like textbooks or encyclopedias. But some of us are still in a bind. It's tough, and

I can only wish you the backbone of a first-grade teacher who gave a talk to a regional teachers' gathering and then fielded questions. One question was, "Are you worried that your students will not do well next year because you teach differently than their second-grade teacher will?"

She answered, "No. I can't justify giving my students a negative experience because I think they'll have one next year." Students learn more about writing when they compose top-quality texts than if they spend weeks on dull reports. The format isn't the crux of writing—the content is. We write to display our information, not doom it to the back corner because no one ever chooses to read it. When all teachers want well-written information, our task is easier, as Pete Schiot learned.

Pete teaches fifth grade in Durham, New Hampshire, where his students will go on to a middle school with teachers who know about writing. In the 1984–85 school year Pete broke away from traditional reports. For their animal unit, his students each chose an animal, researched it, held conferences about their information and how they'd present it, wrote drafts, and produced final products, like this piece by Amy Burtelow:

My Life as a Mustang

Where was I? There was soft grass under me and a big blue sky above. Was I deserted? I realized that I was very wet and that something warm and dry was licking me. Slowly I lifted my head and looked beside me. My mother, seeing that I was awake, paused for a moment and nuzzled my neck.

Clearly from instinct, I tried to get up. My legs would get tangled and get in the way but soon I was up on my long wobbling legs. . . .

During my time leadng the band, I had to lead my band away from enemies, such as cougars and wolves. At times, I would fight a wolf with my strong hooves and easily win. They were after the newborn foals. I saw the airplane many times too.

One day another stallion came along and screamed. I was 16 years old in a mustang's short life of about 20 years. I was also much weaker. It wa a stallion's place to fight to his death, so I screamed back. The younger stallion rushed at me with his teeth fully bared. I knew I would be the one to die in this fight.

Amy and the other students read a variety of material, sought response while they were in the process of writing, learned from others about their animals, gained ideas from classmates about genres to use, and produced interesting writing in which they incorporated what they learned. By not requiring a format for his students to follow, Pete demanded more from them. (See Hembrow 1986 for an article about Pete.) They not only had to learn about an animal, but they had to choose an interesting way to present their knowledge.

Pete was impressed by the quality of his students' writing, but it was not quality alone that convinced him to use his new approach to report writing again the following year. The students' excitement about what they were learning overrode, in Pete's mind, their ability to write well. The children remained interested in their report topics for months after the unit ended. Not only did Amy maintain her interest in mustangs but other students continued to bring her articles and tidbits of information throughout the year. The entire class continued to learn about everyone's specialty.

References

BENEDICT, SUSAN. 1985. "Emily Dickinson's Room Is as Old as Grandfather Frog": Developing the Basic Skills. In *Breaking Ground: Teachers Relate Reading and Writing in the Elementary School*, ed. by Jane Hansen, Thomas Newkirk, and Donald Graves. Portsmouth, N.H.: Heinemann.

EVANS, CHRISTINE SOBRAY. 1984. Writing to Learn in Math. *Language Arts* 61, no. 8 (December).

FIVE, CORA. 1985. Children Recreate History in Their Own Voices. In *Breaking Ground: Teachers Relate Reading and Writing in the Elementary School*, ed. by Jane Hansen, Thomas Newkirk, and Donald Graves. Portsmouth, N.H.: Heinemann.

FREEDMAN, RUSSELL. 1986. Pursuing the Pleasure Principle. *Horn Book* 62, no. 1 (January/February): 27–32.

HANSEN, JANE. 1984. Readers Talk Like Writers. In *Changing Perspectives on Research in Reading/Language Processing and Composing*, ed. by Jerome Niles. Rochester, N.Y.: National Reading Conference.

HARSTE, JEROME C. 1985. Portrait of a New Paradigm: Reading Comprehension Research. In *Landscapes: A State-of-the-Art Assessment of Reading Comprehension Research, 1974–1984*, ed. by Avon Crismore. Bloomington, Ind.: University of Indiana.

HEMBROW, VERN. 1986. A Heuristic Approach Across the Curriculum. *Language Arts* 63, no. 7 (November).

LEVINE, DENISE STAVIS. 1985. The Biggest Thing I Learned but It Really Doesn't Have to Do with Science. . . . *Language Arts* 62, no. 1 (January).

MATTHEWS, KATHY. 1985. Beyond the Writing Table. In *Breaking Ground: Teachers Relate Reading and Writing in the Elementary School*, ed. by Jane Hansen, Thomas Newkirk, and Donald Graves. Portsmouth, N.H.: Heinemann.

NEWKIRK, THOMAS. In preparation. *Archimedes' Dream*.

ROBERTS, JANICE. 1985. Excellence in Language Arts. Article distributed in Mast Way information package.

The Teacher's New Role

We place the reins in the child's hands. I didn't fully understand why until I read an interview that Kim Stafford, a poet and writer, conducted with Makoto Imai, a Japanese wood worker. Imai said, "If first workbench you see as a child has a vise, then you need it all your life. You think you cannot work without it."

We have been led to think we cannot teach without manuals, and we remain in their grip for years. They seem so comprehensive and systematic in their coverage of skills that we cannot conceive of the day when we can teach without them. Yet that is precisely what we work toward.

Until we break the constricting security of their grip, response teaching will not become a reality. Books cannot respond, but teachers can. The nature of our new role requires that our students lead us. We must be willing to jump, to experiment, to let go of our security blankets. But this new role is uncertain and it scares us. We must make more decisions than in the past, which places more responsibility on our shoulders.

We must decide what to teach, rather than turning the page in the manual and writing the label of the next exercise in tomorrow's box of our lesson plan book. We may go next door to find out what that teacher intends to do tomorrow, but if our neighbor is helpful, she will ask us questions about our children in order to help us make our own decisions. The teachers at Mast Way learned to generate options and each taught differently, but they used common practices: 1) They helped their students learn to make decisions about reading; 2) They respected and responded to what their students knew; 3) They used more direct teaching methods than teachers have used in the past.

Teachers View Students as Decision Makers

I sneaked some comments about reading instruction at Mast Way Elementary School into my writing course at the University of New Hampshire last summer. One of my students was Judy Velasquez, a sixth-grade teacher in Healdsburg, California, and she returned home with her head buzzing. By April she not only had a classroom full of writers but also of readers. She says the most noticeable difference between her present students and those of former years is the additional control they have. "This control is very important to them. They guard it. As I see how much they value their control I look for ways to let them make more and more decisions."

Once students recognize all the doors open to them through topic choice in writing, they don't want to be placed in the straight jacket of rigid assignments. They find ways out. Restrictions become challenges to overcome. Similarly, book choice brings the world of reading into their laps, and they insist on time to read the books they want to read. Time away from their books brings frustration. But as we give students more power to make decisions, we feel their independence and may become uncertain about what role we, as teachers, are to play.

Our new role begins when we view ourselves as decision-makers. It may be difficult not to have a prescription to follow, but this is the position we place our students in when we teach them to make decisions for themselves rather than following our dictums. Their decision-making begins, however, only after we give ourselves the authority to change our role.

We may decide to change because we have become bored with teaching, or maybe we want to try something new because we want to decrease the number of unsettling days we have with our students. Most of us know we are good teachers, but we are constantly searching for ways to grow, and we want a new horizon to explore, one where we and our students will move forward with even more energy. We realize the view of teaching described in this book is different. It's not to be taken lightly because it involves a decision to change.

Initially, we don't know what the specific change will be. If we have become comfortable with our ability to recognize what our students know about their topics in writing, we may become uneasy about how infrequently our goal during reading is to find out how their knowledge extends beyond ours. Therefore, we may decide to give our students the responsibility for generating their own response to what they read rather than answering our questions. But this may not work too well and we realize that in writing, their commitment is somehow tied to the fact that they choose their own topics. This gnaws at us and we wonder if they will become more involved in their responses during reading if they respond to books they like, books of their own choice. Although we didn't realize it at the time, the initial decision to teach writing was to lead to many other decisions, many of which go beyond writing.

We can make the changes we feel are necessary in reading if we have a strong enough desire to do so. In many workshops, teachers come to me and say, "I can't do this because of . . . the curriculum . . . my principal . . . my supervisor. . . ." However, at each of those very same workshops, there is always someone who is determined to change and has already outlined the first steps. The decision to change is personal. We make it for different reasons, and each of us follows different paths afterwards, but we must have the confidence that the information we will need to figure out what to do is available.

We cannot learn only from books like this one. We must read journals, such as *Language Arts*, and *Horn Book*, attend conferences, workshops, inservices, classes, and summer institutes, visit the classrooms of other teachers, invite visitors to our class, and talk about our teaching. When we move out of our classrooms, we become aware of new options. We find ourselves less secure, but we take a deep breath and leap—only after we've spread a safety net below ourselves.

The most fundamental way to learn about teaching writing and reading is to write and read (Matthews 1984). We write and read enough to say to others, "Yes. I write. Yes. I'm a reader." This credential allows us to say the next words, "Yes. I teach writing and reading." We write and read on our own and share it with our friends. We know firsthand about the decisions writers make when they get stuck or have too many ideas. We also make decisions when we read about which book to read next and why we do or don't like it. We learn about decisions others make when we talk about our writing and reading with our friends. Also, our students know we are writers and readers.

Most of the Mast Way teachers wrote in their classrooms, some more frequently than others. Daily writing may not be necessary, but our students do notice our participation. Phyllis Kinzie's fourth-graders commented on the writing she did. "It's encouraging. . . . It shows she cares when she doesn't just go off and do something else when we write." The teachers at Mast Way not only wrote, they shared their writing with their students. This overture on their part admits them to the community of learners and gives them credibility as advisors about writing. The same may be true for reading.

The more books we read, the easier it is to talk about books. The words come. One book reminds us of another and one writer brings another to mind. The ideal reading teacher loves to read and can't resist books. This sounds like something I heard decades ago, but it's more relevant now when we rely less on guidebooks and more on ourselves as resources.

Our own reading and writing becomes enriched when we share

with our colleagues. Such group conferences serve three purposes. First, as it turns out, a very important reason for the sessions is one of personal involvement. We become increasingly interested in the books we read and the writing we hear. In addition, we become acquainted with our colleagues in a personal dimension, beyond what we knew from coffee room chat. This helps us to work closely as we explore new teaching avenues. Finally, our sessions become a laboratory for learning how to respond to our students as we gain a sixth sense about what to say from the kinds of comments we appreciate receiving from others. A weekly gathering keeps us busy, but it also helps us grow.

Teachers in many parts of this country, from Miami, Ohio, to Fresno, California, meet to share and learn. Teachers in Canada, from Edmonton, Alberta, to Halifax, Nova Scotia, also come together to meet and share their own writing and reading. Once we put forth the effort to learn about the basic principles of writing and reading instruction, we have a sufficient knowledge base at least to begin. This knowledge gives us the support not only to start but to continue to learn.

We give our students new decision-making power. Our students need information on which to base their decisions, or they, too, get nervous. Like us, they begin to realize that the more they learn, the more options they become aware of and that a certain amount of risk and anxiety is usually a part of the responsibility of making a decision.

We may want to protect young children from this anxiety. Florence Damon, kindergarten teacher, says her children think everything they do is good, and she wants to accept everything. In order to decide how to get better, you have to admit something is not good, and she wonders at what age this critical decision making should begin. In June her children know they're getting better, but she doesn't think she wants to promote comparative thinking where they say, "I can't do this." Her students will try anything, and she wants this behavior to continue. However, they can tell if a library book is easy or hard, or why they like it. Maybe this is preparation for a way to look at reading decisions.

When Mark tries to decide whether he will share *The Man Who Lived Alone* by Donald Hall or *Arthur, For the Very First Time* by Patricia MacLachlan, he says, "If I share *The Man Who Lived Alone*, I could read it all, but *Arthur* has some funny parts and they might like it better. Did you know he had a pet hen? But I'd like to read a whole book. I think I'll share *The Man Who Lived Alone*." Mark has clear reasons for his decision. When children and teachers talk regularly about options and choices, the teachers learn about reasons they didn't even know their students considered. We expect them to decide what to do and to generate their options, but we see ourselves as the people who help them generate options. This is why we also make decisions about our teaching. We can say, "My students learned to read because of me," rather than, "I just did what the program outlined and they learned to read. Anyone could have done it." We try harder when we make our own decisions because if we fail, we know we must take "credit" for that. But when we make decisions successfully, our enthusiasm for our teaching increases. Like us, whether children's decisions turn out to be good or not, they know they made them and will make their next ones in light of them. Their progress rests on their own shoulders. Students become more involved in their work when they make more of their own decisions.

Teachers Become Learners

The notion of the teacher as learner catches us off guard.

In some ways, it's the opposite of what we've traditionally thought when we labeled the adult the teacher and the youngsters the learners, but it's not quite the opposite. The teacher continues to teach, but she becomes more of a learner (Five 1986, Boutwell 1983) than in the past. She learns from the students in order to know what they know and thus, what to teach, how to extend their knowledge into new territory. Because our goal is to create independent learners the teacher serves as the number one learner in the classroom. The students see a learner in action (Susi 1984), and in this way, they learn how to learn.

Ruth Hubbard learned from David in Pat McLure's first-grade class (Hubbard 1984). As she walked about the room during writing, she noticed that David simply wrote *C-A-T* on several pages. This disappointed her, and she pulled a chair up beside David. "Tell me about your writing, David."

David beamed, "I'm writing and thinking about all the different cats I know." He proceeded to tell her about the cats, their names, who they belonged to, and anecdotes about some of them. He concluded, "That's eight cats I've remembered today."

Ruth focused on what David did know, rather than on what he didn't know. This is the key to the teacher as learner. The teacher's focus is always on what the child knows—about his writing or a book he's reading. Children soon sense the teacher's respect for their work and look forward to telling her what they know.

David was undaunted by Ms. Hubbard's stop at his desk. He chatted freely about his cats, and she enjoyed their conversation. David will write tomorrow. He knows his teacher is interested in his work. Similarly, we carry this notion into reading. We learn when we stop beside a student who has a book we've never read, and we learn how books we have read affect them differently from us, as well as differently from each other. When we learn from our students, they respect and learn from each other.

Similarly, in reading conferences we come to learn from the child who is sharing a piece of writing, her own draft or a Patricia MacLachlan book. Sometimes, several of us may meet together to share what we think about a book we've all read, but we gather to learn from each other. We are curious to find out what we each know and think. By focusing on the knowledge of the child who shares, we set the tone for learning.

Our students see us as people who believe they know something worthwhile. When we come with open ears, open eyes, and closed mouths we hear what our students know and learn how to enlarge that knowledge further. We teach in response to what our students display as needs, or edges of their knowledge, rather than use a prescribed list as our guide, and plan our contacts with our students differently than I did when I taught.

I would come to class with a list of questions to check whether the children knew the things I had selected as important. I didn't find out what else they knew. But now we let them see us as learners, and, also, teach them to ask us questions about our reading and writing. In January of 1985, Phyllis Kinzie shared one of her drafts with her fourth-grade class. It was fiction based on experiences of her own children when they were young. When she finished, the students not only responded to her, but back and forth among each other. The first comment came from Jon: "I like the story. It seems like a real kid."

Phyllis: "Thank you. I tried to make it real."

John: "Especially the part about the stuffed animal."

Matt S.: "I liked the relationship between the girl and her stuffed animal. . . ."

Eric: "Was the elephant her only stuffed animal?"

Phyllis: "No, but Sydney [Sydney is Sandy in the story] only used one at a time and she cried when each wore out and we bought a new one."

Allison: "I like it when you said, 'Think of your friend when you fall asleep.' "

The children talk back and forth about sleeping with stuffed animals.

Then Josh says, "My sister is lucky. Her bed is against the wall so her stuffed animals don't fall off."

Gabrielle: "Once when my mother kissed me goodnight she kissed one of my stuffed animals by mistake."

The class laugh and talk among themselves.

John: "I had a big teddy bear and slept on his lap."

The children laugh again and swap stories.

Matt S.: "I wondered if you'd put looks in."

Phyllis: "You know why I didn't? I know you kids love to but I like to have everyone picture how the characters look."

Matt S.: "Yes, before I went to John's camp I pictured it but it was different."

Phyllis: "Are different pictures wrong?"

Matt S.: "No, you can picture characters the way you want. . . ."

Eric: "Like in *Chronicles of Narnia*, I picture them. . . ."

Phyllis: "When you picture a professor do you picture your dad?"

Melinda: "I liked how you made Lisa nice to Sandy. . . ."

Mark: "I liked to see Sandy run down the hall. I could just see her. I do that after a scary movie."

Phyllis: "Well, I debated whether she should scream or run."

Ms. Kinzie's students see her as someone who makes decisions about her writing, someone who is learning how to write, someone who respects their thoughts, someone from whom they can learn how to respond to writers, and someone from whom they can learn about writing.

Teachers Use Direct Teaching Methods

In the Mast Way classrooms the teacher's role is so different from the norm that it's often difficult to see it as teaching. One day in 1984, when I met with three visitors who had spent two days observing at Mast Way, one of them asked, "If we try to teach this way, what do we say to those who pressure us for direct teaching?"

I didn't know how to answer her. Now, I think I know what she meant, but it's still a confusing issue. We need to reconsider what direct teaching means. The kind of teaching the Mast Way teachers do is direct teaching in the most literal sense. They teach directly to the child. They teach what the students need, when they need it, in the context of their own reading or writing, wherever the problem arises (Graves 1984). On the contrary, the kind of teaching usually labeled "Direct Teaching" is not as direct. Direct teaching most commonly applies to the overt use of a specific plan to teach a skill, such as the /ch/ sound. This definition also applies to a session in which the teacher brings a kindergarten class together on the carpet and teaches them to say /ch/ whenever she holds up a card containing the letters *CH*. In these situations, however, many of the children either already know the skill or are not yet ready for it. Only a few are being taught, and they are not being taught in the context of their own reading or writing. They have to transfer this learning to appropriate tasks. We may need to reconsider what direct teaching could mean.

The direct teaching of content. Trevor read *The Man Who Lived Alone* by Donald Hall and commented aloud to his friends, "The old man had a friend named [pause] Grover Cleveland. Grover was an owl and the man caught mice with his bare hands for Grover and he stayed up all night talking to Grover."

The teacher had noticed the allusion in the owl's name, but none of the children appeared to have her interest. They responded to staying up all night, talking to an owl, and catching mice with bare hands. Eric commented, "He could never catch mice with his bare hands; besides, what if they had rabies?"

Trevor: "We can catch gerbils with our bare hands."

Eric: "But they're our pets."

Trevor: "The old man probably thought all animals were his pets. He maybe sat still for nights, and the mice in his basement became his friends. If he could talk to an owl, he could catch a mouse."

Angie: "But if the mice became his friends he wouldn't feed them to Grover."

Trevor: "I guess he liked Grover better than the mice. Owls really are interesting."

Bert: "They mostly sit and sleep and sometimes hoot. When we read about owls, it always just says, 'Who-o, Who-o!' but if the man talked to Grover, they must say something else."

Trevor: "I think they say 'Who-o, Who-o!' in different ways, like we don't always say, 'Word, Word!' "

Everyone laughed and Trevor started to think, "I wonder how their different words do sound."

The teacher took her cue: "I don't know, but you're probably right that if we listened carefully their 'Who-os!' would sound different. I wonder if you could learn to make two different kinds and talk to us."

Trevor studied owls for seven days. He began the topic, his friends extended it, and he accepted his teacher's challenge to continue. But his teacher helped him focus on the aspect of the content that struck him as important. This same principle holds for skills instruction.

The direct teaching of skills. Florence Damon, the kindergarten teacher at Mast Way, found that her students learned their sounds at the writing table when they sat with one to five friends and requested help from each other. Their queries were specific: "What do I put for 'water'?" and the teaching was direct: "It's an upside-down M." Both Florence Damon and the first-grade teacher who received her students the next year attested to the higher proficiency of these children than previous classes whom Florence had taught by her traditional "grunt and groan" lessons. This is worthwhile evidence, but it's still difficult to describe what Florence Damon and the other Mast Way teachers do.

Once, after I'd given a one-hour talk about response teaching, a teacher said to me, "I agree with you. Children can learn to read by themselves." I felt awful. How could I talk for an hour and give my audience the impression that I think children can learn to read by themselves? That's not what I meant to say. I don't think children can learn to read by themselves. Precocious children who read at the age of three didn't teach themselves to read. They live with readers, people who read to them and/or respond to their inquiries about print. They couldn't have learned to read so early without someone's influence.

The role of adults in their lives is different from the traditional role of "teacher," but it is no less important. Similarly, the Mast Way teachers' role is different from the typical role, but their task is as major and influential as ever. Their role is to find out what students know, affirm for them what they know, ask what they want to know next, and teach it.

We teach the skills the children know they need. One day, fourth-grader Sarla requested an editing conference with me. I asked her if she wanted help with a particular skill. "Yes. This is the first time I've used dialogue and I need help with my quotation marks. Some of the kids used dialogue in third grade but I never did."

Sarla's comments are interesting. She could have learned this skill the previous year, but because she didn't need it, she didn't learn it. She knew she'd continue writing and would learn the skill when she needed it. Sarla knows that the school, her teachers, and her friends exist to help her with what she wants to learn, and she's aware of what she can choose to learn. She knows she'll get the help she needs when she needs it. School is relevant.

Direct teaching lets school provide a useful service to children. Other children could teach Sarla about quotation marks as well as I could. Several people are available to give her the help she needs, just as several of us could discuss content with Trevor or provide the letter *W* for 'water.' The students determined the direction of their learning and others followed their lead. We didn't teach Trevor about owls, as someone taught Sarla about quotation marks, but because we accepted his interest, he can pursue it rather than leaving it hanging while he reads a story chosen by his teacher. The basic goal of teaching—helping the learner pursue information—inspires us to encourage his interest.

Teachers teach students how to learn. More than teaching information and skills, we teach students how to learn. We work with them while they are in the process of learning and discover what strategies they use to tackle things they do not yet understand. (See Willinsky 1984 for a story about a teacher who has a literate classroom.) When a student cannot think of a workable way out of a dilemma, we focus the child's attention on how to move forward, rather than answering the child's question.

When first-grader Amanda asked me to read the word *thumb* for her in a book about a giant, I didn't. I suggested that she read on. Six pages later, after skipping the word four times, she was able to read it. She had accumulated enough context to figure out the word. When I asked her to explain how she figured it out, she verified what I hoped she had realized. Three days later, when another child asked me to read a word for him, I went to Amanda. Yes, she remembered how she had figured out *thumb* and would teach Christopher this procedure.

Another time I might teach strategies differently. When a fourth grader comes to me and says, "I don't get this," I might say, "Well, you could reread it or you could ask a small group about it. Which will you do?" The student gathers two friends, reads to them, and they talk. I listen and, finally, tell the group to speculate about when they might gather friends together to help them learn.

We teach students to write and talk about what they do, so they know they're learning how to learn. This not only encourages the reader's own awareness, but other students also learn a strategy they may not have used. By following our lead, they teach each other ways to answer these questions:

- What do I want to learn next? What will I write? Read?
- What is more than one way to use this information? What are some ways I could write about it? What are some ways to interpret this book?
- What learning strategies can I teach others?
- How do I decide when a task is finished? How do I determine whether a draft is worth pursuing or should be dropped? Can I explain why a book was important to me and what it might mean to someone else?

When we teach children the process of learning, we assume a new role. We step back and watch them learn, listen to the questions they ask each other, and make only a few suggestions ourselves. We teach them to consider alternatives and make decisions.

References

BOUTWELL, MARILYN. 1983. Reading and Writing Process: A Reciprocal Agreement. *Language Arts* 60, no. 6 (September).

GRAVES, DONALD H. 1984. *A Researcher Learns to Write.* Portsmouth, N.H.: Heinemann.

HANSEN, JANE, AND GRAVES, DONALD. 1986. "Do you know what backstrung means?" *The Reading Teacher* 39, no. 8 (March).

HUBBARD, RUTH. 1984. What's Going on in His Mind? in *Children Who Write When They Read.* Durham, N.H.: Writing Process Laboratory, University of New Hampshire.

MATTHEWS, KATHY. 1984. Are You Willing To Be the Kind of Writer You Want Your Students To Be? *Learning Magazine*, April/May.

SUSI, GERALDINE LEE. 1984. The Teacher/Writer: Model, Learner, Human Being. *Language Arts* 61, no. 7 (November).

WILLINSKY, JOHN. 1984. The Writer in the Teacher. *Language Arts* 61, no. 6 (October).

"A book is a seed that sprouts. One book is the beginning of more and more books, authors and ideas. The more you use a library, the more you use a library," says Marcia Taft, the librarian at Mast Way Elementary School.

Marcia says that since the research project began, the Mast Way students have started to read more library books. "There's a numerical increase," smiles Marcia, "especially in nonfiction. And the children don't just wander in because they have free time. They come because they want a certain book, a particular author, or they come with a friend who has a favorite to recommend. I can hear remnants of the talks they have about books in their classrooms."

These children talk about books differently than the nonwriters who formerly used the Mast Way library did, and this influences the way Marcia talks to them. She has changed what she does when she teaches children about books but, mostly, the environment in the library is new because Marcia now belongs to a reading-writing community.

The Librarian Belongs to the Schoolwide Writing-Reading Community

When the writers at Mast Way started to choose the books for their reading instruction and shared those books, their interest in reading increased. They read more than they had in the past, and the dream of all librarians came true. Students' use of the library increased. However, the teachers also started to use the library more, which shouldn't have surprised us, but this was the first time we had worked in a school of writers, and we hadn't predicted the difference in teacher use. The whole school community wanted to use the library more frequently and Marcia always kept the doors open.

Accessibility of the library.   The Mast Way library had always been open all day every day, but now Marcia's open-door policy became more crucial because the library became an integral part of the reading-writing program. Whenever children wanted a book, they could take a short walk and procure it. A school with a reading program in which children read books needs a library with nonstop hours.

The library at Mast Way buzzes before school and throughout the day. Marcia works Monday through Thursday, and her assistant works on Fridays. The Mast Way students are fortunate to have a librarian present every day; support of the library in the district has, historically, been good. More importantly, however, it is Marcia who has issued the invitation to everyone in the school to come anytime.

Marcia places no restrictions on when children may use the library. The kindergarten children have a scheduled weekly library visit, when Marcia reads to them and they check out books, but they can return at any time between their scheduled visits. Children in grades one through five do not have scheduled visits and use the library whenever they want a book. They not only know it's permissible to use the library, they feel Marcia's warmth and know they are welcome. This warm welcome is not accidental; she wants the library to have a friendly atmosphere and talks about this aspect of her role.

When Marcia asks others to remember their school libraries from years past, they often tell her their library was a cold place, a place where they went to get a book but which they left as soon as possible. This is not what Marcia wants at Mast Way. She sees a library as a place to browse "among people, displays, and ideas—a place where the outside world comes into our reading, writing, talking." Children may come with a specific book in mind or a particular piece of information to find, but she hopes they will peruse other books as well. If they spend time with the interesting books they happen to notice, they may return to look more closely at them. However, Marcia alone cannot set the tone for the library.

The teachers reinforce her desire to make the library the center of the school, by encouraging students to use the library often and listening to them talk about their book choices. Marcia appreciates this and also talks about this support when she meets with other librarians. They contrast this with what happened in the days when they were students and remember teachers who didn't talk to them about their library books. The books their teachers talked about were their reading books. Of course, the big difference at Mast Way is that the library books *are* the reading books. When Marcia, the teachers, and the students talk about books, the books they talk about are library books.

Teachers use the library.   Marcia notes that teachers have begun to use the library more for books they want to read. They have not only continued reading to their classes daily, but they read children's books themselves because they take part in the children's share sessions. They find and read books they want to share and books their students recommend to them. They become part of the reading-writing community in their classrooms. They become learners like their students.

This was a difficult stance to take, but a necessary one if teachers are to let their students read. Marcia generalizes about teachers' decisions to become more informed. "Children's books are legitimate. It used to be, maybe teachers were embarrassed because they didn't know about a book or, at the other extreme, embarrassed to be an expert on children's books. If you are someone who spends lots of time with children's books, you hesitate to let people know because they might think you waste time. Why don't teachers know more about children's literature? It's just not important."

Initially, some of the Mast Way teachers felt deficient in what they knew about children's literature. As their students started to read more and more, the teachers went to Marcia for authors' names to suggest to their students. They also wanted titles of books to share—books their students might like but might not find on their own. The teachers often prepared for reading class by reading books and interacting with Marcia.

Gradually, Marcia and the teachers have started to talk about books in a different way. Now Marcia doesn't only tell the teachers about books, they talk about books together. Teachers come to her excited about a book they've read and share their insights with her. They also share the children's responses to books. (Samway 1986 writes about how awful children's response can be with traditional book reports.) Marcia says she used to dispense information, but now she's not the only book expert. However, she still has the greatest access to books and makes her knowledge available to the teachers.

When the teachers met during weekly sessions to share their writing, Marcia closed each meeting by sharing a children's book. This increased the teachers' awareness of children's books both they and their students might read. But Marcia says the greatest impact of the teachers' group was not her opportunity to share new additions to the library; rather, the personal knowledge she and the other teachers gained about each other changed their relationships within the school. They realized that they were all in this reading-writing effort together.

The librarian has an overview of the school. Marcia sees a cross-section of the school every day. She has an overview of what the teachers and children are reading. When one student came to learn about coins because he was writing about his coin collection, she suggested that he talk to a student in another room who was also writing about his coin collection. Marcia is in an ideal position to bring the writing and reading of the school together, and she does this in more than one way.

The library has a special section in which the writing of Mast Way writers is available for others to read. Here the students can read hardcover books, books stapled together with construction paper covers, and single sheets of paper taped to the wall. The corner is labeled "Mast Way Writers" and has tables where children can share their writing. The library has become a place where students get to know each other, both as authors and as people.

As children become better acquainted, they can more easily become members of the schoolwide community of writers and readers. Partly because this community is new, Marcia knows the joy of sharing with her peers and wants the children to feel this same spark. The wider the diversity among readers who interact in the library, the richer a student's view of books may become. When the children know students in other grades, and they all talk books together, they start to realize that reading books makes them part of the community at Mast Way.

The Librarian Teaches Children to Respond to Books

Librarians want students who love to read. As writers, children become interested in the writing of other authors and gravitate toward the library. Their writing and sharing stimulates their interest in books, and this interest, coupled with the librarian's welcoming response to them in the library, results in an increase in the number of children who use the library.

Students read lots of books. As more students come to check out books at the Mast Way library, Marcia Taft spends more time with students than she used to. She also has more books to reshelve and in general, more to do than she did in the past. However, the children also use classroom and community libraries.

The well-stocked classroom library doesn't take away from use of the school library (Cullinan 1986 writes about the importance of lots of books.) The collection in the classroom makes selection more convenient for most children during writing and reading, but it also serves to stimulate their interest in authors and topics, which they pursue in the school library. The classroom library whets their appetites but cannot satisfy voracious readers. Neither does the school collection. As children and teachers become more interested in books, they also visit community libraries more often.

Some teachers at Mast Way regularly checked out as many books as they were allowed to from their community libraries and brought them into the classroom for the students to read. The children themselves started to make trips to the Lee Town Library or the Durham Library. These libraries were not places the children went because they didn't like the Mast Way library. Rather, they learned that libraries differ, and they wanted to find out what other collections contained. And libraries became nice places in which to spend time. Much of the children's involvement originated in their classrooms, but the Mast Way library and books from other libraries supported this interest. Marcia, in turn, worked to keep their interest alive.

The librarian encourages informal response in the library.   The children show their excitement about books. (See Hyman 1985 for an essay on the importance of letting children's responses remain alive.) So does Marcia. She is a gentle person with a quiet voice and teaches the children to use a similar tone. The library is a place for sharing, not silence. The children respect those who study there, but they also approach Marcia with "Look what I found!" or, "Listen to this," and begin to read.

Marcia responds, "You really like the way the girl talks to her father, don't you?"

"You know, it sounds like me and my grandpa sometimes."

"You mean you talk about things that happened a long time ago?"

"Sort of. My grandpa leans back and tells long stories and he sounds different when he tells stories than when he just talks."

Marcia says her ways of responding to children have changed. When children used to come to the library, they met an "expert" and asked her to suggest a book or requested her help with information. Now they usually make their own book choices and she responds to their choices. She tells them what she enjoys about the books they intend to read, and when they return books they tell her what they thought. She knows much more about what children think of the books in the Mast Way library. Marcia knows why they read certain books, and she selects books for the collection more in accordance with their interests now than she did in the past. "The children think of themselves as idea sources for me for books to buy."

For their writing, the children often want specific information, and so she purchases larger numbers of well-written information books than in the past, although the children also find a lot of information in fiction books. Mainly, they read interesting books and try to write like real authors instead of textbook or encyclopedia compilers. In the library, they talk about which books are the most interesting to read. (See Adamson 1983 for a reflection on different emphases in the treatment of children's literature.) They share their enthusiasm with Marcia and with each other. "Listen to the way this author describes the mountains. It's like a poem in the middle of the writing."

"You could really write a poem in the middle of your report. You could."

The children learn to recognize good writing and think of ways to improve their own.

Marcia lets the children know she likes book talk in the library, but she goes a step further than simply talking about books: she lets the children share with each other. It she didn't, not only would she have a line waiting to talk to her, but children would get the impression that she is the expert through whom they must filter their knowledge. Children get to know each other better when they talk about books, and when they respond to each other, they find out that readers are readers. They can talk about books with students from any class, and this enhances their notion of themselves as readers in a school full of readers. They can see their former selves in the younger children when they talk about books they remember from previous years, and they get a sense of where they are going from the older students.

The librarian organizes formal response in the library. During the 1984–85 school year, Marcia started to set aside two forty-five minute blocks of time each week for children from kindergarten through fifth grade to come to the library to share their writing or reading. Children who participated in the group responded to whatever others shared, whether it was a draft, a final product by a Mast Way writer, or the final draft of a professional writer.

An expansion of their first session, on October 2, 1984, shows us what researcher Lorri Neilsen saw. Seven children attended: two first graders, Roger and Jill; three second graders, Melissa, Sara, and Jenny; and two third graders, Jenny and Derek.

Derek, who apparently suffered stage fright at the last minute, asked Marcia to read the poem he brought.

Roger read his story about the new book he had on spiders. It was not a library book, he was careful to add. It was his very own to-keep book.

Sara introduced the group to a book she was currently reading about a young boy's adventures with dolphins. She gave the group an overview of the story line, with appropriate embellishments, and then read a page.

Jenny (third grade) read a funny story about a hippo that ate the teacher. As she read, she could barely suppress her grin and made sure everyone had a chance to see the pictures by slowly and deliberately displaying the book to the semicircle in front of her.

Jenny (second grade) came as a listener to give Melissa a boost of confidence when she read her first published book, a book she had written the previous June about a unicorn, a girl, and a bird. Before she read, Melissa apologized, "The pictures aren't that good. I can draw a unicorn much better than this now." Immediately after she finished reading, she explained, "At first I had it so the girl slid down the side of the unicorn's head, but I didn't like that. I changed it a lot as I wrote it. . . . I wanted to do this right because it was my first published book." In answer to a question about why she chose to write about a unicorn, she said, "I picked a unicorn because it's an animal that everyone likes. Everyone would want to read it." Later, when someone asked what she was writing now, Missy took a deep breath and began a retelling of her adventure at the Lee town fair, where she and her family built and became a large worm using hula hoops, blankets, and paper.

The diversity displayed in this first session and the variety of comments from only one of the seven children who talked, provided the impetus Marcia needed to continue these meetings. The session had proceeded smoothly, and although this had worried Marcia, she knew how to respond to the children because she was part of the teachers' writing group in which she had learned how to respond and receive response to her writing. In those sessions, she had faced head-on her own fears about sharing her writing. Marcia valued the supportive comments her peers gave her, and she responds accordingly to the children when they share in the library. But she attributes the success of the sessions to the children's ability to respond to each other, which they have learned in their classrooms. As the sessions continued, they revealed even more diversity. At the February 4 meeting:

John read a piece about his trip to Pennsylvania, which focused on seeing M & M's being packaged.

Matt and David read their report on mink, which included strong verbs, and they delighted in reading them together: "spit . . . hiss."

Amanda read her detailed expository piece on the snowy owl.

Buddy read about sea treasures in a piece that used sophisticated vocabulary, including words like *obliterated*.

Stacy read a short report about birds that go south.

Andy read his own "Gobots." His writing had an introduction and a colorful, detailed account of each of the kinds of gobots he owns. His illustrations were well-drawn and meticulously colored.

The children sometimes considered their wider audience when they wrote, as we see in the January 29 session, when Aaron read the information book he had written about the sun. In the book he used the word *mirage* and provided a definition. He said he did this "in case a younger reader would look at the book—I did that on purpose." However, during the 1985–86 school year, Marcia decided to have one session each week earmarked for upper grades and one for lower grades. This arrangement continued to capitalize on a wider audience than the children experienced in their classrooms but permitted children from somewhat similar ages to share among students with whom they had more common interests. In all cases, these formal sessions were different from the type of formal session we commonly associate with libraries.

Marcia says librarians most often think of sessions on library skills when they recall their former notions of what librarians should do in planned lessons. Marcia does teach library skills, but she thinks the most important skill is excitement about reading books, if that can be termed a skill. It's the most important thing she wants to teach, and therefore, she spends the majority of her time fostering children's enthusiasm. However, she does teach research skills.

She teaches them in response to children's needs, the key teachers also use when they teach skills. Some may think that this is inefficient, but in a response system, we see it as a more direct way to teach. Marcia says, "The children learn skills because they need them, and they learn many skills from each other." She supplies help when a child requests it, but she often refers the child to another student. Marcia knows who can use the card catalogue or vertical file and fields requests for help to other students who can teach their peers. Again, she tries to dispel the children's view of her as the only expert and helps them see each other as authorities with their own areas of expertise. They work together in the library in much the same way they do in their classrooms. (Five and Rosen 1985 show how children work together on research projects.) Marcia thus supports the learning procedures of the teachers, and she in turn appreciates their support as she explores new ways for students to use the library.

At the end of the Mast Way research project, when I interviewed the teachers, Marcia said that one of the best parts of the project was that "I've learned about risk-taking. I don't feel too bad if something fails." Marcia can't enumerate the steps someone could use to develop the kind of library she has now. Instead, she says the main change is the atmosphere in the library, and this hinges on new relationships within the school as a whole—from the teachers' group, to the classrooms, to the library. Now, all hallways lead to the library.

References

ADAMSON, LYNDA G. 1985. And Who Taught You Children's Literature. *Horn Book* 61, no. 5 (September/October).

CULLINAN, BERNICE E. 1986. Books in the Classroom. *Horn Book* 62, no. 4 (July/August).

FIVE, CORA, AND ROSEN, MARTHA. 1985. Children Re-create History in Their Own Voices. In *Breaking Ground: Teachers Relate Reading and Writing in the Elementary School*, ed. by Jane Hansen, Thomas Newkirk, and Donald Graves. Portsmouth, N.H.: Heinemann.

HYMAN, TRINA SCHART. 1985. Caldecott Medal Acceptance. *Horn Book* 61, no. 4 (July/August).

SAMWAY, KATHARINE. 1986. And You Run and You Run to Catch Up with the Sun, But It's Sinking. *Language Arts* 63, no. 4 (April).

The Chapter I
Reading Teacher | Eighteen

Millie Woodward, who taught the Chapter I reading students at Mast Way from 1981 to 1985, says her first major change in the research project was "experience with choice." When her students "read books they were interested in, they read a lot more." They initiated their own discussions about their books, and for their seat work, they decided what to write about from those books rather than writing answers to Millie's questions. This response system, both oral and written, gave her "a much better idea of their comprehension than questions." In general, she emphasized "meaning" more than in the past. Choice encouraged this emphasis because the students became more involved in books they had selected themselves than in stories their teachers assigned.

Millie explored her new ways to teach reading after she let one-third of her students write for a year. She was one of the teachers who had taken Don Graves's writing course before the research project began, and some of her students learned about writing with Millie before their classroom teachers explored response teaching.

When I work with Chapter I teachers in workshops I tell them about Millie, and they often wring their hands because they feel constrained by regulations about what they are supposed to teach. Even when Chapter I teachers feel free to teach writing, it's difficult to figure out how to manage it in the splintered blocks of time they have with students. However, the initial question Chapter I teachers ask is, "How can I justify spending time on writing when I am a reading teacher?"

Readers Read Writing

When we started the research project in Ellen Blackburn Karelitz's classroom, my most recent job had been a Title I reading position. But some of my students didn't know what reading was. They "read" one word after another:

The man drove his car into the garbage.
Then he shut the garbage door.

A student read *garbage* for *garage* and didn't even stop. He didn't insist on making meaning when he read.

The first way I noticed that writing benefited reading in Ellen's class was that the children were determined to make a story make sense (Hansen 1983). They created messages with pencils from the first day of school and assumed that other writers also created messages. They wanted to know what those messages were.

Writing is the foundation of reading; it may be the most basic way to learn about reading. An analogy that works for me is photography. A photographer often understands other photographers' work better than a nonphotographer. When she looks at a print, she sees it through a lens. She twists her body as if she were taking the shot. She wonders what light setting was used and how many shots the photographer took to get this particular photo. She wonders what the photographer would like to do differently to make it even better. Her head is full of thoughts and insights that go behind the surface of the picture.

Similarly, when writers read, they use insights they have acquired when they compose. They can read behind the lines. They wonder what kind of people other authors are and what decisions they made when they wrote. They wonder what information authors discarded and whether they had trouble deciding how to sequence their information. They think about how those authors chose their title, lead, and ending. They even wonder what questions their friends asked them about their drafts. Writers speculate about what other writers would like to change, even after a book is published. They often have more thoughts about print than nonwriters.

As reading teachers, we want our students to know about writing because everything they read is writing. Students who compose accounts of their thoughts and deeds, reports about topics of interest, fiction, and poetry, are writing reading. Show a printed page to writers and they say, "That's writing." A nonwriter says it's something to read. When I taught Title I students, neither my students nor I treated printed pages as writing because none of us wrote. When our students become writers, they change.

They gain insights into reading that extend beyond what our former students knew about reading, because when they write, they write the kinds of things people read. They write reading. We have always used writing in our reading classes, but we have kept our students a step removed from it. We have only used the writing of others. However, when our students write, they learn how reading is put together because they do it. They learn the essence of print.

"But, teachers ask me, do students really become better readers when they write?" Yes, teachers of poor readers can support their students' reading growth when they include writing in their reading program (Fleming 1986; Hayes and Bahruth 1985). These students understand their skills. Students who write about topics of their own choice, read daily from books they want to read, and spend their time sharing with their entire class, can generate more meaningful accounts of what they read than my students did when I taught.

Chapter I Teachers Make Decisions About Their Teaching

When I meet Chapter I teachers across the country, I find great discrepancy in their roles. Many have administrative status and possess authority. At the other extreme are aides, who are regarded as babysitters. Millie's status was neither. She had always been one of the teachers and, during the research project, she was part of the teacher's group that met weekly to share their writing and reading. She is an avid reader who convinced some of us we'd enjoy *The Mists of Avalon*, and at the end of the project, she confessed she'd like to get a piece of her writing published in *Modern Maturity*.

As a writer and reader, Millie knows she makes decisions. She must decide what to write about and when, or with whom, to share it. Her ability to write rests on these decisions. Most of us never learned what to do as writers, and we don't write. She can call herself a reader because she always has a book going. She has learned how to choose books and shares her excitement about them. During the project Millie learned to approach her own reading differently. For example, when she reads fiction she doesn't skim as much. She may reread paragraphs because she wants to write better description. She wants to teach her students to do the things she does.

"But," I hear, "as a Chapter I teacher I can't make decisions about my teaching. I not only can't decide to let my students write, I have to use the same materials as the classroom teacher." Or in some places I hear, "I have to use materials different from the classroom teacher's, and the materials must cover certain skills I check off a list."

People who don't want children to write are often people who don't write. Knowledgeable administrators and classroom teachers will not keep us from letting our poor readers learn about reading through writing. Sometimes we gain control over what we do by educating those who have not yet had a chance to learn about writing.

In New Hampshire, we had a fortunate situation with Dr. Mary

Gile as state director of Chapter I. Mary wanted to learn about writing, and she and I organized a workshop for twenty-four Chapter I teachers. Mary participated fully throughout the four three-hour sessions and at the close made a surprise announcement. "I will ask that the state guidelines be changed for next year. We will encourage Chapter I reading teachers to include writing in their programs."

It is important that we be allowed to make this decision. When we decide what kinds of changes we want to make, it is our commitment to our decision that contributes to our success. We are not going through the motions of teaching a certain way because someone says we have to. As Millie said, the changes she brought into reading from writing began with choice, but she did not only mean topic choice in writing and book choice in reading. She knew of more options to choose among when she decided how to teach.

Millie wrote about choice—Control—in a piece of writing she shared with the teachers' group:

> . . . I have observed or been part of new directions in reading—more exposure and discussion of varied types of readings and authors, choices of reading material, and a different emphasis on meaning.
>
> Are we seeing in action an important writing component? Control —not the teacher of the children, but her own control of a search for new ways of teaching reading because she wants to work with interested and involved readers?

Ways Chapter I Teachers Can Help Their Students Read Writing

The Chapter I programs in various states and local districts vary tremendously. Therefore, it's difficult to suggest plausible ways for teachers to structure their learning environments. Millie's teaching of writing and reading covered a three-year span, from 1982 to 1985, when she retired. She taught differently during each of these years, and I'll outline the three years in the hopes that other Chapter I teachers will see themselves within her experience and adapt what Millie did to best help their students in their very different schools.

During the first year, Millie began to learn about reading and writing by letting some of her students write. These students did not write in their classrooms; their Chapter I reading centered on their writing. During the next year, several additional classroom teachers started to set aside time for daily writing, and Millie began to experiment with reading, using the same stance toward learning that she used during writing. Finally, during her third year, she worked more closely with teachers in both writing and reading.

Year One.   Writing is not easy for most of us, but it is especially difficult for Chapter I students. Millie had started to teach writing the year before the project began. Most of her students did not write in their classrooms, and it was hard for them to write in the Chapter I room. Mainly, they didn't value themselves, what they did, or what they thought. They didn't think they knew anything, and if they did, they didn't think anyone else was interested, particularly their teachers. When student's don't think they know anything or think they will be rebuffed if they tell about something they do know, they can't write.

We start at the beginning. We share ourselves with our students. Millie told her poor readers about the new canoe she and her husband had bought. She asked them about themselves, their families, and what they did. Her students talked to her and each other about things that happened to them and what they thought about them. Millie's response was that of a genuine learner: "I don't know much about race cars. You taught me what a supercharger is."

Her students needed to realize that they knew something, and they needed to learn specifically what they knew. They needed to consider themselves persons who had information to share. When Millie sensed that her students realized they possessed information, she and her students wrote. Bruce wrote one sentence and asked, "What do I do now?" Millie answered, "I'm writing. Please don't bother me." She continued to write. She didn't look up. Her students wrote, too.

When the students read their writing to Millie and each other, their listeners told them what they had learned and asked questions to learn more. As one Chapter I teacher told me, "I learned the first day that there's always more than is on the page." The students learned this also. They liked one another's support and continued to write and share.

Sometimes Chapter I teachers wonder how to set up writing within forty-minute time blocks. A couple of practical suggestions about the structure may be helpful to teachers. One is to maximize the forty minutes so they really have forty minutes. When the students enter the room, the Chapter I teacher can be writing. The students go straight to their writing folders, sit down, and write. There is not a wasted minute.

Another suggestion is to look at the forty-minute periods as one never-ending block of time. A child writes, confers with one person or with the class, which in Chapter I classrooms is a small group, continue to write, eventually chooses a draft for publication, edits, and celebrates. One child may write several drafts while another writes a few. On any day, one child may start a new draft, another child may be working for the third day on a long draft, another child may be reading about Porsches for his report, and the fourth child may be editing for spelling. When the forty minutes end, the children put away their folders and resume the next time they come.

They no longer fear failure in writing. Initially, our students often balk at writing because they have had negative experiences. However, when they learn that we respond to what they know and do not try to find errors, they don't hesitate to say, "I like writing." Seventh-grade Chapter I students in Lynne Wissink's class in Dover, New Hampshire, want to continue writing when the bell rings. "Can I stay here and write?" they ask.

Chapter I teachers confirm the worth of what their students know about frogs, fish, bikes, and race cars. By asking questions about these topics, they learn more about their students than they have ever known before. Students respond to our interest. By valuing their knowledge, we help them to value themselves. This improvement in their perception of themselves was the first noticeable result of writing that Millie observed in her students. She says the importance of this change must be emphasized. (See Mosenthal 1986 for an essay on the importance of setting goals in reading.) Both she and her students became excited.

Year Two.   Millie's second year of working with writing, the first year of the research project, was a transitional year for her. As her students started to write more and more in their classrooms, she either adjusted the amount of time they wrote with her or they brought their classroom writing with them. Previously, the writing they did with Millie was often their only writing, but now, since most of them wrote in their classrooms, Millie needed to cut back. She rethought how to teach reading to capitalize on what her students had learned about writing.

Millie's decision to change the way she taught reading was basically a decision to focus on meaning in reading as she now did in writing. This new emphasis affected the way her students used their time. Never before had they read stories or books of their own choice. Now, when they shared with Millie and their friends, everyone made comments and asked questions about content. Millie used the same supportive response system she used in writing.

Our never-failing initial response to what our students know whenever we ask about the books they choose assures them that we value what they know. This is a shift for us. We have usually directed our students to spend the majority of their time on isolated skills like phonics and spelling of prechosen vocabulary words, rather than on the heart of reading: meaning. Even when we did focus on meaning, we asked questions—questions whose answers we already knew. We tested. Under that system, poor readers who came to us found out, for the nth time, that they were poor readers. However, when we change our approach, as we do in writing, to find out what our students know, they gradually change their attitude toward reading, toward us, and toward themselves. Response is the revolutionary key to writing instruction and, similarly, the center of what we do when we teach reading.

Beyond general comprehension, students sometimes need help

with vocabulary. If a child couldn't read a word or couldn't use a word in a discussion, Millie taught this new vocabulary word. A child, for example, who talked about the "stuff they put on the driveway" found the word *gravel* on the page, and Millie taught the child the label for a word that, in this case, represented a known concept. It's extremely hard for us to trust vocabulary instruction to a response mode, but if children show no vocabulary deficits when they share, we can trust that they have understood the words. Children who want to learn seek help with words they need. Our task is to create an environment in which they want to compose meaning when they read and seek help when they need it.

Millie also taught skills, but she taught them very differently than she had in the past. "I used to use phonics sheets not necessarily coordinated with a story. There were so many for each story. Plus, I used extra phonics." However, Millie developed her ability to hear when she needed to teach a child a skill. For example, when a student read to her and attacked a *ch* word with a /k/ sound, Millie considered a lesson on *ch*. It is as hard for us to teach skills in a response mode as it is to teach comprehension and vocabulary this way. However, if the children's skills needs are real, those needs will be evident when the children read.

When her students stumbled, Millie waited. She listened to what strategy the student tried and later taught the word-recognition skill she thought would be most helpful. She did not teach when the student was reading for meaning. When the school had its Language Arts fair, Millie and several of her students demonstrated for parents the discussions they have about different methods of working with unknown words. They sat around a table and read to each other. If they had trouble with a word, they later explained how they figured it out. Students who can tell others whether they skipped a word and came back to hear it make sense, sounded it out, divided the word into parts, or asked a friend, have several strategies at their disposal. Poor readers become more and more adept at explaining what they do, which increases their repertoire of what to do when they falter.

Everyone rightfully expects us to teach comprehension, vocabulary, and skills, but we must have the right to teach them the way we think is best. We can teach our students to choose their books and respond to those choices. We, in turn, respond to what they know, and when we sense a need, we teach something new. We have the authority to point out constantly to our students what they know rather than what they don't know.

Year Three.   During Millie's third year, the second year of the research project, she noticed the biggest change in her students' reading, especially for those she did not isolate.

She followed the pattern of the classroom teachers and did not separate some children from others of different achievement levels. She fostered the community feeling the teachers strove to create. In writing the teachers did not establish low, middle, and high groups. They didn't establish permanent groups at all, because writers learn most when they interact with many different writers. The teachers wondered if this would also be true in reading. They thought their poor students would learn more if they interacted with good students than if they met only with each other. Millie also worked with her students in heterogenous groups when they met with their classmates to "talk books."

She listened, learned, and responded as the classroom teacher did. Both had the same goal: to help the students realize what they knew. Some of Millie's students worked best alone, and either teacher might stop beside Jeremy, for example, and say, "Oh, you're reading *Corduroy*. I've read it, too. What do you think of it?"

Jeremy, when this response system is new to him, may say, "It's OK."

The teacher has yet to find out what Jeremy knows, so she pursues, "Show me a part you think is OK."

Jeremy shows the page where Corduroy emerges, shrunk, but doesn't say a word.

The teacher still hasn't found out much about what he knows, so she continues, "Yes, he shrank. Tell me about that."

Jeremy simply says, "The dryer was too hot."

The teacher starts to get excited, "You know heat can cause things to shrink. That's important. Do you have anything else to tell me?"

The child may or may not answer, but before the teacher leaves the child, she refocuses him, "Where were you when I came. . . . Please read just a bit to me."

When Jeremy is on track, the teacher moves on.

Over time, the student contributes more and more to the conference, usually starting to talk the moment the teacher pulls a chair up beside him. He knows she wants him to tell her about his book. Her goal is to find out one thing the student knows and restate it in specific terms. Often, when we respond to a student, he comes to understand his book better as he tells us about it.

The Chapter I students also share with their classmates. We hear them tell about their delights and concerns. Remedial readers can be full-time members of their classroom (and school) community of readers and writers (Five 1985). Other students can respect, appreciate, and want their insights.

Chapter I students' notion of themselves as readers is stronger when they are taught along with the other readers in their classroom rather than being relegated to a lesser status. (Bloome 1985 writes about the social contexts of reading.) Millie worked with the students in whatever format fit in with their classroom teacher's schedule. She conducted individual conferences, responded in Big Conferences, and responded when a few children met to share. They learned more when they interacted with more proficient readers, and she facilitated this in whichever situation she worked in.

The other students also learned from the Chapter I students. The Chapter I teacher helps good readers realize what they learn from their Chapter I classmates because the Chapter I students' perception of themselves comes primarily from the other students. Therefore, the remedial reading teacher takes on still another task and is present when the other readers respond to her students.

Millie did not, however, work in all her students' classrooms. But regardless of the pattern of consistency she and each teacher designed, Millie no longer assigned basal stories. If her students used a basal, they chose which story they read. Also, she assigned fewer written comprehension questions than in the past and, for those she did use, she focused on the meaning of her students' answers rather than spelling. (See Hull 1985 for research on errors and correction.) And she used no phonics worksheets.

The collaboration between Millie and the teachers gave Millie an idea for a presentation at the annual University of New Hampshire spring writing conference. She suggested to Leslie Funkhouser, one of the second-grade teachers, that they prepare a handout to show how they both treated their students similarly. They wanted to share information about the roles their students and they, as teachers, played when they wrote and read. This chart was their handout.

Choice

Writing	Reading
A child:	A child:
will choose his or her own topic.	will choose a book.
may get an idea from a friend.	may get an idea for a book from a friend.
may brainstorm with one or two friends.	
may write about something that really happened.	may read nonfiction.
may write fiction.	may read fiction.
may, at first, draw a picture and tell about it.	may, at first, get information from the pictures.
may, later, draw and write a small amount of information to go with the picture.	may, later, get information from pictures and read some of the information about the picture.
may, still later, write a lot and use pictures to illustrate the information after writing.	may, still later, get information from the words, cover, title, and pictures.
may write a chapter story.	may read a chapter book.

will choose a story to share.

will choose a story to publish.

will choose a book to share.

will choose books by authors
they know.

Sharing

Writing

A child:

may read a draft to friends,
listen to their comments and
questions, and decide whether
to add more information.

may read a draft to a small
group; ask for comments and
anything the draft reminded
them of; and answer questions.

may pick his or her best story
to read to the class; ask for
comments and reminders; and
answer questions.

will pick a story to be
published and edit it with a
friend and the teacher.

may read his or her published
book to other audiences, in the
library, or in other classes.

will listen to other children
read their writing; make comments, offer reminders, and ask
questions.

Reading

A child:

may read part of a book to a
friend—an exciting or funny
part or a good word picture.

may read part of a book to a
small group; ask for comments
and anything the book reminded
them of; and answer questions.

may read a book, or part of a
book, to the class; ask for
comments and reminders;
answer questions; and tell
something about the author.

will write about a book.

may read a favorite book to
other audiences.

will listen to other children
share favorite books; make comments, offer reminders, and ask
questions.

Teacher's Role

Writing

A teacher:

listens and receives a child's
piece of writing, "Tell me what
you're writing about."

questions a child to learn more
information about the child's
topic.

accepts the child's writing—
tells the child what she likes in
the writing.

Reading

A teacher:

listens and receives a child's
book, "Tell me about your
book."

questions a child to learn more
information about the child's
book.

accepts the child's reading—
tells the child what he or she
was able to do, what he or she
read well, and what he or she
knew.

shows the child ways to solve problems in the writing. Refers the child to peers for help.	shows the child ways to solve problems when reading—e.g., context clues, picture clues. Refers the child to peers for help.
provides opportunities for children to share successes and knowledge in small groups, with the class, in other rooms, with parents, by tutoring in lower grades, and by publication in the classroom, school, and local newspapers.	provides opportunities for children to share successes and knowledge in small groups, with the class, in other rooms, with parents, by tutoring in lower grades.
models own writing for the students. Provides opportunities for other adults and children from other classrooms to model their writing.	models reading daily for the students. Provides opportunities for other adults and children from other classrooms to model their reading.
helps the children evaluate their writing, e.g., helps the children choose pieces for publication.	helps the children evaluate their reading progress, e.g., discusses choices of books with children and helps them evaluate what they write about their reading.

It's significant that Millie and Leslie's chart doesn't outline a separate role for Millie. Their long list gives me a new look at Chapter I reading. Children with problems sometimes suffer from our lack of cohesiveness, but they are the last students who need two different teachers with separate reading programs. Millie and Leslie both teach the children to choose and share, and they assigned themselves a unified role. They listen, question, accept, show, provide opportunities, model, and help their students.

At the end of the project when Millie interviewed her students, they labeled themselves readers because they read a lot of books, chose their own books, and their reading was like everybody else's. Millie's own comment was, "I wish I had learned this years ago. This is the best thing I've ever done in my career. . . ."

References

BLOOME, DAVID. 1985. Reading as a Social Process. *Language Arts* 62, no. 2 (February).

FIVE, CORA. 1985. Teresa: A Reciprocal Learning Experience for Teacher and Child. In *Toward Practical Theory*, ed. by Jerome Harste and Diane Stephens. Bloomington, Ind.: Language Arts Department, Indiana University.

FLEMING, PAULA. 1986. The Write Way to Read. In *Understanding Writing: Ways of Observing, Learning & Teaching*, ed. by Thomas Newkirk and Nancie Atwell. Portsmouth, N.H.: Heinemann.

HANSEN, JANE. 1983. The Writer as Meaning-Maker. In *Teaching All the Children to Write*, ed. by J. L. Collins. New York: New York Council of Teachers of English.

HAYES, CURTIS W., AND BAHRUTH, ROBERT. 1985. Querer Es Poder. In *Breaking Ground: Teachers Relate Reading and Writing in the Elementary School*, ed. by Jane Hansen, Thomas Newkirk, and Donald Graves. Portsmouth, N.H.: Heinemann.

HULL, GLYNDA. 1985. Research on Error and Correction. In *Perspectives on Research and Scholarship in Composition*, ed. by Ben W. McClelland and Timothy R. Donovan. New York: Modern Language Association.

MOSENTHAL, PETER. 1986. Research Views: Defining Progress in Reading Research and Practice: The Theorists' Approach. *Reading Teacher* 40, no. 2 (November).

Administrators | Nineteen

John Lowy, the Mast Way Elementary School principal, knows all the students by name and visits classrooms regularly. Heaven help you if you expect to find him in his office. When John steps in the door of a classroom, he braces himself. "Mr. Lowy, listen to this." "Mr. Lowy, can I read you my writing?" "Mr. Lowy, I just started a new book. Look, it's by the same author as the one I read to you last week."

John stops and listens. Then, one day he arrived late for a meeting with us. "I only wanted to give the teacher a message. What was I going to do? I couldn't just walk out when the children wanted to read to me." John has noticed a change in what the children want to share with him. When the project began, they held crumpled sheets of paper in their hands, but now they also extend books. John Lowy feels the excitement about reading in his school, but when I give presentations about Mast Way, some teachers respond with hesitation.

I often hear, "But my principal won't. . . ." Teachers tell me their principals keep them from growing, from exploring the new knowledge in reading/writing, from changing. However, several of us at the University of New Hampshire have traveled to forty-eight of the fifty states, and we have never yet heard of a principal who, having spent one entire reading/writing period in the classroom of a teacher whose reading/writing program clicks, came away saying, "I refuse to let any of my teachers try this." Principals and supervisors need to see something work.

Administrators will support our new undertakings, as we do those of our students, but this requires a new look at administration just as it requires a new look at teaching, because we are taking a fresh look at learners. These are all major changes.

At least three of the perennial concerns of administrators may mesh or interfere with a reading/writing program that focuses on what students can do: They are: 1) the definition of on-task behavior, which sets the learning environment for a school; 2) the tests that determine what administrators push and what teachers teach; and 3) the evaluation procedure that administrators use to assess teachers, which reflects the authorities' view of teachers' status.

Administrators Want Students On-Task

At the beginning of our study, John Lowy counted on-task students when he visited classrooms. This made teachers nervous because, for one thing, they were afraid that John did not understand the oral component of their writing instruction: the talk that must occur when we learn to place importance on the children's work process as well as their finished work. The teachers taught their students to request responses from each other, but they worried that John would not count interactions among children as on-task behavior. (Smith-Burke 1985 writes about the importance of oral language.) These new behaviors lead to a revised definition of what it means to be on-task.

Talking is on-task behavior. All kinds of conferences—spontaneous and planned, informal and formal, unstructured and structured, two-way and whole-class, small group sessions, and sessions with and without the teacher—have a place in a reading/writing program. John Lowy took part in these conferences at Mast Way. He held individual conferences with students and listened to them share with their friends. He recognized "writing talk," "reading talk," "book talk," and "talk about what I know," and realized the positive influence of all this talking on children's writing, reading, and attitude toward learning.

He understood that the three boys who are writing about "Star Wars," "My Dog Clarence," and "My New Bike" while they jabber about Gobots, what they'll play at recess, and Dungeons and Dragons are involved in writing. He knows this when he hears them use words from one another's speaking vocabulary in their writing, sees their quick steps toward the box of writing folders when they arrive the next morning, and detects the same differences between Barry's quiet tone and Cheryl's boisterous voice in their writing that he heard in their voices at the table. We don't want to silence the writer's voice.

Our collective encouragement—that of administrators, teachers, and students—reinforces the writer's hope that she is a person who has something to say. When teachers have to find out what their students are doing in order to respond, their physical location in classrooms changes. Administrators expect teachers to be among their students, listening. Principals and supervisors expect students, as well as teachers, to be talking.

Decision-making is on-task behavior.   Administrators used to say, "I'll come back when you're teaching," if they came to observe and didn't find the teacher lecturing. I had this happen to me years ago, but supervisors now look for evidence that students are making decisions, not simply paying attention. They look for instances when children choose among options and decide their own learning course. These behaviors become part of a new understanding of on-task behavior.

We want students to make independent decisions about their learning, and we want them to be able to explain their options and decisions to administrators who stop beside their desks. Reading supervisors and consultants, however, often have a harder time than teachers in coming to grips with what students need to do when they write and read, because they don't work with children every day. Teachers, on the other hand, can see within a few weeks the change in students when their teachers expect them to initiate plans rather than complete the teachers' plans.

Students rise to meet the teacher's higher expectations. The teacher stops thinking, "I'd better choose Bruce's books because he'll choose some that are too hard." Instead, she thinks, "I'll teach Bruce to choose his own books," and Bruce, who at first wonders what's going on, selects his books. It takes him a while to figure out what he likes, but then he starts to think reading is OK. We notice changes most quickly in our poorer readers, especially when we offer them more than book choice.

We also provide occasions for Bruce to share his books and respond when others share theirs. And we minimize or discontinue worksheets. Bruce writes an open-ended response to what he reads. He hated worksheets and thinks it's better to decide for himself what to write about the books he likes best. He, his friends, and his teacher share some of their written responses when they talk about their books. In general, Bruce reads more and with a better attitude when we give him the responsibility of making more decisions about what he does and wants to do.

Asking someone for help is on-task behavior.   Learners can't reach their goals alone. That's what learning is all about. When we are learning something new we become frustrated, don't know what we're doing, and need help. Thus, on-task students become anxious, don't know for sure which book they want to read next, and ask friends for ideas. Administrators recognize these behaviors as appropriate and necessary when they spend time in classrooms where teachers have created reading/writing communities.

Sometimes, if local teachers have not yet started to change their teaching, there is not a classroom to visit to see how this works. Videotapes may provide help. A reading supervisor from Oregon called me: "I'm in a meeting with the other reading staff and we want to support our teachers when they try some of the changes we experienced in your workshop, but we need to show our principals how this works. They think this kind of teaching is chaotic. Could we show the video you showed of Johanna [Whitney and Hubbard 1986]?"

I don't know where administrators get the impression that reading/writing classrooms are disorganized; they can't be, as we saw in chapter 6. However, this impression is common. Therefore, administrators need to see orderly classrooms, where more children are working productively than in our former classrooms, where we called "Draw lines, circle words, and color the picture" on-task reading behavior. In classrooms like those at Mast Way, administrators see children read, get help if they need it, and initiate written and oral responses to their books.

Teachers and children do things differently now than we did when we were students and when many of us began our teaching careers. Not only that, but many administrators gained their current positions because they were recognized as good teachers by traditional standards. Now we find it hard to reevaluate a learner's behavioral characteristics and admit that a good classroom may look very different from the kind we led (Newkirk 1985). We often need to experience interactive learning ourselves.

More and more supervisors enroll in the UNH Summer Writing Program. They write, share their work with their peers, and respond to their colleagues' writing. They learn the value of talking in a writing program and, similarly, in a reading program based on the same principles. Talking is inherent if we teach responsively. The children often respond to their reading through talking, and our response also is in the form of talking. However, we talk less than in former days, because we base our talk—our teaching—on what we learn when we listen to our students.

Thus, our teaching is more focused, to the point, specific. Because we listen more, we say less. We don't have to give a lesson on quotation marks in second grade, third grade, fourth grade, ad infinitum. We may never give it. A student may figure out how to use quotation marks from his reading, and because one of our goals is to help the students realize how much they know, that student may teach quotation marks to others who, in turn, teach. However, there are many times when we do the teaching.

When an administrator observes, he may see a teacher working with individuals, small groups, or the class as a whole. The teacher may call together a small group because she has written her first poem and wants to share it; the teacher may help a child cut apart his writing and paste it in a new sequence; or a child could read a trade book to the class, ask for response, and call on the teacher. Her question provokes thoughts the children didn't mention and stimulates a new line of discussion. The supervisor learns to recognize what the teacher does when she teaches and understands the extra responsibilities she confers on her students.

We expect the students to open the discussions about their reading, and we expect them to get help with their work any time they need it. Our expectations say, "If we see you quiet all the time, you must be doing things you already know how to do. You must not be learning anything new." Administrators are right when they sense that a different kind of classroom will result from this way of looking at learning. If a major new role for the students is to talk more, then administrators need to expect this.

Administrators learn, as teachers do, to watch students carefully. Administrators assess on-task behavior when they ask students, "What are you doing? Why? What will you do next?" We expect students to be able to explain their entire process, not just what they learned, as might have been the case in the past. Our expectations are higher than they used to be. Students are not only on-task, they determine their task, know how to pursue their task, and want to pursue their task.

Administrators Worry About Test Scores

Administrators' anxiety about standardized test scores can blur their vision of the larger picture of reading. Mast Way students scored lower on the Word Study Skills section (within stanines four through six) of the Stanford Achievement Test than on any other section when John Lowy arrived in 1969; those scores were still the lowest in 1983. John wanted those scores to go up. He wanted his teachers to focus on teaching those isolated skills. His concern is common. We worry about both skills and comprehension scores and look at how we might generate additional ways to document the new behaviors we see in our students.

Tests on isolated skills interfere with reading. In 1978, the International Reading Association passed a resolution against the assessment of subskills in reading (Bartoli 1985), and the Mast Way teachers tried to heed this resolution. During the first year of the project, the teachers were learning to create the overall environment they wanted for writing and reading to flourish. When teachers learn to teach via response, they often shift much of their belief system. It's not just an "activity" to "do" with the class. As Janet Emig (1983) has found, responsive teaching often requires a paradigm shift in an educator's thinking. It takes time to base our instruction on what each student knows rather than the teachers' guide.

At the end of the first year, John Lowy's anxiety about skills had risen considerably. He feared that teachers were teaching skills less, and he was right. They were figuring out how to find time for their students to write and read more. They were learning how to help their students make choices, how to have conferences with a focus on information, how to teach their students to rely on each other, how to create a supportive community, and how to listen to children's individual voices sing through their writing. The teachers were learning the basics.

The teachers started at the beginning, where writers start, with the information and strong voice that give a piece of writing its potential. Polish and technical skill come later, when a writer decides a piece of writing has enough merit for publication. We all need to deal with one thing, or only a few things, at a time. Teachers would learn to teach skills after they had learned how to teach what undergirds writing. At the moment, they were learning the aspects of writing that were newest to them.

Later we can learn how to teach isolated skills, although we could argue that we don't want to teach them, and we will probably teach them as I showed in chapter 12. But this still leaves administrators' concerns unattended. We do need to teach children test-taking skills. It's not fair for them to have to circle words with matching sounds on an important test if they've never practiced. Also, the comprehension test may cause problems if we don't give students some experience with it. We might set aside a block of time, other than the reading/writing time, and give children worksheets that look like the tests.

Multiple-choice comprehension questions limit reading. Multiple-choice questions can tap either literal or inferential information. As far as literal questions go, research shows (Wixson 1983) that children who practice inferential questions become better at literal questions than children who practice literal questions. Therefore, in order for children to handle this type of information, we should focus on broader concepts. However, even multiple-choice inferential questions limit children's comprehension by confining the readers' thoughts to those of whoever wrote the question.

In contrast, the Mast Way children generated their own questions, which went beyond the information in the text, and when they discussed one another's questions, they came away with more meaningful insights than they found in set answers like a, b, c, or d. More importantly, they learned that it was their own responsibility to initiate a response to what they read. Their purpose in reading was not to find answers to someone else's questions.

But children need to do well on the tests. They need to practice. Again, this does not mean that they need to take time away from their real reading. The Mast Way teachers handled this either by giving the children practice with multiple-choice questions for a couple of weeks shortly before the test or by having them practice once a week for an extended period of time. An important point about these practice sessions is to keep them separate from the reading/writing time because they interfere with our goals (Ohanian 1984), and we don't want to confuse our students.

Extra documentation is necessary. We want the values of our reading program to be reflected in the overall evaluation plan. Administrators ask us to develop ways to show children's ability to use time, to generate options and choose among them, to use their reading as a springboard for thinking, to show the discipline of a learner, and to celebrate their accomplishments. We want this information to supplement the test scores, because, as I wrote in chapter 10, it is central to our program; it tells us how much more our students know than test scores measure.

We shortchange our students if we don't include all they can do on their record—answer questions, generate questions, look at published print as drafts, glean ideas for their writing when they read, choose appropriate reading books for themselves, and share a book with the entire class. Not only can the children do these things, they can give us specifics about what they do. And it helps them to plan when they realize their present level of expertise. The administrator supports the children's need to document their learning.

Administrators Evaluate Teachers

Just as we evaluate children differently than we used to because we have additional expectations, administrators alter their expectations of teachers. They expect teachers to assume more authority, and make more decisions than in the past. Like the teacher-child relationship, the principal-teacher relationship changes. The staff works together differently, and their collective wisdom continues to move them forward as they make new decisions.

Administrators expect teachers to work together. Evaluation of teachers sometimes has as dismal a record as the assessment of children's reading progress. When Phyllis Kinzie, a fourth-grade teacher at Mast Way, served as the district representative on the district performance-based pay committee, she said the teachers wanted a plan that would pull them together, not pit them against each other. Phyllis said, "I don't need anyone to tell me what I don't do well. I think about that every night." Teachers want support for ways to grow. Administrators are learning how to support what teachers do well just as teachers are learning how to support their students. It's a shift for all of us.

Before the research project, John Lowy's working definition of a principal was typical. He set himself up as the power figure for his teachers to listen to and obey. The project gave John's ulcer a heyday, but in the interview I held with him two years later, he announced, "I've changed 180 degrees."

John's change came about slowly, as most do. He started to learn about writing two years before we approached Mast Way about the project. He took a one-week writing course for administrators at the University of New Hampshire, but he says, "I didn't get excited about writing. I didn't really write. I wrote curriculum."

The following summer, Pam Bradley, one of the fourth-grade teachers, convinced him to enroll in the full three-week UNH Summer Writing Program. Almost all the participants were teachers. John was the only principal, and he says, "I loved it. It was the best course I ever took. Better than any I ever had for my bachelor's, master's, or PhD. I wrote. It was wonderful."

John learned for himself the importance of a writing community. As with almost everyone else, he had a hard time at first, but once he let himself go and wrote, he understood why the teachers and children like writing, and later he could transfer this into reading. However, the connection between his own learning and that of his faculty came much later.

He started to see and hear their support of one another in the sessions of the teachers' writing group. John was part of the group. He wrote, read his writing to the teachers for their response, and listened when they read theirs. He leaned forward to hear specifics so he could tell a teacher what struck him in her writing. He worked hard to listen to the teacher expand her topic. He relearned, in the environment closest to him, the ramifications of response for unlocking the potential in students' writing.

Teachers who receive support for their writing are like children in a supportive classroom. They can take risks with their writing. They can stretch themselves because they don't fear criticism. They know that a new genre may not work as well as an old, familiar genre, but that they will only learn if they try. They and their fellow workers, including their administrator, expect unpolished performance. This view becomes especially significant when it extends beyond writing.

Principals who support new attempts at teaching will see unpolished performances take on a lustre rather than dullness. Teachers bring their teaching drafts to each other. They receive a wide range of support and suggestions. Just as in a writing classroom, where everyone struggles with drafts that gradually improve, the staff all know they're working at new teaching ideas. They get excited, try new things, and stretch even more.

The administrator values at least two abilities that influence teachers' professionalism. He values teachers' ability to share their successes, because this helps good teaching spread throughout his school, and he values teachers' willingness to ask for help from each other. These two values show themselves within the evaluation plan.

Administrators expect teachers to make decisions. In order for it
to be worth their while to ask each other for help, the teachers need
to have the authority to make decisions about what they'll do. The
principal's role becomes one of encouraging teachers to share options
and choose the path each of them wants to follow. If the teacher
doesn't arrive at her own goal, she has no one to blame but herself,
and if she makes progress toward her goal, she can take credit. The
teachers say, "It's my classroom; I decide."

This sounds strikingly familiar to what the students say about
their writing; "It's my piece; I decide." The author decides and shakes
up our definition of the word "authority." We try to reconcile authority with response, with keeping responsibility in the hands of
the writer, or, in the context of teacher-principal, in the lap of the
teacher. The leader responds and teaches the others to respond to
each other, but the principal must begin to take on the behaviors of
the writing teacher, one of which is listening. When I asked John to
be a guest at my 1985 summer writing class he said, "I'm going to
tell them I listen more."

John's notion of "A Principal" was tested by the response method
of leadership inherent in the way we work with writers and readers.
As the teachers became a writing community and altered their ways
of teaching, they made demands on John. They learned to listen to
their students, to tell a student, "This, specifically, is what you know,"
to nudge, and to step back so the students relied on each other. In
turn, the teachers expected John to treat them similarly, as teachers
elsewhere will expect their principals to do.

They want their principal to listen to what they want to do, to
tell them about their strong points, to support them when they choose
something to work on, and to trust them to rely on each other. They
want him to view them as learners (Harste and Stephens 1985).

When John has to write a report for the board, he shares his draft
with individual teachers. That's new for John and the teachers realize
this, but it's hard for them to see John's changes. At the end of the
research project he made an announcement to the staff about teaching
assignments for the following year. He had put together three options
and wanted the teachers to look them over and tell him what they
thought. However, he had assigned teachers' names to particular
grade levels in one of the reorganization plans and, therefore, they
assumed that John was telling them this would be the plan for the
next year. For years they had known John as someone who did not
give them very much decision-making authority, and this old perception of him prejudiced their thinking. They saw the teaching
assignments and John says they thought, "John is going back to his
old staff style."

It takes several years for us to sort out what we believe, match
it to what we do, and become consistent enough for others to perceive
us the way we want to be seen. To complicate matters, not only do
we change slowly, but John says, "It's hard to maintain the change."

We regress somewhere, progress in another area of our work, and remain stable—sane—in other areas. Ultimately, the leader who fosters independence sets the tone for a nonperfect pattern of forward motion. This administrator listens to the teachers' excitement about their new accomplishments.

References

BARTOLI, JILL SUNDAY. 1985. The Paradox in Reading: Has the Solution Become the Problem? *Journal of Reading* 28, no. 7 (April).

EMIG, JANET. 1983. *The Web of Meaning.* Upper Montclair, N.J.: Boynton/Cook.

HARSTE, JEROME, AND STEPHENS, DIANE. 1985. Special Education: An Agenda for Negotiation Toward Practical Theory. Bloomington, Ind.: University of Indiana.

NEWKIRK, THOMAS. 1985. The Hedgehog or the Fox: The Dilemma of Writing Development. *Language Arts* 62, no. 6 (October).

OHANIAN, SUSAN. 1984. Achievement Test Scores: Facts That Distort the Truth. *Family Learning,* March/April.

SMITH-BURKE, M. TRIKA. 1985. Reading and Talking: Learning Through Interaction. In *Observing the Language Learner,* ed. by Angela Jaggar and M. Trika Smith-Burke. Newark, Del.: International Reading Association; Urbana, Ill.: National Council of Teachers of English.

WHITNEY, JAMES, AND HUBBARD, RUTH. 1986. *Time and Choice: Key Elements for Process Teaching.* Videotape. Portsmouth, N.H.: Heinemann.

WIXSON, KAREN. 1983. Effects of Different Question Types. *Reading Teacher* 37, no. 3 (December).

It's embarrassing to admit, but I was a researcher in Phyllis Kinzie's fourth grade because I wanted to get her to quit teaching reading the way she'd done it for twenty years and start doing it my way. Phyllis and I liked each other and chose to work together, but she sensed my mission and told me early on, "Jane, there's one thing you must know. You'll never tell me what to do." The knots in my stomach pulled tighter each day as I watched Phyllis's skill when she taught writing, but I couldn't see a consistent approach when she taught reading. Finally, toward the end of my fall semester in Phyllis's room, the first three-and-a-half years of our reading/writing research began to gel for me.

I was supposed to start where Phyllis was. Simple. "Support what the writer knows" underlies all our research. My task was to find out what Phyllis could teach me. I knew several things about Phyllis that made her stand out among the Mast Way teachers. She was the resident expert in children's literature—she not only had a master's degree in children's literature, but she read children's literature voluminously. She designed and directed Mast Way's program for the gifted and talented. She was the district's elementary representative on the performance-based pay committee, a committee that met weekly until 6:00 P.M., an extensive time commitment. She knew how to teach writing; her concern about her students as individuals helped her respond to them in a supportive way. From this list, I started with children's literature.

Phyllis knew much more than I did, and both of us were aware of this. I asked her about books and authors, and she shared books with me. I also learned from the children. Before December vacation, I asked them to recommend books for me to read over break. When I returned, I could share Lloyd Alexander with Todd and Joan Aiken with Matt. I could talk books and became a member of their community of readers. My relationship with Phyllis and the students took root, but during the months it took me to figure out my role, I learned about the snail's pace of change.

I came from a viewpoint in reading that saw the teacher as the authority, and even though I had worked with teachers who believed that the writer is the authority since 1981—it was now 1984—I was only beginning to understand this basic premise. (See Kearney and Tashlik 1985 for another account of a teacher and researcher.) It must be terribly hard for teachers to look at their students as sources of knowledge from whom they can learn and thus see learning in their classrooms as a collaborative enterprise. I spent two days a week with teachers who set as their goal "I want my students to become learners." These teachers set themselves up not as the authority but as the number one learner in their classrooms and demonstrated for their students what learners do. I, in turn, as a professor who works with teachers, must see my role as that of someone who learns from the teachers. If I can't, I can't profess that teachers should teach this way.

My own courses had been a testing ground for new ways to teach, but they now became labs to an even greater degree. In this chapter, I'll tell the story of how my research on teaching necessarily changed my own teaching. I'm self-conscious about writing it, but my own teaching has helped me understand what happens in elementary classrooms. Our purpose at Mast Way Elementary School was to test consistency in the teaching of reading and writing, but for me the purpose became broader. If I believed what I saw at Mast Way, then my teaching needed to change. I needed to view my students as persons from whom I would learn. At Mast Way the teachers wanted each student to recognize what he knows as a person, writer, and reader. I, in turn, wanted my students to step forward as writers, readers, and unique persons.

My Students Grew to Know Each Other as Writers

The class I'll describe most frequently throughout this chapter is EDUC 706, The Introduction to Reading Instruction course for pre-service teachers. At the University of New Hampshire we don't have a bachelor's degree in education, only a master's, and our students complete an internship as part of the requirement for their master's degree. Before they work as interns, they take several education courses; EDUC 706 is one of those courses. The course meets twice a week for fifteen weeks, for two hours per meeting.

We wrote and responded to each other.   My students and I wrote personal narratives the first time we met. Everyone explored topic possibilities and drafted, and during the second session I organized conferences so they could give and receive responses within a small group. Before they shared their writing, I read mine to the class and they responded to me. Throughout the course, whenever they wrote, I did too. We not only wrote narratives, we also wrote responses to professional reading. Whenever a written assignment was due, I also completed the assignment and distributed copies of my work to them. I did this because the Mast Way teachers write and share with their students, and I needed to know how it worked. I had done some of this during the last few years and found that these demonstrations catch students off guard.

They surprise students of all ages. When the eighth-grade students of Linda Rief in Durham, New Hampshire, responded to questions from teachers about their writing class, one teacher asked, "Of the various things Mrs. Rief does when she teaches you to write, what is the one most important thing?"

"She writes," was the immediate response.

Linda Rief hadn't expected this. The students had never talked about it in class, but they had noticed. Her presence as a writer made an impact. I doubt that my writing made that much of an impression on my students, but it was important for them to know I valued their response to my work. I valued their thoughts and their knowledge, and they gained confidence from this. In one small group in another class I taught, when I asked for a certain type of feedback to a draft about one of my Peace Corps experiences, one of my students couldn't help but say, "I'm not used to this. This is a real switch."

This kind of environment is a "real switch," but it's important for us as teachers to write. Of all the things we teach, writing is often the one we hate most. More than once I've had teachers walk out of workshops when I ask them to write. When Mary-Ellen MacMillan, a PhD student at the University of New Hampshire, taught a summer course on Prince Edward Island, the teachers in her class wrote, but with reluctance. She asked them to talk about their fears, and they complained about their writing teachers. I hear the same stories, but even though we complain, we teach the way our teachers did. Now, although we have new data about writing instruction, it's hard to learn how to teach something for the first time when we're products of a system that uses a different model for teaching. Also, when we try something new and become insecure, we may revert. Our new attempts, however, rest on what we now know about writers (Neilsen 1986).

My students and I learned from each other.   Authors have something to share. As teachers, we read what our students write, but writers do not write for an audience of one and, thus, we are not the only readers of our students' work. My class and I learned about calligraphy, how to organize a sorority to sponsor a child for Save the Children, the sensitivity of an elderly neighbor who brought muffins when a student's first child was born, and the travels of a ghost—as only dwellers in old New England houses can document. We possessed the interesting information writers need, and when I, as well as their peers, wanted to know as much as possible about their topics, the students could feel what it's like to be a writer. The stage was set for them to request help about how to put their messages together into compelling manuscripts.

My students sought insights about their new craft from the other writers in the class. This included me, but they received many ideas from each other. One student's paper about an article on teacher expectations shifted from an account of a negative second-grade experience in one draft to an exchange with her parents when she was an adolescent in another. Both renditions had merit, but the student couldn't decide which to use for the assignment. A poem of a classmate led her to try poetry, and she alternated verses with every other verse about her second-grade teacher and her supportive parents. I had never tried poetry and didn't until two semesters later in the summer program. It was harder for me to take risks in my classes with adults than with children. Many of my students are excellent writers, and I couldn't help but wonder how much credibility I'd lose when they saw my feeble attempts, but I did write. Thus, I could share with my students what I learned about writing and what I learned from them.

Mainly, I learned the importance of all of us writing something so that it's interesting to read. I told my students I didn't want to be bored when I read their papers; that by the end of the semester I expected to be able to hear their voices. They shouldn't need to put their names on their papers because each piece of writing would sound like its author. When we recognized one person's sense of humor and another's dreaminess, I knew my class caught a glimpse of what it's like to be a member of a community of writers. Maybe they would want to create this climate in their own classrooms and establish the interaction patterns we used in the university class.

My Students Grew to Know Each Other as Readers

We shared children's literature.   I opened the first session by reading a children's literature book to my class, and either I or one of the class members read to the group as part of each successive meeting. When we shared the books, or sections of them, we responded in the ways I've described in previous chapters. I had always professed the importance of children's literature, but in former years, when I taught the course, I devoted only one session to children's literature, and that was in the form of a lecture. Over the years I had included children's literature in more sessions, but this was the first course in which we shared literature at each session.

Besides the oral reading, each student brought a children's book every time we met and put it in the center of the tables where they sat—browsing material for break and before and after class. Most of my students knew very little about children's literature; a separate course in children's literature is not required at the University of New Hampshire. Thus, the exposure to books twice a week, for a total of at least 30 books per student, plus those they learned about from others, gave them a starting point for using literature in their future classrooms. (See Vaughan 1983 for a child's account of what reading is like when children don't read books.)

By the end of the course, they felt comfortable with children's books. They liked them. Their assessment of which ones were good for which occasions evolved over the semester. They started with familiar books from their childhood, and their familiarity with books grew as they read and shared.

We shared adult literature. It was necessary to share children's literature because my students need to feel comfortable with it if they are going to use it for reading instruction, but the most realistic way for us to touch each other as readers was with adult books. Occasionally, each of us brought a book—a "real" book, not a textbook—to class. One man carried a Stephen King thriller, someone brought a Leo Buscaglia softie, another person brought Ken Follett, and one student displayed Norman Mailer. We sat in small groups and shared our books.

Some members ripped off corners of paper to jot down a title they hoped to read, others opened their notebooks, folded back the appropriate page, and added an entry to "Books I Want to Read." Everyone talked. "Oh, I've read several of Michener's. I liked *The Covenant* best." "*The Knights of Avalon*—everyone's read it but me." "*Cancer Ward* was great, but I liked *The First Circle* best of his." "I couldn't stop reading *The Class*. I stayed up way too late." These rapid comments evolved into more detailed thoughts about each book.

Students compared characters to people they knew, family members, and themselves. People shared information about Africa, nutrition, and the Middle Ages. As the professor, I was a member of one group and learned about dimensions of my students I hadn't known in previous classes. I knew Margaret didn't care for *The Color Purple*, liked her writing course in the English department, and brightened when she talked about her daughter. At the end of the session, students not only had ideas for books to read, but they also commented on what happened among them, "I was surprised at how fast we got to know each other." As we repeated these sessions and changed the composition of our groups, we learned more about each other and from each other.

We also had sessions in which each member of a group had read the same story. I used a book of short stories for our class reader and assigned the entire book. On a few occasions, we each chose a story we wanted to discuss and gathered into groups with others interested in that same story. We learned, of course, that the story carried a different significance for each of us. The wider we opened the discussions, the more diverse thoughts we wove into our interpretations of each story. My students routinely saw meanings in a selection that had never occurred to me. We came to class conferences curious to find out what we had found, and responded to each other.

We learned, through our responses to each other, about reading comprehension. The meaning of a story is not on the page, nor is it in an interaction between the reader and the print. Each person composed a meaning based on what she knew, what she read, and what the others said about the text.

We listened. The response to all writing—our own drafts, Anne Tyler's latest book, or a Shel Silverstein poem—can only happen if we have listened. Maybe I taught listening more than anything else. The writing and reading program rests on the response system, and it in turn rests on listening. Again, I had to demonstrate. I couldn't give a lecture on the importance of listening if my students didn't see me listen to them. I listened more than I talked. I had to, in order to be able to respond to all of them. In addition, I set up situations in which they listened to their classmates and learned from them. If they knew they learned from their peers, then I hoped they would set up their classrooms so their students would learn from each other. Listening, however, develops only when class members have something to tell each other.

We talked. Again, my students' primary way of learning about oral language was not by listening to me lecture on its importance. My students talked a lot. Instead of listening to me tell them what I hoped they had learned, they explained their thoughts to others. They could sense for themselves how their struggle to explain a point exemplified the importance of talking in a learning environment. (See Dillard and Dahl 1986 for a similar college course.) In order to tell others what they learned from a book, they had to understand the print and recognize their own perspective. When others questioned them they heard themselves clarify what they thought they knew. Also, their own viewpoint became more distinct when they could compare and contrast themselves with their peers and professor. When their talk helped their own learning, they could sense the probable value of oral language in an elementary classroom.

I told them about Gail Barstow, the resource teacher at Mast Way.

At the end of the project when I interviewed each teacher, Gail said that the greatest benefit to her students was the improvement in their oral language. They talked much more, and their talk was about topics of their own interest from both their writing and reading. When someone didn't understand them, they tried again, because their messages were important to them. Oral language and listening are embedded within writing and reading lessons, regardless of grade level. Leslie Funkhouser, for example, could easily visualize a lot of sharing in classrooms of little children, but she worried about it in her second grade. It's important, therefore, for teachers to experience the benefits of sharing books with their peers.

My adult students and I hear the life in one another's voices. When I read at home I can imagine the expected responses I'll hear in class, but I can never predict entirely what my students will say. Nor can I predict what they will read next. I can tell you which students would be most likely to enjoy Farley Mowat or Margaret Atwood, but they continually introduce me to new books. These suggestions reflect the readers and help us all become better acquainted with each other. I had never before known my students as readers, and I hoped our sessions might encourage these teachers to set up classrooms in which their students know each other as readers, the teacher knows the students as readers, and the children know their teacher as a reader.

My Students Grew to Know Each Other as People

We heard one another's personal voices.   In addition to children's literature and writing, I did a third thing on the first day of class. Maybe this was the most important one. There were twenty students in the class (the limit) and we all learned each other's first name. More than one student told me later that they had never before been in a university course in which their classmates addressed them as Mary, Tom, or Bernice. However, the learning environment I wanted to establish rests on the value of the individual, and the first form of recognition a person can receive from another is to hear that person call her by name. Then, we wanted to learn more about each other.

In my 706 class in the fall of 1986, my students' knowledge of each other increased each week and showed its power on the last day of class when we ended with forty minutes for four class members to share a piece of writing. Katrin read a poem about abortion, and we talked about the picket lines in front of the abortion clinic. Doug read an analogy between schools and zoos that he had written on four different days when he substituted. We talked about what it's like to be a substitute teacher. Annelisa read a humorous fictional account of a young woman on a hopeless diet and we laughed ourselves into stitches when Lynne responded to it with a story of how she gorged herself on chocolate, scotch, hot dogs, and cheese curls the previous night. Finally, Lauren read her story about what her grandmother did on the day Martin Luther King was shot. Students responded with concerns about the lack of university students' involvement in real-life issues.

Their all-class conference was an occasion to hear one another's voices, a time to think. Our semester had ended with the kind of reading/writing conference they want to hear in their elementary classrooms.

We heard one another's professional voices. The time a university class has together is limited but, in conversations before, during, and after class, we had extended what we knew about each other. I learned from a student senator how the governmental structure of the University of New Hampshire works, but it was hard for me to believe that my twenty-one-year-old students knew much about teaching. Yet I knew I had to look at them as sources of knowledge in the professional as well as the personal realm. This assumption required the biggest change on my part.

I shall return to Phyllis and my comments at the beginning of the chapter. When I stopped looking for a certain kind of knowledge, I realized I could learn much from her. I wanted to demonstrate in my university classes how I learned from the class members and decided to ask Phyllis if she would research me. She came to one of my UNH classes each Monday night from 7:00 to 9:30 for fifteen weeks, the entire spring semester. This class was the seminar for the practicum for master's students who spent fifty hours during the semester working with a reading specialist. Phyllis collected data during the seminars.

She transcribed the discussion into a journal, took part in the discussions, interviewed my students about what they learned, and held a weekly conference with me about the sessions. When we met, Phyllis asked me about individual students. She wondered why someone didn't participate much or was absent. Beyond these concerns, Phyllis was extremely sensitive and careful when she responded to my teaching. She never criticized me or told me what to do. She didn't feel pressured to direct my teaching. I was the one who wanted to learn, and her role was to respond to what I thought went well and to help me wrestle with my problems. Her calm response showed caring because she was interested in me as a person.

She knew I had to sense that I was growing as a teacher, and I didn't want her to provide the direction for my improvements. As I sat on the "teacher" side of these conferences, rather than always being the one to confer with a teacher, I started to sense why response is so hard for me, and probably for many teachers. I always feel a tremendous amount of pressure to lead all my students in a certain way, and this prohibits me from responding to what they know and where they want to go.

Until very recently (and, I'm afraid, I still struggle with this), when I entered a classroom as the professor, I thought of myself as the person who would deliver information and my students as those who would learn what I told them. Their perception of their role matched mine. They came to learn from me. However, I had to convince my students that they could also learn if I did something other than lecture, and I had to convince myself that I was not the only one who could "profess." I needed to be able to walk into my class thinking, "I wonder what I'll learn today from all these interesting people."

I needed to find out what they knew and wanted to know next. Then I could help them figure out how to learn it. I had to learn to view teaching as responding. This notion of responsibility, the response sessions, the conferences, is the hardest part of writing/ reading teaching for teachers, regardless of whether they are fourth-grade classroom teachers or university professors. We think we have certain things we have to teach students, and in order to get it all done we decide to cover it all and hope as many of our students as possible will catch on. If we take time to let the students talk, we not only have less time to deliver information but we fear that the information they give each other may not be as accurate as what we have to tell them.

It is hard to trust the knowledge of our students. It is easy to think that our answers are the best answers to their questions. I know why it's not easy for elementary teachers to set up their classrooms so students ask each other for help. They can certainly get a lot more help that way, but it's difficult to believe that they will learn much from each other. We have to take the risk of trying (Allen & Hansen 1986). Unless we do, our students know we don't have confidence in their knowledge, and that hurts their credibility with each other. I took the greatest chance with this part of my teaching in the summer of 1985.

My group was tremendously diverse. The experience of the teachers ranged from one year to twenty-five, their jobs ranged from a grade-one teacher to a K–12 coordinator of writing to a high school English teacher. They worked in both public and private schools, and they lived in nine states and Canada. There was no way I could pretend to teach this range as a whole, even though I would automatically have done so only five years ago. The more I withdrew, the more they picked each other's minds and the closer we came to being a learning community.

After the course ended we continued to learn from each other, and the participants created new roles for themselves in their local communities. When I recently visited Marla, a high-school English teacher, she told me about JoAnne, another student in our class. JoAnne is an elementary teacher, and Marla knew that a school board member had visited JoAnne's class. Dell, who writes fiction, sends it to others from our class. Janet, who teaches first grade in Illinois, recruited Tom, who taught in Wisconsin, to join her school staff.

Marion started a teachers' writing group. Judy received a grant for herself and several other teachers in her school. Tim presented information about the teaching of writing at a conference in Colorado. Mike sent an article to a magazine for publication. These teachers were not accepted into the course because they had previous records that distinguished them from other teachers. We have no acceptance criteria for summer school. They applied and came. Yes, they were good teachers when they walked in my door, but the activities of the summer school helped them find their voices and strive to learn more. A person can learn if he feels good about what he knows and understands how to learn more. This was my goal, and I tried to focus every session in this direction.

The ever-present task was to make public what made each of us unique. We learned to celebrate each other's contributions, whether these were oral tales, drafts of poetry, or renditions of an article from *The Boston Globe*. As others pinpointed what we knew, each of us started to view ourselves as contributors. We could view ourselves as persons who did know something that others didn't know. And as we learned what the others knew, we identified things we wanted to learn more about. We knew what we knew, felt better about ourselves because others acknowledged our worth, and knew that our learning process had only begun.

I now assume that the courses I teach will affect my students' teaching and base my final evaluation on that assumption when I meet with them to share their answers to these questions: "What did you hope to learn in this course? What did you learn? How will this course affect your teaching?" Naturally, everyone (yes, everyone) gives different answers to these questions, but they have one thing in common. They have plans for what they will do in their teaching. If they go out as learners, then we all move forward. I try to help them see their worth as professionals, which comes from their worth as people.

An incident during the first session of week six in EDUC 706, the Introduction to Reading course, exemplified one common practice in elementary classrooms that I do not think helps students' sense of self-worth. We were in the library at Mast Way for a short session just before my students were to report to their classrooms to spend the next sixteen sessions working with children. Ann Waychoff raised her hand. "Jane, I worked in a classroom last year as a tutor, and the teacher had the children in three reading groups: a low group, a middle group, and a high group. I think that's pretty common, and you haven't said anything about it."

I thought fast. I knew they didn't need experience with ability groups for Mast Way because most of the teachers there felt that segregated groups split the environments they wanted to create. However, this is the answer I gave to Ann and to the class. "You know those papers you handed in just now? That's the second paper you've given me, so this weekend when I read them I'll have a pretty good notion of how well you're doing. I'll divide you into three groups, those of you who aren't doing very well, those in the middle, and those who are performing well. Then, when we work in groups from now on you'll always meet with the others at your level."

They all stared at me.

Finally, Ann said, "You wouldn't."

They all knew how absurd that possibility sounded. I hope they realize that their behavior would be just as absurd if they group their students by achievement level some day.

References

ALLEN, JOBETH, AND HANSEN, JANE. 1986. Sarah Joins a Literate Community. *Language Arts* 63, no. 7 (November).

DILLARD, JILL, AND DAHL, KARIN. 1986. Learning Through Teaching in a Reading/ Writing Classroom. *Language Arts* 63, no. 7 (November).

KEARNEY, LYNN, AND TASHLIK, PHYLLIS. 1985. Collaboration and Conflict: Teachers and Researchers Learning. *Language Arts* 62, no. 7 (November).

NEILSEN, ALLEN. 1986. Knowing by Doing: An Active Approach to Writing Inservice. *Journal of Reading* (May).

VAUGHAN, JOSEPH L. 1983. One Child's Query About Reading Instruction. *Language Arts* 60, no. 8 (November/December).

Teachers as Independent Learners

Twenty-One

A few of the Mast Way teachers read about the 1986 spring NCTE Language Arts conference in Arizona, wrote a program proposal, received an acceptance letter, and went. This was a first for them and they did it on their own. They could do it because they know they're good, which might sound haughty, but it takes a certain amount of confidence to step forward and share what we do with others. The Mast Way teachers felt good about their presentation.

They decided to propose another program entry for the 1987 conference. These teachers not only feel good about what they do, they can show others, and they understand why they teach the way they now do. An independent learner knows why she does something, because without understanding the learning cannot grow.

The Mast Way teachers continue to grow, to change. This is what makes them learners. They see teaching as something they constantly want to learn more and more about, and therefore, they ask themselves questions about what they're doing and whether they might do it differently. Sometimes they, and all of us, become overwhelmed with all the things we think we should change, but we have to choose whatever seems most important to us and later, when we resolve it, we work on something else. To choose one thing to improve means we have to admit that we aren't currently doing it well enough to satisfy ourselves. This is a hard admission, but it opens the door to possible learning.

We Learn About Learning

Many of us began our current study of ourselves as learners by admitting that we knew nothing, or little, about writing and writing instruction. We started by writing, and although in our nervousness we shook, write we did. We shared and continue to share and Respond to other writers. In this way we learned how Time-consuming writing is, the influence of topic Choice, the necessity of a Structured schedule to keep us on task, and the power of a Community to support us. We learned how hard it is to be a learner, to learn about writing, especially, and, to use what we know about writing to learn about reading.

We already know how to read and that may be our biggest problem. When we struggled through the learning-how-to-read process, we weren't analyzing what we did in order to remember it someday when we planned to teach it. Oh well, it doesn't matter, because we weren't writers in those days. If writers' insights into reading differ from those of nonwriters, then when we recently learned to write, we relearned how to read.

We recognize what we do. We think about what we do when we read as writers, write about what we do, talk with other writers about what they do when they read, and notice things we didn't notice when we read as nonwriters. For example, when I read *Very Last First Time* I thought of content area writing and reading because Jan Wallace, the author, used fiction to teach me about the Inuits. I can see a teacher using this book with students as a good example of writing across the curriculum. As another example, in *West with the Night* by Beryl Markham I saw the power of writers' advice—show more than tell—in her personal narrative/autobiography. I don't ever remember analyzing books I read in these ways in former years.

Overall, we now respond to a book as a piece of writing, an approach I didn't have in my repertoire a few years ago. However, my understanding of what I do may be even more important than exactly what I do.

We know why we do it. I think the benefits of knowing *why* can be compared to carpentry or cooking or sewing. If I don't understand how something works, I can only do it if I have the recipe in front of me. When I first started to make my own salad dressings, I used recipes, but now I can shake oil, vinegar and innumerable, unheard of combinations of spices into a dressing. I not only know what different combinations of oil and vinegar taste like, but I know my spices. Similarly, my husband doesn't need plans to build a house. He understands math and geometry, knows where the various stress points would be, and puts in necessary supports. If we are to get away from recipes for teaching, we need to understand learning, become familiar with its essentials, and within those givens experiment with reasonable possibilities.

The more familiar we are with why we learn better under some conditions than others, the more likely we are not to pursue countless dead-end paths. Our knowledge of what we do when we learn to write and read like writers, helps us make reasonable choices when we work with our students and meet with other educators. This knowledge of our emerging understanding is necessary when we are breaking new ground.

People will question us when we do something a little differently than they do or than the majority does. The questions will make us nervous and shake our confidence unless we can explain our explorations. We need to be able to tell others about our own writing and reading, with specific examples, and we need to be able to tell others about books and articles we've read about composition teaching. When we step forward on the cutting edge of research we need to have a firm grip. It's tough to be learners, experiencing the tension of not knowing whether new things will work. Not only must we be able to explain why we do what we do, so must our students, because their process knowledge helps them learn.

Like us, they learn best when they understand what they do rather than just doing as they're told. We give them many opportunities to consider options, make decisions, and share their thinking process. We teach them to respond to each other's plans, which helps them understand what others do and, in turn, articulate their own process.

We enjoy learning. When students have responsibility, they like it. It gives them the confidence to talk about what they do, and they become our best PR agents. When Paul Shaw, principal in Mississauga, Ontario, spoke to the Language Arts Conference in Toronto in 1986, teachers in the audience wondered what the parents of the students in his school think of the way his teachers teach reading and writing. He said, "Their children come home more excited about writing and reading than in previous years. Parents can sense a difference between this year's third grader and an older sibling when he was in third grade. More children like reading and writing, so we have fewer complaints than we had with our former program."

Both children and teachers can like school and enjoy learning (Silvers 1986). We won't all choose to go to national conventions, but we know whether we feel excited enough about our teaching to want to share it with others. When we do, then we learn, because sharing is a two-way process. First, we share because we hope others will find our work interesting and, then we find theirs interesting. We hear possibilities for ourselves to try if we first admit we don't know everything, which is where teaching begins.

We Learn About Teaching

We may rush in and say, "Of course I don't know everything," but traditionally, the teaching profession has based its credibility on the notion that the teacher was the authority. However, if we want our students to become authors, then we must share our authority with them. All of us writers—teachers and students—learn from each other and teach each other.

As teachers, we have two groups in which to learn and teach, that of our peers and that of our students. These two groups help us discover the number one thing we learn about teaching: it can be fun. At first, we feel threatened by our students and one of the new things we gradually learn is how to release the potential in a group rather than trying to control it. This is a centuries-old dilemma teachers face. We will not figure out how to teach a new way in a few years, but we have a lifetime to work on it. We begin with the first step.

We find the potential in the group.   We step out of our classrooms —into contact with our peers. Our research shows that the power of response among teachers has more influence on their teaching than anything else. When we know each other well enough to share personal and professional joys and failures, then we know what it's like to be part of a learning community, and we strive to establish one in our classroom. We decide to teach in a community of learners, and this decision initiates the second step.

We step out from behind our lecterns—into the midst of our students. This is the most scary thing a teacher will ever do.

When Mary Willes (1983) studied teacher behavior during the first few weeks of children's first year of school, she found that teachers turned children into pupils by taking away their voices— the essence of writing. The teachers spent those weeks teaching the children to be quiet. Children could talk only in response to the teacher. In other words, the teachers taught the children not to initiate learning, not to be independent. Also, when children responded to the teacher, they were to give short answers, not complex ones that involved complex thinking. The teachers didn't provide opportunities for children to hypothesize and wonder. The children learned to value short, correct answers, and shy away from uncertain territory. No wonder it's hard for us to give responsibility to our students. It's a model we have not experienced throughout our own schooling, but with the support of our peers we can begin.

As we work on our teaching, the five principles of writing and reading instruction serve as guidelines for us as learners and for our students. We learn how complicated teaching is. It takes a lot of Time to learn about writing, writing and reading, how to work with our peers, and how to transfer what we know from learning with adults into our classrooms. Besides, we always ask ourselves why we are making these changes.

Of all the decisions under the word Choice, the first is, "I decided to change the way I teach." All other changes come from it. Response from others helps us clarify what we think, what we are learning about teaching. We learn not to do everything our peers do and eventually come to realize the value of diversity because we belie the notion of choice if we try to get everyone to do the same thing. If we do strive for conformity, we set ourselves up for failure. Thus, we set the stage for each of us to establish our own agenda and learn from others when we share agendas. We also draw parallels between this and our reading instruction.

When Nathan shares *Stone Fox* he tells the story of his own dog's death. We bite our tongue because we don't think that's the main idea of the book, but Nathan has chosen to share the book because of its meaning for him. Similarly, I remember that *The New KGB* captured and kept my attention for days because I was soon leaving for the Soviet Union, but I've yet to find another person who has read it or whom I could entice to read it. Our reading interests and the meanings we compose are idiosyncratic to us. When we share them, we learn about dogs or the KGB as others tell their stories about their books. But we know it isn't logical to base instruction on situations in which all of us read the same story and answer the same questions about it. Our old ways prevented our readers from becoming involved and didn't give them the responsibility to respond. But we can change, even though to honor diversity of response opens up interaction. Enter now the word Structure.

If our classroom is well structured, parents who visit will leave with this comment: "The students all know what they're doing." This is what we'd like to think of our teaching. We'd like to know what we're doing in the midst of our experimentation. We need a structure to provide us with security, a recurring time to work on what we've decided to change and to reflect on what we do. Otherwise, our new learning will get lost in the press of our daily workload.

We may enroll in a class, meet weekly with friends, keep a daily journal, phone a friend each week, or write to a friend each week. Somehow, most of us need a system to help us know where we've been, where we are, and where we think we're headed. Regardless of the framework in which we decide to learn, we pioneers need other pioneers who can identify with our rutted trails. Our Community, however we define it for ourselves, helps us find our route and see our strengths.

Teachers on a staff can be each other's eyes. In the spring of 1985 Jan Roberts, one of the Mast Way teachers, visited several classrooms while her intern taught. This helped both Jan and the other teachers. Jan could reflect on her own teaching when she watched and talked with her peers, and they realized how unthreatened they felt with

Jan in their rooms. They knew they would have feared the presence of a peer in previous years, but now they could trust each other to look for the good things they did. The response system they used in writing and reading carried into Jan's observations.

The teachers knew that Jan came to learn from them, which meant that she thought they knew something she didn't know. As in writing conferences, where everyone comes as a learner, the knowledge that someone will respond to your work is welcome when you know they haven't come as a destroyer. It's helpful to writers to know what readers hear in their writing, and it's helpful to teachers to hear what the teacher next door learns about teaching from them. The Mast Way teachers also had the researchers as a second pair of ears in their classrooms. When Tom Romano researched in Jan Roberts's classroom, he studied the Big Conferences during the spring. When he shared his data with Jan, she heard herself talk more than anyone else and worried about herself as a listener. The less she listened, the more she didn't know about what her students knew. She not only gave her role in these whole-class shares some serious thought, but she decided to increase the opportunities for small response groups. Data collected by someone else helped Jan see something she already knew about teaching, but it's difficult to see whether we are doing the things we want to be doing.

Another way the Mast Way teachers received feedback was from visitors, and this continues. Jan compared the benefits of researchers and visitors in her final interview with Tom Romano. "One of the things that's been most helpful to me is sharing your daily notes. They gave me another set of eyes. Being in a classroom is a lonely experience in a way. That's why I like to have visitors. When I first started this project, I didn't. It put lead in my heart."

Typically, the only visitors classroom teachers usually have are administrators, and they come to circle errors with their red pens. But visitors come to learn from us, not to judge, and that makes the difference. Jan values the chance to talk professionally with other teachers about her work. This, in turn, makes a difference in her relationship with her students. When she comes to school to learn from them rather than evaluate them, they welcome her.

Our students are not necessarily aware of what they know any more than we are aware of what we know about teaching. However, when we tell our students what we learn from them, their sense of self grows just as ours does when our peers tell us what they learn from us. In turn, our students become better learners because they start to see themselves as persons who know something, and we become more assertive learners about teaching when we realize others learn from our teaching.

When someone has confidence in us, we are more likely to have the nerve to stretch, take a risk, try something new, and if it works we can take the credit. We grow; we change; we get excited!

We rejoice together. We come to the teachers' room and tell about something funny one of our students said during the morning. We sense the power of the group and strive to keep the groups' comments mainly positive. When we have a hopeful attitude toward our teaching, our desire to move forward becomes stronger. Our peers help us realize it's a strength to be on shaky ground. They catch us when we fall, and fall we will. That's a given, and all the possible tension needs humor to keep us going. We all need to have a good time, have fun, laugh. Pat McLure enjoys days when another adult spends time in her classroom, especially researchers. "When it's someone else who enjoys being with children we share funny anecdotes. When the children go out to recess, we sit around and laugh."

We recognize the delight of learning in ourselves and want to foster the same feeling in our students. We know the importance of enthusiasm for forward motion and do everything we can to keep learners' energy high. They, in turn, keep our energy high as we find out new, interesting things from them each day. Our enthusiasm infects our fellow workers, as the children's interest stimulates their classmates.

We Continue to Learn About Learning

One child chooses to learn about poetry and another, whales. They read, write, talk, and listen. Not only do both children learn about poetry and whales, they also learn about Mozart and science fiction from others in the class. After a while the child's line of inquiry draws to a close, and he follows a new interest that has recently emerged. Reading, writing, children's literature, and language arts disappear. They are old terms that conjure up old notions about how children learn. We now know children don't learn in compartments.

Learning is complex. It is much too rich for us to break it apart. The complexity of learning does not bother children, but we have a problem with honoring the child's way of learning. However, when we look at our own learning as we learn to write and relearn to read when writing is on our mind, we realize that we learn the same way children do. Reading is more fun when we meet with others to talk about why we liked a book than when we meet to go over worksheets. I shudder to think that someone would give me four worksheets after I had read Potok's *Davita's Harp.*

Teaching is complicated; learning is complicated. When we compartmentalize it, we lose its essence. One of the major things we learned by studying both reading and writing rather than only one or the other, is that learning mushrooms when we bring more than one discipline together. When we break the barriers between reading and writing in the Big Conferences as well as in the small conferences, the children start to see reading, writing, and sharing (listening and talking) as vehicles for learning.

Learning varies among people.   Variability in the group helps. We strive to capitalize on it, rather than eliminate it. Donald Graves's number one finding in his writing research at Atkinson, New Hampshire (Graves 1982) was that writers vary. He set out to determine stages and found his goal to be impossible because of all the differences among writers. The same is true of teachers as learners. We change slowly and with great variability. As researcher Tom Romano says, "This is as it must be." We have to find our way "in the big split that is American education." We must especially expect variation when we stake out new territory.

We learn our personal strengths and weaknesses, and which tasks it is reasonable for us to try. This goes back to the importance of topic choice and other choices in writing. Writers learn how to choose topics they can write about, and they learn to recognize when a piece of writing won't work. The same is true with book choice in reading. Readers learn to choose appropriate books, to recognize when they need help, to know how to get help, and when to put aside an inappropriately chosen book. These choices underlie our decisions about our teaching. As we learn what kinds of tasks we can do well, we choose ways to change and either work on these improvements or drop them and select others.

Writing teachers need to make their own decisions because they have to teach their writers how to make decisions. They help their writers and readers see options and insist that the writer/reader decide. These teachers need supporters who will help them see options, who will insist that they make their own decisions, and who will recognize them for their accomplishments.

The Mast Way teachers decided whether they wanted to change and how they wanted to change. Ellen Blanchard explained, after the first year of the project, why she liked it, "This is the first time in over ten years of teaching I've felt like a professional." As a profession, we want to make our own decisions.

Marcia Taft, the Mast Way librarian, says the main benefit of the project, for her, was that it kept her in her profession. We expected her to establish the library as the center of writing/reading for the school but we didn't have a plan for her beyond the agreement to write with the teachers' group. She probably feared writing more than anyone else in the school, but, in turn, this may be why she came to understand so readily the value of others' support. Marcia generated the writing/reading share sessions in the library for cross grade-levels, and even though she trembled at first when she sat in the circle to respond with the children, she now looks forward to hearing what they write, read, and say, as the teachers do.

Sometimes when the teachers hear their students share, the helpfulness of their knowledge of themselves as learners becomes especially obvious. One day in the fall of 1983, when I was in Patricia McLure's first grade during their Big Conference, Paula shared with the class. She read a short piece about her father, and the children asked a few questions. Paula smiled as she answered with additional information about her father, and when the children had no more questions, Paula slid onto the carpet next to Pat. They exchanged smiles and later Pat asked me if I'd heard Paula sigh.

I hadn't, and Pat explained, "They're just like us on Mondays when we share. They're nervous."

Pat didn't say more, but I heard her thoughts: "I haven't had the nerve to share yet at our teachers' group." Pat didn't share until February. Two years later Pat shared in Arizona.

References

BRAUSE, RITA S., AND MAYHER, JOHN S. 1986. Learning Through Teaching: Is Testing Crippling Integrated Language Education? *Language Arts* 63, no. 4 (April).

GRAVES, DONALD. 1982. *Writing: Teachers and Children at Work.* Portsmouth, N.H.: Heinemann.

SILVERS, PENNY. 1986. Process Writing and the Connection to Reading. *Reading Teacher* 39, no. 7 (March).

WILLES, MARY. 1983. *Children into Pupils.* London: Routledge and Kegan Paul.

Students as Independent Learners

Twenty-Two

One, two, or three students from Phyllis Kinzie's fourth grade read to the class each day. The children who shared sat in the Author's Chair, the only padded chair in the classroom. The rest of us sat in a circle of splintery wooden chairs, placed in a close trustworthy circle to give someone the courage to sit in the position of authority. The child in the Author's Chair knows what's inside the heads of the circle-sitters because everyone has sat in those chairs. The ordinary chairs show at a glance who is different, but at the same time, their presence prevents the authority from being alone.

John, one of the fourth graders, explains his position when he sits in one of the hard chairs. "I want to get to know the person better and I do when I find out what books they read." Similarly, he explains his position when he sits in the soft seat, "The others want to know what book I'm going to share because they want to get to know me better." The children share themselves, as well as their books.

Both the personal side of reading and the notion of sharing are new at Mast Way School, and both contribute to what turned out to be the number one thing I learned: This kind of writing/reading program lets children become independent learners more than the reading programs I worked with during the previous sixteen years of my career. When we share reading personally, differences among readers become the norm and the support of others helps us value ourselves. We learn the value of others to our growth.

The Reader's Composition

Writing provides insights for readers that they cannot get elsewhere. Initially, they expect writing, regardless of who wrote it, to have an interesting, accessible message. When they share, they learn that different parts of a piece of writing speak to various readers. Over time, they realize that a writer writes to satisfy himself but wants others to find significance in his insights. Thus, when he reads, he knows that although it's his responsibility to think of what might be central to the author, mainly he reads for himself.

Independent readers compose their own messages.   Tradition tells reading and literature teachers to help their students find the author's message, but writers tell us not to look for one meaning when we read. Or, to put it another way, they tell us to look for the one meaning we find significant. Writers think of print as something that will bring forth a response, and if a piece of writing does not stimulate response from a reader, the writer feels that he has failed. No response is the writer's worst fear (Murray 1986), but even a small response bothers him.

Subdued response tells writers that their writing didn't strike a resonant chord with very many readers. They try to choose topics that are not only relevant to themselves but to many others, because they address classic concerns, such as what it's like to be a mother or the new girl in the class. Such questions are complicated and will not bring one response from several readers, nor should they.

Milan Kundera, an exiled Czech writer now living in France, writes about the role of the novel in the totalitarian world (1985). He says, "Totalitarian Truth excludes relativity, doubt, questioning; it cannot accommodate what I would call the wisdom of the novel." Independent readers and writers take the printed word as a springboard for thought. To prevent thinking requires force, because a community of readers can't help but compose a variety of messages from what they read.

Even if the teacher convinces her class that Ezra Jack Keats's message in *Snowy Day* is, "Snow is fun," the child who has just moved to New Hampshire from Minnesota and the one who has just come from Florida will interpret the story differently. Keats hopes that they will both find pleasure in his book, which means that he allows leeway for them. Writers are in control when they write, and thus, readers are in control when they read. This sense of responsibility and independence is a hallmark of the Mast Way writing/reading program. Students learn what it means to compose their own message when they hear about the differences among them.

Independent readers consider other readers' insights.   Their own thinking is not only influenced by what they know, but by the community in which they share. This environment influences what they learn when they write and read. Not only do they hear what one another found meaningful, but they honor diversity. They know each of them is different, expect this, and come together to find out what each has learned from a nonfiction selection or felt about a dramatic novel. It's because of the differences that everyone, including the teacher, can be a learner. The writing/reading program rests on the differences, or to paraphrase myself, the program rests on the independence of each reader's response.

As the children get to know each other, they begin to predict what classmates will hear in a piece of writing. Thus, they can juggle more than one possible interpretation when they read, and later can meet to test their hypotheses about what they thought when they read. In this way, the influence of the community is ever-present and helps each reader have a rich reading experience but still leaves reason to come together. The better we know each other, the more fun we have finding out what we each think. But there are times when we want to be alone.

One way children learn about the advantages and disadvantages of working alone is through collaboration during writing. In November 1984, third graders Melissa and Amy wrote together on some days and explained why. Melissa started, "I like writing alone. In writing alone you can use all of your own ideas and writing together you compromise. But, sometimes it's fun to compromise."

Amy: "I like both [writing with someone else and by myself]. If I'm writing about my kittens or my family I'd rather write by myself, unless a friend was along with me on a trip. If I'm writing a mystery or something, it's fun to have a friend."

These girls can distinguish between times when they'd rather work alone and when they think a collaborator would be helpful. There are times when the other person's insights might be bothersome, but the girls are no less independent on the days they work together. It's their choice to work together and also, their knowledge of writing tells them there are times when they will do better work if they have a collaborator. The ability to make this distinction helps them understand the role others play in writing. They can reject working with others when they write, and they can reject the insights of others when they share a draft.

The ability to consider and decide when to reject is a necessary characteristic of an independent learner, as Matt will soon learn about his friend Chad. In March 1985, Matt and Chad worked on "The Mystery of the Stolen Pants." Matt said it was a comedy and spun an incredibly fast and detailed oral narrative. Chad, as scribe, laughed but ignored the bulk of it and began writing what he had in mind, making the main character a millionaire. In time, they compromised, but the child with pencil in hand felt it gave him control.

Chad wanted to work with someone and liked Matt's contribution, but stuck with his own version. Variations on this scene also occur when writers work with published writing.

Independent readers look for composition starters left by the author. When Daniel reads, he considers himself first because he knows that his readers construct their own meanings from what he writes. He can't please everyone, but he can please himself and chooses which of his classmates to please. If he has one of their books in his lap, he knows whether the book has an entry point for him or not because he's heard the book. If it was one he liked when the author shared it, he may read it several times, but he never reads some books that classmates share. This is also true of books by professional authors.

Daniel likes some better than others. He reads both old favorites and unknown titles he has selected from the bookcase. When he reads the new ones, he wants to find out whether the author left openings for him. This does not mean that he only looks for spaces and doesn't listen to what the author says. He considers the author because he is an author and wants his readers to consider him, but he also realizes that the author wants him to make significant connections between the book and himself. Readers like Daniel look for places where the writer wants the reader to enter into the act of composition.

Writers know the power of print to generate thought, and when they read they think of the power authors give them, which they give each other in their classroom: the power to ask questions. They question each other and extend these questions to the professional authors they include in their community of writers. They wonder about the decisions those authors considered when they wrote. When they read Barbara Steiner's *Oliver Dibbs to the Rescue!* they may wonder whether they should protect endangered animals; or they might take off on the episode in which Bo couldn't get the seal's head off and tell about scary experiences they've had; or they might become interested in white seals, wonder why the author said little about them, and decide to find out about them. We accept any of these three responses. The freedom to make these choices gives readers a sense of independence, which they enjoy.

This joy intrigues me. When I started writing/reading research, I wanted to find out what it was about writing that caused students and teachers to call it their favorite time of day. I found out that it's not because writing is easy. Writers know writing is a series of problems they create and tackle, and some of the things they learn are ways to approach problems. What they thrive on is the power we give them to make decisions when they write and read. They become surprised, for example, at their own insights when they look at print over time.

The Ongoing Nature of Print

Phyllis Kinzie decided to have her fourth graders read a favorite picture book from their early childhood because she wanted even the poorest readers to be able to read to the class successfully and because she wanted everyone to have time to read orally an entire selection written by a professional. She met her objectives, but something more important evolved. The children were surprised to find these books still meaningful and, further, that the significance of the books differed from what they remembered. Children's realization that meanings evolve not only comes to light when they read professionals' books but also in their own writing. Print is by its nature temporary and commits readers to constantly move beyond it.

Writers change over time.   Print is a permanent representation of temporary thoughts. Writers often write on the edge of what they know. They realize that they can't wait to write until they understand something completely because they are constantly rethinking and learning new insights about what they know today. Print is a snapshot of a person at a point in time. Writers feel both good and uneasy about their writing and hope their readers understand. In turn, when writers read, they look for something to learn and seek the edges the author has yet to explore fully.

This book is not the final word on what I know, but it's the best way I can say it right now. Those who tell me what they appreciate in my book and ask me questions are my audience. My writer-readers will not only tell me what they learned and appreciated in my writing, they will also ask me questions. Their questions will be one of the spurs to move me onward and also to move them beyond my text. I'm curious to know what meanings teachers construct from my story. When I declare my book "Finished!" I will be both excited and afraid. I can identify with the teachers in my writing workshops.

Recently, a teacher in a workshop in Healdsburg, California, said to me, "We were all afraid to come and write. No matter what you write, you reveal yourself." I'm no longer afraid to share my writing with teachers in my workshops because I know they won't criticize me, but publishing my first book is another matter. I don't know my audience and I wonder if they'll encourage me to continue my learning. I feel very much like the first graders in Ellen Blackburn Karelitz's and Pat McLure's classes. I was so surprised one day in the spring when Cedric read the book he published in the fall to me. Before I could respond, he quickly said, "If I were to write it now, this is what I'd change." By the time this books comes out, I'll already know how I'd like to change it. I won't have that opportunity, and neither did Cedric. Our books are our final drafts and the key word is *draft*.

Readers change over time. When fourth-grader Mark read Leo Lionni's *Frederick* to his class they talked about how the mouse contributed to his family because he daydreams. Todd analyzed their discussion. "Do you think we would have talked about *Frederick* like this in first grade?"

They stopped. Then Alison said, "No, we just thought he was cute. We didn't really understand it then."

They came to realize that the meaning on the pages of *Frederick* and of other picture books perhaps didn't change, but they, the readers changed. Because the author included elements in his book to appeal to a wide audience, many children liked it, but not all for one reason. After their initial insights, the fourth graders started to wonder about differences more frequently. When a story had two children in it, they thought they identified with the younger when they were little, but now they identified with the older child. Eventually, they wondered if they had changed during fourth grade.

In some ways, children do change within one year. If their grandfather dies, the experience gives them a different view of Donald Hall's *The Man Who Lived Alone*. They realize that they see things when they reread a book that they didn't see the first or second time through. One day Melinda hailed me, "Listen," and she read a poem. Then she read it again and again, with a larger smile each time. "It sounds more and more like my brother and me when we fight!" For years we have asked children to reread in reading class, but when children choose to reread we gain better insights on its benefits. Some of what we know about rereading comes from careful thinking about the habits of young children at home.

They reread books or demand that we reread them countless times. Rather than developing a set pattern of routinely reading stories twice, they reread by choice. Some books they don't reread but the option to choose to reread is ever-present. They may reread for several reasons, but one is that they enjoy a story and another is that they find something new. Pieces of conversation and descriptions of characters enlarge and take on meanings. Overall, the differences children find in rereading help them know there isn't only one interpretation of a text, and that the meaning each of them finds today shows the differences among them, which set the stage for these performers. They all have a part to play and they all compose the audience.

References

KUNDERA, MILAN. 1985. The Novel and Europe. *The New York Review of Books* (July 19).

MURRAY, DONALD. 1986. One Writer's Secrets. *College Composition and Communication* 37, no. 2 (May).

Bibliography

ADAMSON, LYNDA G. 1985. And Who Taught You Children's Literature? *Horn Book* 61, no. 5 (September/October).

AIKEN, JOAN. 1984. On Imagination. *Horn Book* 60, no. 6 (November/December).

ALLEN, JOBETH, AND HANSEN, JANE. 1986. Sarah Joins a Literate Community. *Language Arts* 63, no. 7 (November).

ANDERSON, LINDA. 1984. The Environment of Instruction: The Function of Seatwork in a Commercially Developed Curriculum. In *Comprehension Instruction: Perspectives and Suggestions*, ed. by Gerald G. Duffy, Laura R. Roehler, and Jana Mason. New York: Longman.

ATWELL, NANCIE. 1985. Writing and Reading from the Inside Out. In *Breaking Ground: Teachers Relate Reading and Writing in the Elementary School*, ed. by Jane Hansen, Thomas Newkirk, and Donald Graves. Portsmouth, N.H.: Heinemann.

———. 1986. Making Time. In *To Compose: Writing in the High School*, ed. by Thomas Newkirk. Portsmouth, N.H.: Heinemann.

———. 1987. *In the Middle*. Montclair, N.J.: Boynton/Cook.

BARTOLI, JILL SUNDAY. 1985. The Paradox in Reading: Has the Solution Become the Problem? *Journal of Reading* 28, no. 7 (April).

BECOMING A NATION OF READERS. 1984. Newark, Del: International Reading Association; Urbana, Ill.: National Council of Teachers of English.

BENEDICT, SUSAN. 1985. "Emily Dickinson's Room is as Old as Grandfather Frog": Developing the Basic Skills. In *Breaking Ground: Teachers Relate Reading and Writing in the Elementary School*, ed. by Jane Hansen, Thomas Newkirk, and Donald Graves. Portsmouth, N.H.: Heinemann.

BISSEX, GLENDA. 1980. *GNYS AT WRK: A Child Learns to Write and Read.* Cambridge, Mass.: Harvard University Press.

BLACKBURN, ELLEN. 1984. Common Ground: Developing Relationships Between Reading and Writing. *Language Arts* 61, no. 4 (April).

BLOOME, DAVID. 1985. Reading as a Social Process. *Language Arts* 62, no. 2 (February).

BOUTWELL, MARILYN. 1983. Reading and Writing Process: A Reciprocal Agreement. *Language Arts* 60, no. 6 (September).

BRUFFEE, KENNETH A. 1983. Writing and Reading as Collaborative or Social Acts. In *The Writer's Mind*, ed. by Janice N. Hays, Phyllis A. Roth, Jon R. Ramsey, and Robert D. Foulke. Urbana, Ill.: National Council of Teachers of English.

CALKINS, LUCY. 1986. *The Art of Teaching Writing*. Portsmouth, N.H.: Heinemann.

COOPER, JAMES, ET AL. 1977. *Classroom Teaching Skills: A Handbook*. Lexington, Mass.: D.C. Heath and Co.

CRAMER, BARBARA B. 1984. Bequest of Wings: Three Readers and Special Books. *Language Arts* 61, no. 3 (March).

CULLINAN, BERNICE E. 1986. Books in the Classrooms. *Horn Book* 62, no. 4 (July/August).

DE VILLIERS, P. A., AND DE VILLIERS, J. G. 1982. *Early Language*. Cambridge, Mass.: Harvard University Press.

DILLARD, JILL, AND DAHL, KARIN. 1986. Learning Through Teaching in a Reading/ Writing Classroom. *Language Arts* 63, no. 7 (November).

DONALDSON, MARGARET. 1976. *Children's Minds*. New York: Holt, Rinehart, and Winston.

EMIG, JANET. 1982. *The Web of Meaning*. Montclair, N.J.: Boynton/Cook.

EVANS, CHRISTINE SOBRAY. 1984. Writing to Learn in Math. *Language Arts* 61, no. 8 (December).

FISHER, CAROL. 1980. Grammar in the Language Arts Program. In *Discovering Language with Children*, ed. by Gay Su Pinnell. Urbana, Ill.: National Council of Teachers of English.

FIVE, CORA. 1985. Teresa: A Reciprocal Learning Experience for Teacher and Child. In *Toward Practical Theory*, ed. by Jerome C. Harste and Diane Stephens. Indiana: Language Arts Department, Indiana University.

FIVE, CORA LEE. 1986. Joy in Learning: A Teacher Investigates Her Own Learning Process. *Language Arts* 63, no. 7 (November).

FIVE, CORA, AND ROSEN, MARTHA. 1985. Children Re-create History in Their Own Voices. In *Breaking Ground: Teachers Relate Reading and Writing in the Elementary School*, ed. by Jane Hansen, Thomas Newkirk, and Donald Graves. Portsmouth, N.H.: Heinemann.

FLEMING, PAULA. 1986. The Write Way to Read. In *Understanding Writing: Ways of Observing, Learning & Teaching*, ed. by Thomas Newkirk and Nancie Atwell. Portsmouth, N.H.: Heinemann.

FREEDMAN, RUSSELL. 1986. Pursuing the Pleasure Principle. *Horn Book* 62, no. 1 (January/February).

FULWILER, TOBY. 1986. Journals Across the Disciplines. In *To Compose: Teaching Writing in the High School*, ed. by Thomas Newkirk. Portsmouth, N.H.: Heinemann.

FUNKHOUSER, LESLIE. 1985. Who's the Smartest? In *Teachers and Learners*. Durham, N.H.: Writing Process Laboratory, University of New Hampshire.

GALDA, LEE. 1984. The Relations Between Reading and Writing in Young Children. In *New Directions in Composition Research*, ed. by Richard Beach and Lillian S. Bridwell. New York: Guilford Press.

GOODLAD, JOHN I. 1984. *A Place Called School*. New York: McGraw-Hill.

GOODMAN, KENNETH. 1986. Basal Readers: A Call for Action. *Language Arts* 63, no. 4 (April).

GRAVES, DONALD. 1983. *Writing: Teachers & Children at Work*. Portsmouth, N.H.: Heinemann.

———. 1984. *A Researcher Learns to Write*. Portsmouth, N.H.: Heinemann.

GRAVES, DONALD, AND HANSEN, JANE. 1983. Author's Chair. *Language Arts* 60, no. 8 (November/December).

HALE, ROBERT D. 1986. Musings. *Horn Book* 62, no. 3 (May/June).

HANSEN, JANE. 1983a. Authors Respond to Authors. *Language Arts* 60, no. 8 (November/December).

———. 1983b. The Writer as Meaning-Maker. In *Teaching All the Children to Write*, ed. by J. L. Collins. Albany, N.Y.: New York Council of Teachers of English.

———. 1984a. First Grade Writers Pursue Reading. In *Fforum: Essays on Theory and Practice in the Teaching of Writing*, ed. by Patricia Stock. Montclair, N.J.: Boynton/Cook.

———. 1984b. Readers Talk Like Writers. In *Changing Perspectives on Research in Reading/Language Processing and Composing*, ed. by Jerome Niles. Rochester, N.Y.: The National Reading Conference.

———. 1985. Teachers Share Their Writing. *The Reading Teacher* 38, no. 9 (May).

———. 1987. Organizing Student Learning. In *The Dynamics of Language Learning: Research in the Language Arts*, ed. by James Squire. Urbana, Ill.: National Council of Researchers of English.

———. In press. Listen to Learn. In *Ideas and Insights: Teaching the English Language Arts K–6*, ed. by Dorothy Watson and Ruie Pritchard. Urbana, Ill.: National Council of Teachers of English.

HANSEN, JANE, AND GRAVES, DONALD. 1986. "Do You Know What Backstrung Means?" *The Reading Teacher* 39, no. 8 (March).

HANSEN, JANE, AND HUBBARD, RUTH. 1984. Poor Readers Can Draw Inferences. *Reading Teacher* 37, no. 7 (March).

HARMS, JEANNE MCLAIN, AND LETTOW, LUCILLE J. 1986. Fostering Ownership of the Reading Experience. *The Reading Teacher* 42, no. 3 (December).

HARSTE, JEROME. 1985. Portrait of a New Paradigm: Reading Comprehension Research. In *Landscapes: A State-of-the-Art Assessment of Reading*

Comprehension Research, 1974–1984, ed. by Avon Crismore. Bloomington, Ind.: University of Indiana.

HARSTE, JEROME; WOODWARD, VIRGINIA; AND BURKE, CAROLYN. 1984. *Language Stories & Literacy Lessons.* Portsmouth, N.H.: Heinemann.

HAYES, CURTIS W., AND BAHRUTH, ROBERT. 1985. Querer Es Poder. In *Breaking Ground: Teachers Relate Reading and Writing in the Elementary School,* ed. by Jane Hansen, Thomas Newkirk, and Donald Graves. Portsmouth, N.H.: Heinemann.

HEATH, SHIRLEY BRICE. 1983. *Ways with Words.* Cambridge: Cambridge University Press.

HEMBROW, VERN. 1986. A Heuristic Approach Across the Curriculum. *Language Arts* 63, no. 7 (November).

HEMMING, HEATHER. 1985. Reading: A Monitor for Writing. In *Breaking Ground: Teachers Relate Reading and Writing in the Elementary School,* ed. by Jane Hansen, Thomas Newkirk, and Donald Graves. Portsmouth, N.H.: Heinemann.

HOLDAWAY, DONALD. 1979. *The Foundations of Literacy.* Sydney: Ashton Scholastic.

HUBBARD, RUTH. 1984. What's Going On In His Mind? In *Children Who Write When They Read.* Durham, N.H.: Writing Process Laboratory, University of New Hampshire.

———. 1985a. The Fifth Idea. In *Children Who Write When They Read.* Durham, N.H.: Writing Process Laboratory, University of New Hampshire.

———. 1985b. Monday Morning. In *Teachers and Learners.* Durham, N.H.: Writing Process Laboratory, University of New Hampshire.

———. 1985c. Reading Aloud: Comments or Questions? In *Teachers and Learners.* Durham, N.H.: Writing Process Laboratory, University of New Hampshire.

———. 1985d. Reading Their Way. In *Teachers and Learners.* Durham, N.H.: Writing Process Laboratory, University of New Hampshire.

———. 1986. Structure Encourages Independence in Reading and Writing. *Reading Teacher* 40, no. 2 (November).

HULL, GLYNDA. 1985. Research on Error and Correction. In *Perspectives on Research and Scholarship in Composition,* ed. by Ben W. McClelland and Timothy R. Donovan. New York: The Modern Language Association of America.

HYMAN, TRINA SCHART. 1985. Caldecott Medal Acceptance. *Horn Book* 61, no. 4 (July/August).

JOHN-STEINER, VERA. 1985. *Notebooks of the Mind.* Albuquerque, N.M.: University of New Mexico Press.

KANTOR, KENNETH J. 1984. Classroom Contexts and the Development of Writing Intuitions: An Ethnographic Case Study. *New Directions in Composition Research,* ed. by Richard Beach and Lillian S. Bridwell. New York: The Guilford Press.

KEARNEY, LYNN, AND TASHLIK, PHYLLIS. 1985. Collaboration and Conflict: Teachers and Researchers Learning. *Language Arts* 62, no. 7 (November).

KUNDERA, MILAN. 1985. The Novel and Europe. *The New York Review of Books* (July 19).

LEVINE, DENISE STAVIS. 1985. The Biggest Thing I Learned But It Really Doesn't Have to Do with Science. . . . *Language Arts* 62, no. 1 (January).

LINDFORS, JUDITH WELL. 1985. Understanding the Development of Language Structure. In *Observing the Language Learner*, ed. by Angela Jaggar and M. Trika Smith-Burke. Newark, Del.: International Reading Association; Urbana, Ill.: National Council of Teachers of English.

MATTHEWS, KATHY. 1984. Are You Willing to Be the Kind of Writer You Want Your Students To Be? *Learning Magazine*, April/May.

——. 1985. Beyond the Writing Table. In *Breaking Ground: Teachers Relate Reading and Writing in the Elementary School*, ed. by Jane Hansen, Thomas Newkirk, and Donald Graves. Portsmouth, N.H.: Heinemann.

MAYHER, JOHN S., AND BRAUSE, RITA S. 1986a. Learning Through Teaching: Is Testing Crippling Integrated Language Education? *Language Arts* 63, no. 4 (April).

——. 1986b. Learning Through Teaching: Is Your Classroom Like Your Grandmother's? *Language Arts* 63, no. 6 (October).

MENYUK, PAULA. 1980. What Young Children Know About Language. In *Discovering Language with Children*, ed. by Gay Su Pinnell. Urbana, Ill.: National Council of Teachers of English.

MOSENTHAL, PETER. 1986. Research Views: Defining Progress in Reading Research and Practice: The Theorists' Approach. *Reading Teacher* 40, no. 2 (November).

MURRAY, DONALD. 1985. Under the Lightning. In *Writers on Writing*, ed. by Tom Waldrep. New York: Random House.

——. 1986. One Writer's Secrets. *College Composition and Communication* 37, no. 2 (May).

NEILSEN, ALLAN. 1986. Knowing by Doing: An Active Approach to Writing Inservice. *Journal of Reading* (May).

NEILSEN, LORRI. 1985. Silent Partners. In *Teachers and Learners*. Durham, N.H.: Writing Process Laboratory, University of New Hampshire.

NELSON, KATHERINE; RESCORLA, L.; GRUENDEL, J.; AND BENEDICT, H. 1978. Early Lexicons: What Do They Mean? *Child Development* 49.

NEWKIRK, THOMAS. 1985. The Hedgehog or the Fox: The Dilemma of Writing Development. *Language Arts* 62, no. 6 (October).

——. In preparation. *Archimedes' Dream*.

OHANIAN, SUSAN. 1984. Achievement Test Scores: Facts that Distort the Truth. *Family Learning* (March/April).

PAPERT, SEYMOUR. 1980. *Mindstorms*. New York: Basic Books.

PERL, SONDRA, AND WILSON, NANCY. 1986. *Through Teachers' Eyes: Portraits of Writing Teachers at Work*. Portsmouth, N.H.: Heinemann.

PETTY, WALTER T.; PETTY, DOROTHY C.; AND BECKING, MARJORIE F., EDS. 1984. *Experiences in Languages: Tools and Techniques for Language Arts Methods*. 4th ed. Boston: Allyn and Bacon.

ROBERTS, JANICE. 1985. Excellence in Language Arts. Article distributed in Mast Way information package.

ROMANO, TOM. 1985. How Did You Get That Way? In *Teachers and Learners*. Durham, N.H.: Writing Process Laboratory, University of New Hampshire.

ROSENBLATT, LOUISE. 1978. *The Reader, the Text, the Poem*. Carbondale, Ill.: Southern Illinois University Press.

SAMWAY, KATHARINE. 1986. And You Run and You Run to Catch Up with the Sun, But It's Sinking. *Language Arts* 63, no. 4 (April).

SHANNON, PATRICK. 1985. Reading Instruction and Social Class. *Language Arts* 62, no. 6 (October).

SILVERS, PENNY. 1986. Process Writing and the Connection to Reading. *Reading Teacher* 39, no. 7 (March).

SIMPSON, MARY K. 1986. A Teacher's Gift: Oral Reading and the Reading Response Journal. *Journal of Reading* 30, no. 1 (October).

SMITH-BURKE, M. TRIKA. 1985. Reading and Talking: Learning Through Interaction. In *Observing the Language Learner*, ed. by Angela Jaggar and M. Trika Smith-Burke. Newark, Del.: International Reading Association; Urbana, Ill.: National Council of Teachers of English.

SOWERS, SUSAN. 1986. Six Questions Teachers Ask About Invented Spelling. In *Understanding Writing: Ways of Observing, Learning & Teaching*, ed. by Thomas Newkirk and Nancie Atwell. Portsmouth, N.H.: Heinemann.

SUHOR, CHARLES. 1985. Objective Tests and Writing Samples: How Do They Affect Instruction in Composition? *Phi Delta Kappan* (May).

SUSI, GERALDINE LEE. 1984. The Teacher/Writer: Model, Learner, Human Being. *Language Arts* 61, no. 7 (November).

TAYLOR, DENNY, AND STRICKLAND, DOROTHY S. 1986. Family Literacy: Myths and Magic. In *The Pursuit of Literacy*, ed. by Michael R. Sampson. Dubuque, Iowa: Kendall/Hunt.

TCHUDI, SUSAN. 1985. The Roots of Response to Literature. *Language Arts* 62, no. 5 (September).

TEMPLE, CHARLES A.; NATHAN, RUTH G.; AND BURRIS, NANCY A. 1982. *The Beginnings of Writing*. Boston, Mass.: Allyn and Bacon.

THOMAS, LEWIS. 1979. *The Medusa and the Snail*. New York: Viking.

TORBE, MIKE. 1983. Writing About Reading. In *Fforum: Essays on Theory and Practice in the Teaching of Writing*, ed. by Patricia L. Stock. Upper Montclair, N.J.: Boynton/Cook.

VAUGHAN, JOSEPH L. 1983. One Child's Query About Reading Instruction. *Language Arts* 60, no. 8 (November/December).

VON REYN, JANET. 1985. Learning Together: A Teacher's First Year Teaching Reading and Writing. In *Breaking Ground: Teachers Relate Reading and Writing in the Elementary School*, ed. by Jane Hansen, Thomas Newkirk, and Donald Graves. Portsmouth, N.H.: Heinemann.

VYGOTSKY, L. S. 1978. *Mind and Society: The Development of Higher Psy-*

chological Process, trans. and ed. by M. Cole, V. John-Steiner, S. Scribner, and E. Souberman. Cambridge, Mass.: Harvard University Press.

WALSHE, R. D. 1984. Teaching Writing: Attend to "Skills" as Part of "Process." In *Children and Learning*, ed. by Walter McVitty. Portsmouth, N.H.: Heinemann.

WATSON, KEN, AND YOUNG, BOB. 1986. Discourse for Learning in the Classroom. *Language Arts* 63, no. 2 (February).

WEINSTEIN, RHONA. 1986. Teacher Expectancy. In *The Contexts of Classroom Literacy*, ed. by Taffy Raphael. New York: Longman.

WEISS, JERRY. 1986. Writers and Readers: The Literary Connection. *The Reading Teacher* (April).

WELLS, GORDON. 1986. *The Meaning Makers: Children Learning Language and Using Language to Learn*. Portsmouth, N.H.: Heinemann.

WELTY, EUDORA. 1984. *One Writer's Beginnings*. Cambridge, Mass.: Harvard University Press.

WHITNEY, JAMES, AND HUBBARD, RUTH. 1986. *Time and Choice: Key Elements for Process Teaching*. Videotape. Portsmouth, N.H.: Heinemann.

WILLES, MARY J. 1983. *Children into Pupils*. London: Routledge & Kegan Paul.

WILLINSKY, JOHN. 1984. The Writer in the Teacher. *Language Arts* 61, no. 6 (October).

WIXSON, KAREN. 1983. Questions About a Text: What You Ask About Is What Children Learn. *The Reading Teacher* 37, no. 3 (December).

WOOLF, VIRGINIA. 1932. How Should One Read a Book? *The Second Common Reader*. New York: Harcourt-Brace.

YOLEN, JANE. 1985. The Story Between. *Language Arts* 62, no. 6 (October).

ZINSSER, WILLIAM. 1980. *On Writing Well*. New York: Harper and Row.

About the Author

I wrote this book while on sabbatical in an unfinished house in Bartlett, New Hampshire. By the time you read it, my husband will have completed our house, and it will have become our weekend retreat. I've loved my year in the mountains but enjoy being back at the university.

In 1979 I joined the faculty at the University of New Hampshire with my new PhD from the University of Minnesota, as one of P. David Pearson's advisees. A native Minnesotan, I still look forward to two return trips each year to see my entire family, who all live there. My mother and dad live on the farm my dad has lived on since he was a young boy, my sister Karen farms five miles away, and my brother Neil is the pastor of two country churches only twenty miles in the other direction. My other sister, Shirley, teaches first grade in St. Paul. She gets the first copy of this book.

I taught second and third grades in Minneapolis from 1967 to 1970; first and second grade in Hawaii; second grade and remedial reading in Iowa; second grade in New Jersey; and first, second, and fifth grades in Liberia, when my husband and I joined the Peace Corps after college.

While a student at Grand View Junior College in Des Moines, Iowa, I danced in the Danish folk dance troop, which presented twenty-five exhibitions each year. I had grown up in a Danish Lutheran church and decided in second grade I would go to Grand View, which was a Danish folk school when my father-in-law attended it many years ago. After Grand View I received my bachelor's degree from Drake University and, later, my master's from the University of Iowa.

I've skied in probably ten cross-country marathons, but have yet to set any records. However, I do enjoy the outdoors and allow time for skiing, skating, biking, running, or hiking on most days. During my sabbatical my husband and I skied in a marathon in Murmansk, a city in the Soviet Union.

I guess I'm a perfect Yuppie because I drive a mini-van, wear dusty rose L. L. Bean corduroys, and have a new Cusinart. I love to cook. My husband and I, along with most of our friends, no longer eat meat, but none of us has yet discarded New England seafood. I try a new recipe each week and often have people over for dinner. Please come! And, if you'll sing along, I'll play my old pump organ.

Index